FROM DOPE BUCKET TO ICE BUCKET

A Roughneck's Adventure in the Oilpatch

To Will.
I hope you enjoy
my story

Roy

FROM DOPE BUCKET TO ICE BUCKET

A Roughneck's Adventure in the Oilpatch

ROY HAITES

© Roy Haites, 2018

Published by HYTIS Publishing

A CIP catalogue record for this book is available from the British Library.

ISBN 978-1-9996866-0-4 (Hardback)
ISBN 978-1-9996866-1-1 (Paperback)

Book layout and design by Clare Brayshaw

Production by:

York Publishing Services Ltd
64 Hallfield Road
Layerthorpe
York YO31 7ZQ

Tel: 01904 431213

Website: www.yps-publishing.co.uk

Opa's story, for; Struan, Fife, Amelia and Lara

Contents

Book 2 – Aberdeen Days

Acknowledgements

Many thanks to Allan Jennison for encouraging me to write my stories and to Jill Morris for providing guidance on how to turn my stories into a book.

Book 1 - Roma Days

CHAPTER I

The Dope Bucket

When I was sixteen years old my family moved from Calgary, Canada, to Brisbane, Australia. Once we got settled, I went to Brisbane State High School for two years.

After finishing high school in November 1964, I told Dad that I didn't want to go to university or spend any more time studying. I did not however, have any idea where to find a job or what kind of work I might like to do for the rest of my life. When Dad saw me spending my days lying beside the swimming pool, it didn't take him long to work out that I wasn't thinking about employment so, he decided to put me to work.

Dad figured a few weeks working on a drilling site near Roma, Queensland, might let me appreciate that having a university degree would be a much better option than working eight hour manual labour shifts in the hot Australian sun. His plan was to let me see just how hard oilmen had to work for their living.

My father was a geologist. He had emigrated from Holland to Canada with his family when I was two years old. In Canada he first worked in the coal industry in Sydney, Nova Scotia, and than moved to Calgary, Alberta, to work for an oil company. In 1962 he was head-hunted to manage a small oil company in Australia, hence the move to Brisbane.

The job Dad had arranged was for me to work as an inventory monitor on a drill site where his company was drilling a well. This involved tallying up the empty bags of drilling-fluid additives consumed by the drillers and checking the serial numbers on all the drill bits they used, plus attending to a few minor admin jobs.

I had never seen a drilling rig and had never been to Roma. I think Dad was a little surprised when I accepted his plan with enthusiasm and started looking forward to going to work. I thought it sounded like a big adventure.

The job was due to start just after New Year, on January 5 1965, so Dad booked me a lift to Roma with a driller who was returning to work after his festive holiday. The day before I was due to leave, I packed a bag with some clothes and a few other things I thought I might need. When the driller arrived I was ready to go. I was eighteen years old and headed west.

Roma is just about far enough west to be in the 'outback'. Nearly, but not quite. Australia is over two thousand five hundred miles wide and while Roma is three hundred and twenty miles from the coast, the 'real outback', where very few people live, starts around six hundred miles inland.

The first eighty miles of our drive took us through rich farming country then we climbed up a steep range to Toowoomba. In Toowoomba we passed over the 'Great

Divide', the point from which all rivers flow inland instead of heading east towards the coast. We continued driving west through more farming and grain-growing country. After one hundred and fifty miles, the countryside became progressively drier and more barren.

Having taken seven hours to make the journey, we finally arrived in Roma at 5.00pm. As we drove into town we passed a huge cattle sale yard which was one of the main business activities in the area. In Roma itself there wasn't a lot to see. It was a small town with a population of around two thousand people. The main street was only three blocks long, with half a dozen pubs, one general store, a post office, a chemist, two book stores, a few cafe/restaurants and three or four other shops.

I was booked in at the Commonwealth Hotel located one block off the main street. This hotel was a basic country pub with a huge bar and maybe twenty rooms upstairs.

In Queensland, January is the hottest month of the year. When I arrived it was still 95 °F outside and only a few degrees cooler inside. After checking in, the proprietor invited me to join him for a glass of beer and then told me where I could go for something to eat. I had my meal and returned to the hotel for an early night. From my room I could hear people in the bar until 11.00pm and thereafter, throughout the rest of the night, I could hear the guy snoring in the room next door. As there was no soundproofing and no air conditioning in the hotel, between the noise and the heat, I didn't get much sleep.

As I was under twenty-one I shouldn't have been served any beer and the proprietor should have closed the bar at 10.00pm, but, this was a country pub and no one seemed to bother about these minor details.

Dad had arranged for Doug, his company representative, to pick me up the next morning. Doug arrived bright and early. I was wearing a long sleeved shirt, jeans and trainers which Doug said would do just fine. He had picked up an extra hard hat for me, so we were ready to go.

Off we went to find the drilling rig.

The drilling rig was located some thirty miles east of Roma. We approached it along a dusty track which the drilling contractor had built to provide access.

I got my first sighting of the tall oil derrick a few hundred yards before we arrived. It was a steel lattice construction with big pulley wheels on top and an unusual looking hoist mechanism inside. As we drove on-site, I saw that the derrick was mounted on a sturdy ten-foot tall substructure. Immediately in front of this substructure there was a four-foot wide steel slide, *vee-door*, leading down to a forty-foot long *catwalk*. There were *pipe racks* either side of the catwalk loaded with a couple of hundred lengths of *drill pipe*. To the left of the substructure there were two twenty-foot long steel cabins mounted on top of one another. The floor of the upper cabin was level with the top of the substructure. (This level was known as the *rig floor*.) To the left there was a large rectangular tank. It contained *drilling fluid*, *'mud'*, and was positioned between the rig and a large open pit containing muddy water. Located behind the rig was a bank of three large diesel engines and two big piston pumps. I could hear the sound of these pumps and motors working away, as well as other mechanical noises coming from the rig floor area. Apparently the rig was *drilling ahead*.

The drilling rig with all the equipment round about looked like a huge play-set someone had arranged in the middle of nowhere. It was standing in the centre of a four acre plot which had previously been cleared and levelled. Along the edge of the plot there were three caravans, a large flat-bed truck fitted with a lifting jib and a couple of pick-up trucks. There was also a large reel of cable, various pieces of machinery and many pallets stacked with bags of cement and other material.

Doug took me over to one of the caravans. This was his office. He gave me some general pointers and mentioned a few safety items I needed to be aware of. He then explained what my job as inventory monitor would involve.

After his briefing, Doug took me to meet Barry who appeared to be the man in charge. Barry gave me a quick tour of the rig itself, explained a few more safety issues and then showed me where the drilling fluid, *mud sacks*, were located. They were stacked near the side of the drill site and Barry told me that any discarded drill bits would be dumped nearby. Those were the mud sacks and drill bits I would need to keep track of. Keeping a record these consumables looked like it was going to be a pretty easy task.

As there wasn't any counting for me to do, I spent the rest of my first day chatting and drinking coffee with Doug. Doug was the first of many drilling superintendents

I would meet who loved to chat and constantly drink coffee. By four o'clock he was finished for the day so we headed back to town.

Over the next few days my inventory monitoring took less than half an hour per day. There were usually a few more mud sacks to count and maybe one more drill bit serial number to record, then my work was finished. I spent the rest of my time watching the men on the rig. I found it totally fascinating. I spent hours standing in the *doghouse* just off the rig floor watching what everyone was doing. (Doghouse is the name given to the driller's site-office which connects to the rig floor.) I was trying to understand how everything worked and trying to comprehend the process of drilling, 'constructing', a well in the ground.

By the end of my first day I'd already worked out the hierarchy on the rig. Barry was the *toolpusher*. He was the overall boss and kept an eye on everything. He was at the rig most days and was always there whenever there were problems or difficult jobs, regardless of the time of day. Below him there were three drill crews who each worked an eight-hour shift. The boss of each five-man crew was the *driller*. The driller worked on the rig floor where he operated the main pieces of equipment. His lead hand was the *derrickman* who climbed up to a small platform, called a *monkeyboard*, near the top of the derrick whenever pipe was being *tripped* … lowered into, or removed from the well. On the rig floor, the *motorman* was the driller's main helper. His job was to coordinate his activities with the driller and ensure that the two *roughnecks* working alongside him were also doing what was required.

During every tripping operation, each person operated a particular piece of equipment and the five-man team worked together as a unit.

Doug was the oil company representative and he also came to the rig every day. Like Barry, he would also be there whenever there were difficult or important tasks being undertaken.

Once drilling commenced, different service people showed up to perform specific tasks at various stages of the construction. When they were drilling, a *mud engineer* came to check that the chemistry of the drilling-fluid was correct. The geologists were called, *mud loggers,* and were responsible for collecting the rock cuttings and then analysing these so they could plot the progress of the well through the various rock strata. The *cementers* came with their big pump-trucks to cement casing into the wellbore at various intervals. Once drilling had been completed, the *logging engineers* came with their logging trucks to survey the rock formations. They would determine if any of the rock was porous and establish if gas or liquid was present in this porosity. Should the *mud loggers* or *logging engineers* find traces of hydrocarbons, a *drillstem tester* might be called out to *test* the well and establish the potential for any oil or gas production.

On the rig there were many different pieces of equipment to learn about. They spoke about, *drawworks, elevators, rotary tables, slips, mud pits, stabbing boards, spinning chains* and many other things I'd never heard of. As well as learning what those items were, I also had to learn the meaning of many animal names such as, *doghouse, cathead, catwalk, catline, mousehole, rathole, and monkeyboard*. They had a clever name for everything, and everything had a reason for being where it was and doing what it did. All the bits of kit were designed for a specific purpose and I was very impressed how easily and effectively everything seemed to work.

Watching them working, it all looked like a bunch of big boys getting to play with some very big toys.

I watched for hours and was soaking it up and figuring it out as fast as I could. If I didn't understand what a particular piece of equipment did I would ask Doug or Barry to explain it to me so, pretty soon, I started to have a rough idea how a drilling rig worked.

After my three-week stint, I left Roma, returned to Brisbane, and handed Dad his inventory report. It confirmed that everything was in order and the drilling contractor wasn't robbing him blind. I was also able to tell him that I now knew the career I wanted to pursue. I had fallen in love with life in the oil patch. I wasn't going to university, I was going to get a job working on the rigs.

This wasn't the outcome Dad had expected but, nevertheless, he encouraged me to go ahead. I think he realised if I didn't go to work on a rig, I would probably end up laying beside the pool again and he certainly didn't want that to happen. I immediately applied to the Roma-based drilling contractor, Richter Bawden, and was accepted for work as a roughneck on a drill crew.

The following week I headed back to Roma. (Dad was so pleased to see me go to work he even splashed out for my airfare.) Once I arrived, I checked back into the Commonwealth Hotel and went off to purchase a pair of steel-capped boots, plus more work shirts and a couple more pairs of jeans, then I was ready to go.

The next day, when I showed up at the drilling contractor's depot, I was assigned to work in the yard. Tidying up and moving bits of kit around the depot was not the job I had been hoping for.

I worked there for three days. On the third day a driller came over to introduce himself and arranged to collect me from my hotel at 7.00am the following morning. He said I had been assigned to work as a roughneck on his crew on a drilling rig called a Brewster 55. Perfect! This was exactly the job I was looking for.

The following day, together with the derrickman, motorman and one other roughneck my new driller drove me to the rig. We arrived at 7.45am, in time to start our eight hour shift at 8.00am.

During my very first day on the rig I was throwing *tongs*, as we tripped pipe to change out the drill bit. (Tongs are the large pipe wrenches used to tighten the threaded connection between two lengths of drill pipe. These often feature in photos of roughnecks working on a rig floor.) I then cut open sacks of bentonite to make more drilling mud and finally shifted some drill pipe onto the pipe racks. It was great! During a brief spell when there wasn't something specific to do, I was given a hose and scrubbing brush and told to wash the drill floor and anything else that looked like it could do with a clean.

Apart from the three weeks as an inventory monitor, this was my first real job out of high school. I had never done any hard manual labour before so, when my shift finally finished at 4.00pm, I was completely exhausted. However, in spite of how hard I had worked all day, I had enjoyed it all immensely.

After I got back to town I had one beer, went for a quick bite to eat and then went straight to bed. This time I wasn't troubled by the heat in my room, I didn't hear anyone in the bar or anybody snoring in the room next door. I was out like a light and slept like a baby!

During my next few shifts on the rig I got a lot of stick whenever I made a rookie mistake, however, I was a fast learner and soon became a good roughneck. I got on well with my driller and the rest of the crew and enjoyed the feeling of being one of the team. I really liked being an oilman.

Often when a new roughneck starts work on a rig, they are subjected to an initiation prank. This is usually a harmless task which takes advantage of their total lack of knowledge about the workings of a drilling rig. Possibly because I'd been around for three weeks before joining a drill crew, I missed out on this ritual.

Some of the tasks given to the new boys were actually very clever. I really enjoyed hearing about one task where the new lad had come out best.

His driller asked him to take a tank gauge and measure the depth of the muddy water in the *sump*. (The sump was a large pit constructed next to the rig to store waste mud and water.) The lad was told to lash together two empty oil drums and ride them out to the centre of the sump to get a depth reading. He followed instructions and made his makeshift raft but then, instead of riding the raft, he pushed it away from the edge and floated his hard hat out alongside. He then let out a yell and made a big splash. Before the driller could see what had happened, he quickly hid behind the mud tank. The driller ran to investigate and immediately jumped into the sump thinking his new roughneck had drowned. As he came to the surface the lad stood at the side with a big smile on his face.

One small victory for every new roughneck around the world.

After working on the rig for six weeks I felt like a seasoned hand. I could do pretty much everything a roughneck needed to do without too much instruction or supervision. One day, when my driller picked me up for work, the motorman wasn't there so we headed off without him. Apparently he'd been out drinking the night before and hadn't managed to show up in time for the crew change. On the way to the rig, my driller informed me that I was now promoted to be the new motorman.

I didn't think I was ready for a promotion and certainly wasn't expecting one. I liked my motorman and was sure he would want his job back once he had sobered up. Today, however, I would be the motorman. I knew what the motorman did so that helped. He was the lead hand on the rig floor who 'threw' the *spinning chain*. Occasionally he also pulled the dipstick on each of the motors to confirm that there was enough oil in all the engines … hence his job title.

The spinning chain is a small-link steel chain and was probably the most lethal tool ever invented by the drilling industry. It is singularly responsible for the loss of more fingers than possibly any other piece of equipment in any industry. Forty years ago, you would be hard-pressed to find a rig hand who'd worked as a motorman with a complete set of ten digits.

The motorman holds one end of the spinning chain and throws it in such a manner that it wraps itself around the drill pipe. The other end of the chain is attached to a winch which the driller activates very carefully. Pulling on the chain spins the drill pipe so that the pin-connection threads into the box-connection of the pipe already in the well, held in *slips* in the *rotary table*. These threaded connections are known as *tool joints*. As the pipe spins, the motorman places his hands over the chain to keep it from whipping out of control, all the while trying to make sure that his finger didn't get caught under the chain and that the loose end didn't wrap around his hand or fly out and hit one of the roughnecks. It was a very dangerous, but quick and effective, way to thread together two lengths of pipe.

Once engaged, the tool joint would be firmly tightened using the two powerful tongs handled by the two roughnecks. This would be done, one ninety-foot long *stand* of drill pipe at a time, until all the pipe had been joined together and run into the well.

I was anxious about how I would handle the spinning chain for the first time and I suspect the roughneck was pretty nervous as well. Fortunately for both me and him, I never got to give it a throw. As it happened, I was only a motorman for one day and they didn't need to *trip the pipe* during my shift. I did, however, pull the dipstick on each motor a few times just to show my driller I was handling my new job okay.

I must have impressed my driller because the day after my promotion to motorman I got another promotion. This time the derrickman called in sick so I was now the new derrickman. That day the previous motorman did show up again and managed to get his job back but I got the promotion to derrickman instead of him.

When we arrived at the rig in time for our 8.00 am shift I was told by my driller that we were just about to start 'running' surface casing.

As the newly promoted derrickman, I was instructed to climb part-way up the derrick, put on the safety belt, and secure a narrow wooden platform to stand on. While standing on this *stabbing board* I would push out the top end of a forty-foot length of casing so that the bottom end hung squarely above the previous length already in the well. Once these two lengths were joined together they would be lowered into the well and the next piece of casing would be hoisted up and connected. This action was to be repeated until five hundred feet of casing was securely joined together and all in place.

The driller's explanation of what I was to do once I got up the derrick proved to be a waste of time. I climbed the ladder running up the side of the derrick, grabbed the safety belt, passed out, and fell thirty feet back down onto the drill floor.

Unbeknown to me at the time, I suffer from what I call 'blood-rush'. If I stand up suddenly after working in a crouched position I often feel faint or light-headed. That day it was already 90 °F by 8.00 am and my dash up the ladder had done the trick. I had reached for the safety belt but never got to put it on before passing out and falling out of the derrick.

My career as a derrickman came to an abrupt end at 8.15 am. A short but adventurous fifteen minute career.

Fortunately, this was not the day I was meant to die. Had I landed directly on the rig-floor or hit a protruding edge of the *draw works* or *rotary table*, I would almost certainly have broken many bones and my head would have smashed onto the steel deck. This didn't happen.

In my unconscious state I fell like a sack of potatoes and my head collided with the rim of a large, soft-metal, bucket full of special dark brown grease used to lubricate the tool joints. This grease is known as 'dope' and the bucket is therefore the 'dope bucket'. I had landed in the dope bucket!

My knee also hit the *drawworks* brake handle. This brake handle acted a bit like a shock absorber. With my contact it moved down to take some of the velocity out of my fall.

The fall knocked me out so I was unconscious and it appeared likely that I had been seriously injured. The crew slid me off the rig floor onto the doghouse floor and, once an ambulance had been called from Roma, they carried on running the casing. Meanwhile, I was left lying in the doghouse.

'Lost-time accidents' are a big 'no-no' for drilling contractors as they could face financial penalties or the loss of safety bonus payments so, after my fall, they simply promoted the motorman to derrickman and carried on running the casing. No lost-time was recorded.

The location of the rig was a forty-five minute drive from Roma, near a small town called Wallumbilla. (I always remember the name of this town as it very nearly came to be carved on my tombstone.) By the time the ambulance arrived I had been unconscious for nearly three hours. When they brought me around my very first thought was, "If they find me lying on this floor I'll get fired". Then I tried to move and realised I couldn't.

The first voices I heard were the two ambulance men. They were having a good chuckle. One said to the other that it looked like my head had cracked open and appeared to be full of shit instead of brains! Reference no doubt to the brown-coloured dope still covering my face and head. Nice one fellows, just what I wanted to be the first thing to hear.

I was loaded into the ambulance and taken to hospital. A few hours later, once it had been confirmed by the doctors that I didn't have a serious injury, the drilling contractor was informed and made a note of my accident in the evening drilling report. I had fallen into a bucket and broken my nose. End of story.

After two days in hospital the swelling and bruising had eased enough for me to hobble over to a phone and call home.

As my Dad managed the oil company for whom the well was being drilled, I knew he would have seen the drilling report and wondered why he hadn't come to Roma, or at least called me at the hospital, to see how I was getting on. I asked him about this. He on the other hand couldn't understand why I was making such a fuss over just a broken nose. "You will need to toughen up if you're ever going to make it in the oil industry," he said. Apparently no one had mentioned that I was lucky to be alive and had actually broken my nose after falling out of the derrick.

I eventually recovered, and I guess I must have toughened up as I carried on working in the industry for the rest of my career.

CHAPTER 2

The Painful Leak

Unfortunately, the accident was also the end of my working career with the drilling contractor. Given that I could suffer from blood-rush again, they suggested that I probably wasn't suited for a career on the rigs. I had really enjoyed working with the drill crew and was very disappointed to realise that my roughnecking days had come to an end.

In spite of the setback, I was determined to find another job in the industry.

Barry gave me an introduction to a service company and, on the strength of his recommendation, I was offered a job with Byron Jackson Company, known as BJ Service. 'BJ' is one of the many companies which provide specialist services during various stages of a drilling operation. Their particular specialities were, *cementing* casing in the well using high-pressure pumps mounted on the back of large trucks, *coring*, taking core samples with a core barrel assembly, and *testing* the well to look for the presence of oil or gas, using *drillstem testing* equipment.

Once again, it was pretty much 'learn as you go'. Back in the sixties, there was limited pre-job training available so most of the time you learnt the job while working as a trainee. My manager 'Smitty' gave me lots of advice and made sure I understood the dangers of high-pressure work. One piece of advice he gave me was to never hit a flow line with a hammer when the pumps are pumping at high pressure as the pipe might rupture.

The cement pumps were certainly big and could operate at over five thousand pounds per square inch (psi), so it was easy to appreciate that damaging a pipe under extreme pressure could be dangerous. I was going to remember this instruction carefully.

After only two months working as a trainee, BJ got called out from our Roma base to cement a 'string of casing' in a well being drilled near Eromanga, three hundred miles west of Roma. Smitty and I headed out to do the job. I drove the twenty-two-ton twin-pump cement truck and Smitty followed in his pick-up. It was a long drive. The first half of the trip was on single lane pavement and the last one hundred and fifty miles was on dirt roads, ending with a five-mile graded track to the rig site. It took nearly a full day's driving to get there.

The rig site was so remote from any town that the oil company had brought in a camp made up of eight porta-cabins to accommodate the rig crews. This camp provided all the bunks, toilets, showers, galley, and other facilities to support the thirty people on location. The drilling rig itself was much bigger than the one I had fallen off near Wallumbilla and could drill much deeper wells.

The cement job was a big one. Over four hundred, one-hundred-pound bags of cement were to be carried a few yards over to the back of the cement truck. As each person arrived, carrying a bag of cement, they would place it on a *cutting table*. Two people were standing there, one on either side of this table, and they would slide the bag across a protruding blade and dump the cement powder into a hopper. A high-pressure water jet at the bottom of the hopper would then draw in the powder, instantly mixing it into a slurry. The process was continuous, as soon as one bag was emptied another would arrive.

From the hopper, the slurry would be pumped through a sixty-yard, two-inch steel, discharge line running from the back of the cement truck and attached to the *cement head*, (A large manifold for connecting the discharge line to the top of the casing.) fitted on top of the eight-hundred feet of casing in the well.

The object of the cement job was to mix and pump cement slurry down the inside of the casing and back up the annulus between the casing and the wellbore.

When the cement head was being installed I was instructed not to go anywhere near the derrick. (Apparently my reputation for climbing derricks had preceded me.) I stayed on the ground and helped to rig-up a water supply line and the steel discharge line.

Once the job started, every able-bodied man, including the camp cook, came out to help lift and carry the cement bags, one by one, over to the cutting-table. I was given the job of clearing away the empty bags and generally helping to keep things moving.

We were in central Queensland, it was early May, and it was very hot. For the first fifteen to twenty minutes everything was going fine. However, by then the cook was 'gassed', as were a few others. The cooks and camp staff were not used to manual work in 100 °F heat and it showed.

I was doing my best to keep everyone working, but as the pace slowed, Smitty, standing on the control deck at the back of the cement truck saw the need to shift both pumps down into a lower, slower, gear. Smitty did everything with exuberance. He dropped back both throttles, jumped on two clutches, and simultaneously shifted two gear levers.

From a selection of three gear levers, Smitty grabbed a wrong one and shifted one motor out of pump drive, back into road drive. He jumped off both clutches and hit the throttles, causing the truck to suddenly lurch forward. Instantly realising his mistake, he jumped back on one clutch and shifted this lever back into pump drive. He then grabbed the correct gear lever to shift the second pump into a lower gear.

All of this happened in just two or three seconds, but not before Bill, the company rep who stood on the deck beside him, grabbed the handrail and shouted, "Jesus Christ, we're goin' to town!"

I and everyone else, stood back in amazement at this sudden, dramatic, move by the truck. But, as if nothing had happened, Smitty yelled, "Get back to work …. you still have two hundred sacks to go!"

I was concerned that the sudden tug could have disturbed something so I quickly went along to check that the flow line was still okay.

Much to my horror there was evidence of fluid at a *Weco-union*. (A Weco-union is a pipe coupling, manufactured by a company called Weco, which joins together two sections of steel discharge line. It is designed to be hand-threaded and then sealed to withstand 5000 psi or more by belting one of its 'lugs' a few times with a sledgehammer). It was leaking. I stood there looking at the leak remembering Smitty's one important piece of advise, the bit about hitting a line under pressure, trying to figure out what to do.

I quickly grabbed my sledgehammer and tried to get Smitty's attention on the back of the truck. If I could get him to shut down the pumps momentarily, I could give the union a couple of whacks and the line would be pressure-tight again.

Well, I didn't attract Smitty's attention but did get noticed by big Bill. He watched me for a while, then climbed down off the truck and walked thirty yards over to where I was standing looking at the leak.

He looked at me and asked, "What in hell's name are you doing?" I explained that there was a leak at the union and under no circumstances should I hit the line when it was under pressure.

Bill listened to me, then took my sledgehammer and gave the union two of the hardest belts it had ever been struck. I dove to the ground covering my head from the impending explosion.

There was no explosion. The leak had been sealed. Bill walked over, looked down at me, and while holding the sledgehammer handle near its business end announced,

"A man ought to ram this hammer, this far up your butt! There is no pressure on the line, it's practically on a vacuum you dumb-ass."

With that he walked back over to the cement truck.

Pretty harsh words I thought, for just trying to follow one of the key pieces of safety information I'd been given. How was I to know the line wasn't under pressure?

In spite of the little hiccup with the leak, the job went well. By the end we managed to empty all the cement bags and the cement slurry was pumped into the casing and forced up the outside. The drilling mud was displaced from the annulus and cement returns arrived back at surface just as planned. The casing was well and truly cemented in the well.

When the job finished we rigged down the flow line and other equipment, flushed out our pumps, and cleaned the cement dust off everything. The next day, after a good night's sleep, we headed back to Roma. This was the first big cement job I'd experienced and I had really enjoyed being part of it.

Sometime later Bill happened to meet my Dad at an oil get-together in Brisbane. Realising that I was his son, he recounted the story about me and the sledgehammer. They both had a jolly good laugh.

CHAPTER 3

The Mud Mask

On a few occasions we had to go out to a job after a rainstorm or while it was still raining. If we got stuck on a wet road we would have to dig ourselves out, and then, after finally getting to the rig, we would need to rig-up our cement unit on a boggy rig site. Spending hours digging our truck out of the mud or lugging big lumps of iron and hoses around with mud up to your knees, these were the days when we really earned our money.

More often than not however, it was dust, not mud, that we had to contend with. These jobs could also be tough, just for a different reason.

In Australia, when it doesn't rain for a long time it gets dry – very dry. When it's like that, the roads can break up into a talcum-powder-like dust known locally as *bull-dust*. This bull-dust is very fine and plumes up in a cloud behind a vehicle as it drives along. It takes so long to settle that any vehicle following behind would usually stay half a mile back.

On these road conditions the pick-up truck always drove ahead of the cement truck.

A few months after the Eromanga job, Cliff and I were heading out to do a cement job on a rig near Roma. I was driving the cement truck and he was driving ahead of me in his pick-up. As well as providing us with an extra vehicle, the pick-up carried all of the extra tools needed for the job, such as cement heads and casing fittings. Cliff was the cementer for the job and I was his trainee.

On a section of dirt road, Cliff's pick-up was stopped when I drove up behind him. He said that his battery was dead and without electrics his vehicle wouldn't go.

We were only fifteen miles from the rig and needed to carry on as they were awaiting our arrival. We also needed all the tools in the pick-up so we decided to tow it behind the cement truck.

We fixed a tow line, Cliff got back in the pick-up and I drove the cement truck. Within a few miles we were off the main road onto a rough dirt road and then, eventually, onto the graded track the drilling contractor had made. This track was badly broken up so I was driving through nearly a foot of bull-dust for the last three miles.

I knew there must have been a big cloud of dust behind me, but, we needed to get to the rig so there was no point stopping. Anyway, Cliff could not have sounded his horn to attract my attention because his battery was dead.

After thirty minutes we arrived at the rig.

By the time I got out of my cab, Cliff had already leapt out of his pickup and was beating dust off himself. He was covered in red dust from head to foot; hair, arms, legs, shirt, shorts, everything, and his face looked like he was wearing a 'mud mask'!

He was shouting something in my direction to do with my intelligence (stupid), my ability (useless), my mental soundness (crazy), and my parentage. I thought he would have been pleased that I'd managed to get us to the rig on time. However, being pleased didn't appeared to be his first reaction.

"I could have choked in there! I could have died!" he shouted.

Fair enough, as we bumped along through the bull-dust at fifteen miles per hour I hadn't given much thought to the fact that he might be suffocating in a dust cloud. I just focused on getting us to the rig as quickly as possible.

Fortunately for Cliff we always carried water in the cabs of our vehicles so he had been able to soak a rag to cover his face. Using the wet rag enabled him to keep breathing okay but it did leave him with a rather nice mud mask.

After finishing the cement job, the mental image I had of Cliff with his muddy face, and covered in dust from head to toe, kept me chuckling to myself the entire time I spent dusting out the cab of his pick-up with a small brush and an air-hose.

When the job was completed and got back to Roma, we discovered that the pick-up needed a new alternator. Once this was fixed it was ready to go again.

On another occasion we had a different problem with his pick-up.

A few months later we had driven out to a drilling rig with our cement truck and found that the job was delayed. We decided to leave the cement truck and the casing tools on location and then headed back to town for a meal. We had just got on to the main road when suddenly Cliff's pick-up spluttered to a stop. We eventually concluded that the fuel pump must have stopped working as we'd had a fuel pump problem with a similar vehicle once before.

Back then the fuel pumps were mechanical so we thought, 'we can fix this'. I attached a sturdy wire to the fuel pump lever and as I pumped, Cliff tried to start the vehicle. It worked! Cliff had no throttle control but the engine would rev just as fast as I could pump up and down.

Thinking that we could probably make the last twenty miles to town we removed the bonnet and placed it in the back.

I perched myself on the fender with one leg inside the engine compartment and the other one outside. Once I started pumping Cliff started the engine. He put the pick-up in gear and let out the clutch. Off we went, me doing the pumping and him doing the steering.

At first we drove very slowly to make sure everything was okay, then Cliff moved up a couple of gears. As I became more confident I pumped a little faster.

There were generally few vehicles on that road and we only saw one coming in the opposite direction. He slowed right down and gave us the strangest look as we passed by.

Another vehicle came onto the road from a cattle property just ahead of us. He clocked us in his mirror and slowed down to see what we were doing. I started to pump as fast as I could. We passed him doing nearly thirty miles per hour! He gave us a big smile and a shake of the head. I was pumping so fast I nearly lost my balance. I was probably lucky not to fall off!

Those pick-ups really were great little trucks. Out west, running repairs such as these were often an essential part of the job, and important for our survival.

CHAPTER 4

The Long Drive

The longest drive I ever had to a drilling rig was from Roma out to the newly discovered Palm Valley gas field in central Australia. It was one thousand six hundred and fifty miles each way and took nearly four days driving.

Having only been with BJ for nine months, I was still a trainee, so I was driving the cement truck while another cementer, Ben, was following in his pick-up as he normally did when there wasn't any bull-dust to contend with.

Our first overnight stop was in Longreach. On our way there we passed two cattle trains. These are big trucks pulling three trailers fully loaded with live cattle. They were probably heading to an abattoir somewhere.

Over a year, these cattle-train drivers would cover enormous distances. Occasionally, accidents happened when a driver was too tired to concentrate or fell asleep at the wheel. Apart from a few small towns there wasn't much to see, so it must have been hard for them to stay alert and keep their attention on their driving. There had even been a report of one collision involving two trucks where it was assumed both drivers had fallen asleep, hence the new regulations about driving hours which were being strictly enforced.

From Longreach we headed four hundred miles north-west to Mount Isa. There are only three small towns along this stretch of road. After driving for four hours we stopped at a garage/general store in Kynuna. This town consisted of no more than a few houses plus the store. The temperature outside was well over 100 ˚F. Inside, the store contained an array of different items: some groceries, a few racks with clothing and various household items. There were also bags of candy, possibly wine gums or jelly beans hanging on a rack. These were just big multicoloured blobs in the bottom of plastic bags. Everything had melted.

Also, everything, absolutely everything in the store, was covered with a fine layer of dust. Apparently there had been a dust storm through town a month or two before and no one had bothered to clean up. There probably wasn't any point, there would no doubt be another dust storm coming sometime soon. The store wasn't air conditioned and it certainly wasn't dust proof. How they could live like that I don't know.

After driving for another four hours we arrived in Mount Isa. At the time this was one of the biggest mining towns in Australia. Everything in town appeared to have been recently built. There were numerous hotels, staff housing facilities and warehouses with big yards full of mining supply and support equipment.

We stayed the night at a Mount Isa motel.

The next day we continued heading north-east. For most of the way the main road beyond Mount Isa was even more bleak than the Kynuna stretch. However, one or two bits were actually quite interesting. Heading towards Camooweal, we passed the biggest termite mounds I had ever seen. Some of these were up to ten feet tall and ten feet in diameter. They stretched across the outback in every direction, often only twenty or thirty paces away from one another with nothing but a few shrubs or the occasional tree in between. I can't imagine how many termites lived in each mound, but when you consider that the nest extends underground for some distance as well, there must have been millions of them. As I drove past, I wondered what they did with themselves all day and how they managed to survive in such a barren place. They must have lived on something.

In Camooweal itself, the few houses I saw were all covered, walls, windows, fences and everything else, with some kind of flying insect. These were less than an inch long and looked like a cross between a moth and a beetle. They weren't harmful but there were an awful lot of them. Australia often has plagues of: insects, locusts, mice, frogs, and many other bugs and reptiles. This was probably just another localised plague.

On the road from Camooweal to Tennant Creek in the Northern Territory there is a long stretch of nothing.

Along that stretch of road it was so hot in my truck cab that my eyes kept getting dry and it was hard to keep them open. Fortunately I was carrying water in the cab so, every few minutes, I could wet my face with a cloth to apply some moisture.

A little further along we passed an area called the Devil's Marbles. These are huge, rounded, granite boulders, which appear to be balanced on top of one another. Some of the big ones are fifteen feet in diameter. They had been shaped that way by millions of years of erosion. They are very unusual and were quite amazing to see.

We spent the third night in Alice Springs. 'The Alice' as it is known, sits pretty much in the centre of Australia. It is a unique and interesting town, populated by an eclectic mix of locals, Aboriginals, tourists, and truck drivers.

After our night in town we drove due west for the last eighty miles to Palm Valley. The purpose of our trip was to cement production casing in a successful gas well. Unfortunately, on this occasion, the well hadn't encountered any gas-bearing formation so no casing was required. The job we ended up doing was to *plug and abandon* the well.

Completing this work only took half a day. After we finished the job we rigged down our equipment, loaded everything back on the truck and headed home.

The trip back to Roma was just as far but took even longer. On the last leg from Augathella to Morven, we chose to take the direct route along a dirt road as opposed to the longer route on the paved road via Charleville. Halfway along, I discovered that a recent rain storm had turned a mile or two of road into a bog. Three trucks had already tried to get through and failed. Each of them was stuck at a different point along the road. I had a go and made it a little further than the others but then I got stuck as well.

Ben managed to make it all the way through in his pickup. As it was late at night and he was only one hundred and twenty miles from Roma, we had agreed that, should he get through, he would carry on driving home and come back to help me get out the next morning.

A little while after Ben left, a farmer from a nearby cattle station was coming home after a night on the tiles in the Augathella pub. He was in his pick-up and also managed to drive through the muddy bits. As he drove past me he called out to say he would come back and pull me out.

I assumed that I would never see him again.

I was really tired after the long day's drive so I made myself as comfortable as possible in my cab and fell into a deep sleep.

Sometime later I awoke when my truck was given a jerk and started to move. I had been sleeping so soundly I hadn't even heard the farmer return in his big tractor. By the time I sat up he had already attached a tow line to the front of my truck and we were off! Quickly I grabbed the wheel and started the engine. Half a mile later I was back on dry road.

The farmer disconnected the tow line and came over to my cab. "That will be ten dollars for your tow please," he said.

I would happily have given him that and more, but I didn't have any money whatsoever. Ben carried most of the money for our expenses on the trip and what money I had I'd used for my last meal. I was expecting to be back in Roma that night, so I hadn't bothered to ask Ben for any more cash.

No ten dollars to give the farmer meant he wasn't happy. He thought I was withholding his payment. He was still a bit tipsy from his night in the pub so he climbed up into my cab to look for his money.

Once I convinced him that I didn't have any cash he settled down. He wrote down his address and asked me to send the money the next day.

When I got back to Roma in the early hours of the morning I called Ben to let him know that I'd made it home okay, then, first thing in the morning, I took ten dollars, plus a carefully wrapped bottle of Bacardi, to the post office and sent it to the farmer.

I do hope my helpful friend received the money and the gift okay. I had certainly been most grateful for his assistance.

CHAPTER 5

The Two Fires

On one of my occasional trips back to Brisbane to see my parents, I asked Dad to explain how the oil industry worked. I found his explanation most helpful. In Australia, all the underground natural resources are owned by the Australian government. Oil companies could apply for a petroleum exploration permit to undertake geological studies and conduct seismic surveys. If they identified potential oil or gas prospects and wanted to explore these further, they then had to apply to the government for permission to drill a well. Typically, the drill lease they were granted covered the entire surface area above the subterranean structure they were interested in. Once permission to drill was received, the oil company would contract a drilling company to drill a well at some prime location on this drill lease.

After engaging a drilling contractor, the oil company would also select the various speciality service providers: mud engineers, mud loggers, and cementers, and also choose some of the drilling consumables such as the drill bits. This is much the same as engaging a building contractor to build a house where the contractor brings the skilled workers and all the tools to do the job while the client selects the kitchen and bathroom fittings plus other bespoke items.

Finally, if the well was successful and became a producer, the oil company would apply for a petroleum production licence and the government would take a share of the profit. Sounds simple, however, the odds are that only one well in five will be successful so it was always a big gamble.

Shortly after my trip to Alice Springs, I was once again the trainee on a drillstem testing job helping Jon, one of BJ's *testers* to test a well which had been drilled for the company my Dad was managing. The well was being drilled thirty miles to the north-east of Roma.

The well was, nearly, a 'discovery' well. The sandstone formation which had been penetrated with the drill bit contained a small reservoir of oil. During the twelve-hour flow period it produced around forty barrels of very light, almost clear liquid, known as *condensate*. This oil was collected in a big open-top tank located at the end of a flow line, some fifty yards away from the rig itself. During the test, the flow of oil decreased from a strong flow down to a trickle. This meant that the well didn't flow enough oil to be commercially viable and therefore wasn't classed as a new discovery.

Doug, who was Dad's company rep on the job, had befriended the owner of the cattle property on whose land the well was being drilled. During the testing operation, the farmer had come over to see what was happening.

The farmer asked Doug, "Does this stuff actually burn?"

What happened next became the most important piece of oilfield education I would ever have. Never, ever, allow anyone with an open flame anywhere within one hundred yards of an oil rig … particularly when there is a test in progress.

Doug took a stick, dipped it into the tank, then walked thirty yards away from the tank and lit the stick with his lighter. As well as the condensate on his stick, the air and ground all around the tank was ripe with gas and oil vapour. Immediately the flame leapt from his stick onto the ground. The light blue flames then quickly spread, heading towards the tank.

Within seconds a big circle of flames were dancing on the ground surrounding the tank when, suddenly, the oil in the tank ignited with a huge whoosh!

By then Doug, the farmer and everyone else was running as fast as they could away from the fire. I was on the rig floor and, along with the drill crew, leapt down to the ground and ran off towards the scrub.

After twenty or thirty seconds the flames on the ground died off and the fire continued burning in the open tank.

After the first dramatic ignition, the oil in the tank burnt quietly, a bit like a flame you would get on a gas stove, only ten foot high and ten foot in diameter! The blue flame actually looked quite beautiful as it illuminated the night sky.

With the exception of the company geologist, Harold, who had been taking an oil sample from the tank at the time, everyone else escaped the flames. Harold was severely burnt on his hands and face.

Doug loaded Harold into his car and raced off to Roma Hospital.

When we all finally got back to work and recovered our tools and instruments from the well, the pressure charts confirmed that there wasn't any big reservoir of oil. All the oil this well would ever produce had been recovered during the twelve-hour test.

The fire burned for three more hours, after which the tank was empty.

As expected, a few days later Doug was summoned back to head office to file his report. He didn't survive the inquisition, left his job and left the oil industry.

For sure, Doug would have known the hazard of having an open flame around a rig, particularly during a test. I can only assume this is a classic example of someone having a total brain-block. After thirty years working in the industry, this one careless mental lapse cost him his career.

Harold survived. His condition was stabilised in Roma and then, a few days later, he was transferred to a hospital in Brisbane. Years after the event and many skin grafts later, evidence of that night and the fire damage would still be painfully obvious.

To this day, whenever I think back to that night, I can still visualise the scene in vivid detail.

A year or two later when I was qualified as a tester myself, I had another fire experience on a well in South Australia.

When drilling this well, an oil-bearing formation was encountered at a depth of around eight-thousand-five hundred feet. The company rep was hopeful oil would be found and had given instructions that as soon as there was a *drilling break* (a sudden increase in the penetration rate experienced when the drill bit penetrates a softer rock formation), they were to stop drilling and 'circulate up' the rock cuttings.

This duly happened. Once the mud logger examined these rock samples, he confirmed that they were saturated with oil.

The drill bit was tripped from the well and replaced with a core barrel fitted with a purpose built *core bit*, (a drill bit with with a hole through the centre). A ten foot section was then cored. After the core barrel, plus the core it contained, were tripped from the well, the mud logger examined the core samples and found further evidence of oil saturation.

Next the *drillstem test* tool assembly was made up and tripped into the well to test the section which had just been cored.

Beautiful black oil was produced during this test and flowed into a large open-top tank. By the completion of that twelve-hour testing period around sixty barrels of black oil had been produced. The test tools were then recovered from the well and another ten foot section was cored.

This was followed by a second test.

After completion of the second test, a third core was cut and finally a third test was undertaken.

Shortly after the first test had been completed, when most of the oil was produced, head office had been given the information and the MD decided to announce that the well was a new 'discovery'.

When I recovered the pressure charts from the downhole recorders, I could see that the reservoir pressure had decreased over a flow period of just six hours. I showed the charts to the company rep and he could also see that the pressure was declining. This meant that it may be an oil well, but it certainly wasn't going to be a big one.

During the second flow period the reservoir pressure declined even further.

Anyway, back in Adelaide, the MD of the oil company made arrangements for a little promotional event with the Premier of South Australia, Mr Don Dunstan. Together with Mr Dunstan, the MD and a press team were coming out to the rig for a photoshoot.

By the time the third test was completed, the flow of oil had nearly stopped. This well was definitely never going to become an oil producer, however, one must not let reality get in the way of a publicity opportunity!

I discussed the test results with the company rep and he was not happy. "What are we going to do? We have people flying in tomorrow for a photoshoot and press release. What can we show them if we can't show them any oil flowing into the tank?" he moaned.

He had already decided that the test-tools should be left in the well so we could try to show Mr Dunstan a flow of oil while he was at the rig.

"If we leave everything shut-in overnight, surely the pressure would build up enough so we could release a surge of oil into the tank?" he suggested. Then added, "We could even let Mr Dunstan crack open the valve … and, we could also set the tank alight so there would be a big cloud of black smoke for him to see when he flies in."

So that was the plan. Just before the plane was due to arrive, the rep lit a torch and, from twenty feet away, tossed it into the tank. As the well had produced heavy black oil, this time there wasn't any problem with associated gas or condensate. The tank caught alight and immediately sent up a big cloud of black smoke. There was no fire on the ground and no risk of any injury.

One hour later as his plane circled the rig, it must have been quite a sight for Mr Dunstan to see.

After landing on a nearby airstrip, he and his party were driven over to the drilling rig. He came up to the rig floor and I got him to crack open the valve. Sure enough, there was a surge of oil down the line into the tank. The flame immediately leapt up another thirty feet! Mr Dunstan was amazed.

Ten minutes later, all the photos were taken and the group retired to the camp mess for tea and sandwiches. (I had stood proudly beside Mr Dunstan for a photo which made the front page of an Adelaide paper the following day.)

Later, as the party flew back to Adelaide, there was still a plume of black smoke coming from the tank. It burned for four more hours and then died out. The entire production of another well had been consumed by fire in less than half a day.

I was the only service engineer on this job, just myself without a helper or trainee, providing all the coring and drillstem testing services. After each coring and testing operation it took me several hours to place rock cores in properly labelled boxes, read the pressure charts, service all the equipment and make out the job reports.

When the test tools were finally removed from the well and my work was all done I got into my bunk and thought, "I will sleep forever", I was so tired! I hadn't managed to get out of my coveralls for five days and hadn't had any more than ten hours' sleep. I had only managed to catch a few hours here and there when they were tripping my tools either in to or out of the well.

I was exhausted.

It felt like an hour before I actually got to sleep but was probably only a matter of minutes. Six hours later I was wide awake. I couldn't sleep anymore so I got up and finished making out my job reports and invoices.

The next night I went to bed early and slept for twelve hours straight.

In Australia, those two wells turned out to be the only ones I was ever involved with which produced oil. Plenty of gas wells, but no more oil wells. Unfortunately there wasn't a single barrel of oil remaining from either well.

Two oil wells and not one cent of income, but I guess we did have two pretty spectacular fires to show for my efforts.

CHAPTER 6

The Flying Pig

After two years with BJ I was no longer a trainee. I was a qualified 'service engineer' and could carry out cementing, drillstem testing and coring jobs on my own. I liked testing jobs the most as they were generally more exciting than cement jobs and coring jobs. Coring was pretty straight forward, while cementing was repetitive with the main variable being the amount of cement to be mixed and pumped. Testing jobs were never predictable, whenever I went out to test a well I never knew what to expect. The well could produce oil, gas, water, a combination of these, or nothing at all.

Not long after I had finished testing the well in South Australia, BJ got called out to test a well in Timor, an island country to the north-west of Darwin, Australia. Smitty decided to send me to do this job. I was delighted to get the assignment as it sounded very interesting. It subsequently proved to be one of the most unusual assignments I have ever been on.

The well was being drilled near the small village of Suai on the south coast of East Timor, the opposite side of the country from Dili, the capital.

After I had flown from Brisbane to Darwin and then from Darwin to Dili on commercial flights, in order to get to the rig site I had to fly in a small *Dove* charter plane. The plane was probably twenty years old at the time and with a pilot and six passengers onboard it didn't seem able to fly very high. In order to get to the other side of the island, the pilot had to pick a route between, rather than over, the mountains separating the north of the Island from the south.

In a straight line the distance was only eighty miles so it wasn't a very long flight. When crossing the two ranges we bounced through various up-draughts and down-draughts eventually getting to the other side some forty minutes later. The pilot then made a bumpy landing on a grass runway. We had arrived.

After being at the rig for four days, no formation worthy of a test had been encountered so I was released from the job. The charter plane was coming that day so I was told I could catch a lift back to Dili on his return flight.

When I boarded the plane I discovered that I was the only human passenger onboard. Two fighting cocks in wicker baskets were carried in the front hold. Some boxes of fruit and vegetables were stacked on two back seats and I got a seat in the front row across from a pig.

She was not like a big European pig. She was only around three feet long, and had all four trotters bound to a pole. The pilot had put some soil protection under her backside and fitted a wicker muzzle over her snout. When I took my seat she had already been strapped into the seat across from me in an upright position. Our heads were at about the same height, roughly three feet away from each other.

Whenever you sit next to a first time flier, understandably, they can be a little nervous so, you try to give some reassurance. There I was looking across into her piggy little eyes offering a comforting smile, hoping she would be okay.

Anyway, it all went well. Once airborne we both relaxed and enjoyed the flight, although Miss Piggy kept grunting and snorting a lot. I assume she was disappointed with the lack of cabin service.

When we landed I spoke with the pilot and expressed surprise about my travelling companion. He was a bit sheepish about the pig. Apparently he hadn't been expecting anyone for his return flight and said he normally only took a pig when there weren't any passengers. The pig would then be laid out on the floor at the back of the plane. With a passenger on board, the pig had to occupy a seat in order to keep the exit clear.

The pig, fighting cocks, and certain fruit and vegetables were all worth a little more money in Dili than in the village, so flying them north was a little earner for him.

I waited at the airport a few hours, and then flew back to Brisbane that evening.

After standing by for a week I got called back to Timor for a second time. On that trip I flew to Dili on the same commercial flights and then down to the rig with the same pilot in the same charter plane. It was another bumpy flight.

This time the company rep decided that there was something worth testing so I had some work to do. During the test I did find traces of oil, but nothing which could be producible so, after the test, I serviced my tools, wrote up my report, and then my job was finished. The well was then *plugged and abandoned*.

Unfortunately, for my trip back to Dili this time, there were other people booked on the charter flight so I had a choice: I could wait two days for the next flight or get a ride to Dili on the back of a Toyota pick-up.

I chose the drive option. Two rattan deckchairs were strapped securely onto the back tray of the pick-up for a rig-hand and me to sit in. We then left the village, together with our driver and his assistant.

Off we went. Within a couple of miles the road became a track and the terrain became very hilly. Up we climbed, first this way then that way, following a track as it headed up towards a pass in the mountain range. From this elevation the scenery was stunning, but mostly we kept our eyes on the track watching out for bumps, rocks and ruts.

The track was so rough and some of the hills so steep it was difficult to stay in our seats so a lot of the time we just stood holding onto the rail at the back of the cab.

On the very steepest hills, the driver's assistant would reel out a winch cable and attach it to a tree, a rock or simply secure the grapple. The driver then engaged the winch, selected the lowest four-wheel drive gear, and slowly crept up the steep incline. Some of these sections were too steep for us to stay onboard. We then had to get off and walk up the hill.

There were three lots of winching to get us over the first range. In the valley between the two ranges we also had the challenge of fording a small river. It was fairly narrow, but fast flowing and just deep enough at one point to have water splashing over the bonnet. That time we stayed onboard and held our luggage on our laps to keep everything dry.

The second mountain seemed easier than the first but was probably much the same. 'Been there, done that' so it just felt less difficult.

After eight hours' driving we arrived in Dili having covered nearly one hundred and twenty miles, half as far again as the distance in a direct line. It was a tough drive but easily the best four-wheel drive experience I've ever had. It was amazing to see what could be done when you had the right vehicle and the right gear.

Back then East Timor was a Portuguese Trust Territory with around six hundred thousand inhabitants. Shortly thereafter, it was annexed from the Portuguese by Indonesia who already controlled the western half of the island. (I guess they figured that it just made sense for them to have the whole Island.)

In 2002 East Timor finally gained independence from Indonesia and became the first new country in the twenty-first century.

Although the well I was involved with didn't find any producible oil, some years later another oil company did discover a big gas field offshore. Since independence, revenue from this field has generated around seventy-five percent of the country's gross national product. It is expected to be depleted by 2020, so there will be difficult times ahead.

I wonder if, with independence the price of livestock throughout the country has now stabilised, or whether the occasional pig or fighting cock still gets airborne?

CHAPTER 7

The Passenger Pilot

There are many stories in the oil industry about oilmen and drink. It seemed to be a common denominator everywhere I went and really was a part of the industry culture.

My taste for beer started on the day I arrived in Roma and the publican first offered me a glass. I never became much of a drinker but I did enjoy a beer with the boys. After working hard in the heat all day I soon discovered that there was nothing better than a cold glass or two of the amber nectar to revive the spirit.

Many oilmen I met enjoyed a lot more than just one or two beers. Some couldn't survive without a regular intake of large quantities plus the occasional all-day binge.

One drinking story involved a mud logger working with another service company. About two months after the Timor job, I was on a well being drilled two hundred miles west of Roma. BJ had the cementing contract and had positioned a cement truck on location for the duration of the well. I had flown out to the rig to cement a string of casing and had been there four days. The mud logger had been there four weeks and was overdue for relief. He finally got word from head office that his relief was coming on the crew change the following morning and, as he wouldn't be needed on-site over the next 24 hours, he could leave that day.

He boarded the twin engine Piper Aztec along with four others and headed to town.

After arriving in Roma around lunchtime he went straight to the pub. Four weeks without a drink had been a long time!

His relief was scheduled to fly from Brisbane to Roma that afternoon and would make the crew change the next morning. He didn't get to see his replacement but wasn't bothered, he was busy catching up with his drinking.

Well, as it happens, his replacement fell ill and hadn't made the flight from Brisbane so he wasn't in Roma to make the crew change flight the next morning.

The boss had no choice but to send the first chap back to the rig.

First he had to find him. He called the one and only cabbie who offered a taxi service in Roma and offered him one hundred dollars if he could find his man and get him on the next flight back to the rig.

After checking out a few pubs (Roma had around a dozen), the cabbie found his man, well the worse for wear, asleep in a chair at the School of Arts Hotel. After checking with reception, he found that his man was also booked to spend the night there. He helped the drunken mud logger upstairs and dropped him on his bed.

Early the next morning he went back to collect him from his room. He took him downstairs and drove him to the airport, making sure he boarded the flight his relief was supposed to have been on.

Apparently the mud logger slept most of the way back and, once he arrived at the camp, immediately went to his bunk to sleep it off.

Sometime after lunch he appeared in the mess room. We all acted as if he'd never left. No one asked him about his night in town or anything and, when he mentioned it, we just pretended he hadn't been away. He, on the other hand, kept asking what had happened. How had he ended up back at the rig? He was certain he'd left the day before and was supposed to be flying to Brisbane that afternoon.

He remained confused until his boss eventually called to apologise for sending him back to work. His relief man was recovering and would definitely be on the flight in three days' time.

A few days later, when I left to come home, I got onboard the same Aztec plane. On that occasion the pilot found that he could only get one of the engines to start so, with one propeller going full tilt, he raced up and down the runway trying to jump-start the second engine. Eventually it started and we all flew back to Roma without any problem. The starter failure hadn't worried the pilot unduly as it had happened a time or two before. It didn't affect the flight but it certainly didn't do much for the confidence of the passengers.

On one other occasion when I was flying west, there

were just the two of us on-board, myself and the pilot. I fell asleep, as did the pilot who was supposed to be flying the plane. I'm not sure how long we slept but we awoke when the plane hit a sudden bump. Apparently we'd flown through a small thermal.

We spent the next ten minutes looking for the glint of a tin roof. Out west many properties have their station name painted on the roof of their house or steading so, once we found a property, we could work out where we were and the pilot could plot a new flight path from there. That's how it was done before the days of satellite navigation.

One other thing some pilots occasionally did, which they probably wouldn't do today, was to get a passenger to fly the plane. "Just keep it on this heading and at this altitude and she'll be right," they would say and then have a twenty minute kip.

With the sun shining through the cockpit windscreen it was really hard for the pilot, or a passenger flying the plane, to stay awake.

I don't think there were ever any accidents attributed to the use of passenger-pilots, but I'm sure it didn't comply with any best-practice flying procedures.

A year later, when I was working on the Glomar Conception drillship, I even got to fly a helicopter once. This wasn't so that the pilot could have a sleep, he just thought I might enjoy giving it a try. He told me what to do and handed over the controls.

It was really very difficult. I managed to keep us on course without losing too much altitude for about one minute. The pilot then took back control and flew us safely the rest of the way from the rig to the coast.

From my very limited experience, flying a helicopter is a lot trickier than flying fixed-wing. For sure, no one would ever fall asleep flying one of them.

CHAPTER 8

The Curious Kangaroo

The average rig hand was male, young, and virile. They worked hard and they played hard. When they weren't working on the rig they were always looking for the next party. In Roma, apart from these occasional weekend parties, there just wasn't an awful lot for a young bachelor to do.

One Saturday night, a house party in town made it all the way out to the rig. A 'girlfriend' who was 'a bit of a goer', didn't want the party to stop so she rode the crew car out to the drilling rig with the rest of the *graveyard* crew for the midnight to 8:00 am shift.

When they arrived at the rig, the girlfriend was secreted into the camp caravan. As the rig was *drilling ahead*, there wasn't a lot of work for the crew to do other than to add one more length of drill pipe every twenty or thirty minutes so, from time to time, each crew member came over to the caravan where she would keep him entertained.

Typically the night shift is long and boring, the least enjoyable of the three shifts. On that occasion however,

I suspect the crew might even have been disappointed when it came to an end. The toolpusher wasn't around but, had he been aware that the boys had a girl on the rig, they would have all been in trouble. At 8:00am when the day-shift crew arrived, the graveyard boys managed to smuggle the girlfriend back into the crew car and everyone went home happy.

For me, life in Roma wasn't quite so adventurous. There was the movie theatre where they screened a new movie twice a week and there were a lot of pubs where I could have a beer with friends after work. Other than that there was the Roma Squash Court and the Roma Golf Club. I was a member of both clubs. I didn't like sitting on a bar stool for hours on end, so mostly I would have dinner with one of my workmates then go to the cinema, play squash or just stay at home and read some training books.

In Roma the big day at the pubs was Saturday afternoons. Australians love betting on horse races and on Saturday all the races from across Australia were broadcast live on TV and radio. The punters would place their bets at the nearest TAB betting shop and then sit in the pub drinking endless glasses of beer while checking their results.

In order to keep everyone at the pub as long as possible, many publicans held a raffle late on in the afternoon. The prizes were usually a couple of steaks, a tray of sausages, or a cooked chicken.

It was therefore not uncommon between six and seven on a Saturday evening to see a 'bloke' weaving down the road with a greasy chicken or a string of sausages stuck under his arm.

I can just imagine how pleased his wife would be to see her man come staggering in with his greasy 'chook'. He would be expecting nothing less than a hero's welcome … after all, he had won the raffle, and, brought home the dinner!

When I first arrived in Roma I managed to rent a flat for myself. It wasn't a very large flat and it wasn't very pleasant so, after nine months, when I got an opportunity to rent a house, I did so immediately. This was my first ever house rental. Although I was living there by myself, I really enjoyed having my own home. It was an old 'Queenslander' style house, one-storey, built on short two-foot high stumps, with a veranda running along the front and down one side. There was a lounge and kitchen/dining area, plus two bedrooms and a bathroom all coming off the lounge area. There were lots of windows facing the veranda plus a set of French doors leading onto the veranda itself. It was all designed to catch any breeze that might be available. The windows and the French doors were often left open and were rarely locked.

One night I awoke to become aware of someone standing at my bedroom door. There was enough moonlight to see his outline and I could hear his breathing. I pinched myself to make sure I was actually awake. I was definitely awake. This wasn't a dream.

I lay there thinking, "I'm going to die!" (it's worth mentioning that the town of Roma only had two thousand people and is the last place in the world anyone might be concerned about a murder or violent crime). Anyway, as I lay there, I decided that I wasn't going without a fight. I would spring from my bed, charge straight at the intruder and knock him to one side. I would then leap over the sofa, burst through the French doors and run for my life!

That was the plan.

"Its now, or never," I thought. I sprang from my bed and fell flat on my face with the bed sheet tangled around my feet. Quickly I tried to stand but stumbled forward and fell again at the doorway. No stopping now … I was wide awake. I surged forward on my hands and knees past the intruder heading towards the sofa. I crawled up and over the sofa and got as far as the French doors.

Getting that far had only taken ten seconds but felt more like two minutes, and, I hadn't made any contact with my assailant whatsoever.

About then it occurred to me that if this guy wanted to do me harm he would probably have already done so. He'd certainly had plenty of opportunity.

I looked back to see what was happening.

The 'man' hopped away from the bedroom door, hopped around the sofa, through the French doors in front of me and down the veranda. Four or five more hops and he disappeared into the night.

I had been in a blind panic over nothing.

I had seen the neighbour's pet kangaroo about many times before. I guess he was just curious to see what I looked like in my pyjamas and had come by to pay me a visit.

CHAPTER 9

The Deadly Gas

After I'd been with BJ Service for nearly three years, the company secured a long-term contract on a new drillship, the Glomar Conception, which was coming to work in the Gulf of Papua off the northern tip of Queensland in six months' time. Ken, the regional manager in Brisbane, told me he intended to assign me to this job and said that I had six months to become fully trained to perform all the services BJ had been contracted to provide.

I was already reasonably qualified and Ken felt that I had enough cementing experience for the work I would need to do on the drillship, however, in spite of testing two oil wells and a bunch of gas wells, there was a lot I still didn't know about *testing*.

Ken decided that I should go overseas to broaden my testing knowledge. I was to travel to Canada where the first part of my training would take place in northern Alberta during the Canadian winter. I also needed to learn how to operate some casing tools so, after I finished in Canada, I would travel to California to learn about those.

A number of years after my family moved to Canada from Holland, we eventually moved from Nova Scotia to Calgary when I was ten years old. We lived there for six years. In Calgary, as a schoolboy, I played a lot of ice hockey and had a paper round, so I knew what it was like to be outside in the cold. The thought of working on the rigs for hours at a time, sometimes in temperatures as much as 30 °F – 40 °F below zero, would however, be a different matter altogether. Still, I was very excited about going back to Canada and was sure I would manage. I thought the cold weather would just add another exciting dimension to the experience.

When I left Australia in October 1968, I was twenty-three years old. I arrived in Edmonton just as the winter drilling season was getting underway. In northern Alberta they tended to drill wells over the winter months because the dirt roads are far better to drive on when they are frozen. It was also easier to get staff during the winter as a lot of farmers worked on the rigs when they weren't needed on their farms.

From Edmonton, together with Mel, a qualified tester, I drove five hundred miles north. After ten hours we arrived at a small town called High Level, not far from the border with the Northwest Territories. BJ had a workshop there and were providing services in an area around thirty to forty miles west of High Level called Rainbow Lake and Zama Lake.

When I arrived in, I moved into a trailer home and went to work at the workshop. I spent my time there servicing various bits of kit while I waited to go out on testing jobs with Mel.

The first call-out came after only three days.

Mel and I left High Level early one morning in his test-truck laden with five tons of drillstem test-tools. We drove out to Rainbow Lake and found our drilling rig. Once we arrived, the first thing we had to do was make sure our tools were ready to be assembled.

All the rigs had big boilers and they used steam to melt ice off the drill pipe tool joints and other equipment. Ice on tools joints was not good, as it could prevent them from being made-up properly. If our test tools were not properly tightened they could disconnect downhole and a *fishing job* to recover them was never going to make us very popular with our client.

We stuck a steam hose into the tools on the back of our truck. After thirty minutes any ice had melted and the tools were nice and warm, making them easier to handle.

Testing a well was cold, hard work and there was one additional problem. In some wells hydrogen sulphide, H_2S was present in the gas. H_2S is deadly, very deadly. Normally, gas containing H_2S has a rotten egg smell, however, above a certain concentration the H_2S affects the nerves in your nose. When these nerves become desensitised the H_2S doesn't have any smell whatsoever. We therefore constantly needed to check for H_2S using a detection kit and, should any traces of H_2S be found, anyone on the rig-floor had to put on protective clothing and use breathing apparatus. It made working on the rig floor very slow and cumbersome. Typically a normal task such as tripping pipe would take over twice as long.

In Rainbow Lake, the rig sites were often in the middle of a forest. Although they were generally flat, if there was a hollow and there wasn't any wind to move the gas along, the H_2S would settle on the ground. Because people couldn't see it and often couldn't smell it, they wouldn't know it was there. Also, because H_2S is heavier than air, if some were inadvertently vented from the drill-pipe during or after a test, it would remain on the ground. This could be very dangerous.

I heard one story where the camp dog had run through a low area a few days after a well had been tested and died shortly thereafter from H_2S inhalation. That story certainly made me respect the potential danger I was dealing with. Having seen two fires, I had come to Canada with a lot of respect for the flammability of oil and gas. I now had even more respect for the lethal danger of H_2S. It certainly upped the ante!

After a few jobs as a trainee working alongside Mel and getting a lot of instruction on how to test these dangerous wells, I was given a test-truck and deemed to be ready to go out testing by myself.

The wells I tested were often producers of oil or gas and a few of these did, in fact, have small concentrations of H_2S. Fortunately there were no mishaps. Either I was very lucky, or I had been properly trained. I learnt a lot and with this added experience I thought I was surely ready for any eventuality on my next assignment in three months' time.

Little did I know what danger lay ahead. H_2S wasn't to be a problem, but I would need to do some more climbing....

CHAPTER 10

The Lonely Wife

While working in northern Alberta I lived in a trailer-home just outside High Level. This was very different from my 'Queenslander' back in Roma. It certainly wasn't as big and, instead of looking to catch the breeze, everything possible had been done to keep the heat in and the cold out. All winter long there was at least two feet of snow around the trailer and a big snowbank along both sides of the road where the snowplough had cleared the road.

When I moved into my trailer home I was given two important instructions. The first was to take a lot of care when using the gas appliances and not use the gas cooker to supplement the central heating, and the second was to only put rubbish into one of the bear-proof bins placed around the park.

Apparently there were a few bears hibernating in the forest nearby. Although I didn't see any around, one night I did wake up in a bit of a panic after dreaming there was one standing at my bedroom door!

High Level was a real boom town. The town had been built in just a few years to support the nearby drilling activity. There was only one hotel which had a big lounge bar. Other than that, there wasn't anywhere to go. No cinema, no clubs and just a couple of cafes plus a garage.

There were thirty or forty rigs working in the Rainbow and Zama lake areas, so all the service companies had staff living in High Level. It was a busy oil patch and once or twice a week I would get a call to go out to test another well.

As there wasn't a lot to do in town, it was just as well that I was kept so busy.

During the week, the hotel was a good place to go for a beer with colleagues and on Saturday night it was the place to be. Saturday night was different from other nights. Saturday night was fight night!

There was an Indian reservation near High Level and Saturday was the day after the Indians received their wages or social security cheques. They were ready to have some fun and, for them, this usually involved having a few beers and a good fight!

The fight took place inside the hotel bar. Everyone expected it to happen and the whole thing was sort of pre-planned. The bar staff cleared away all but a few of the tables and spectators, those wanting to watch and not wanting to fight, came in early and stood along the wall.

Those not too bothered about having a fight, or actively wanting to fight, occupied the chairs around the tables. These groups were usually made up of a locals and a few oil workers.

Nothing much would happen until eight or nine o'clock. The Indians were somewhere drinking beer and the 'cowboys' were inside enjoying their beers. Then, all of a sudden, a few Indians would storm into the lounge. They would head for the nearest table and each grab a cowboy. Once they pulled their man off his chair and wrestled him to the floor, the fight had begun.

There were no rules, mostly just wrestling with a few punches thrown in for good measure … nothing very violent. If more than one Indian was beating on the same cowboy or if someone was losing badly, after first handing their beer glass to a spectator, other cowboys would join in the fray. It was pretty much just a brawl with more cowboys than Indians.

The first Saturday night I was there, one lone, fully charged Indian came storming into the lounge. He pulled the nearest guy from his chair, looked around and realised he was on his own. He jumped back and shouted, "Back-off, I'm off to get more Indians!", then raced out the door.

Twenty minutes later he was back with three more from his tribe. All hell broke loose for around five minutes. Four Indians and the same number of cowboys were all on the floor taking hits off one another. Finally one Indian called a retreat and 'whooping and hollering' they fled from the room.

There was a lot of cheering and lively discussion about what had just happened. The chairs and tables were then put back in place and everyone went back to drinking beer. The Saturday night fight was over for another week.

By the end, there were usually one or two black eyes and maybe a broken lip but, everyone seemed to have enjoyed themselves immensely. It looked a lot too painful for my idea of fun, but for entertainment in High Level that was pretty much as good as it got.

One other occasional source of entertainment was the two-way radio. These were fitted in most vehicles up north and provided a means of making contact in the event of an emergency.

Mostly, however, the two-ways were used to make calls back home, usually to a wife or girlfriend. The interesting thing about these radio calls was that you could only hear one side of the conversation. The side of the person being called … the wife or girlfriend. You couldn't hear what the caller was saying.

I often had my two-way on and enjoyed listening to one or two of these exchanges.

While driving out to a drilling rig one day, I particularly enjoyed one conversation I happened to hear. Listening to what the lady on the other end was saying, I worked out the gist of the story. Her husband had been away for over a month and was calling to say that, yet again, he would not be coming home that week. She was very annoyed and started to give him a piece of her mind. There was a long silence. I assumed he was trying to calm her down and reminding her that everyone in northern Alberta could hear what she was saying.

Once he finished talking, the long silence was finally broken when she came back on the line. She said, "Well this is how it is. My address is: 604 16th avenue SW Calgary. Sex starts here at 9:00pm this Friday night. If you're not here, you won't be getting any." With that she hung up.

I do hope he managed to get there for 9.00pm that Friday, or at least in time to join the queue!

CHAPTER II

The Bear Necessity

Whenever I was driving in the wilderness on my own at night, it was a frightening experience. The winters in northern Alberta are extremely cold and I was always aware that I could be at risk of freezing to death if my truck stalled or I got stuck outside.

Finding my way to a particular rig location was never easy. Each time I was called out to test a well it was always at a different rig from any previous job. To get to where the rigs were I drove along the main road for twenty miles and then turned off towards the oil fields. Along this newly constructed road I would eventually come to an intersection where there might be as many as five signs displaying drilling contractors' logos and rig numbers. If the rig I was looking for wasn't on one of these signs I would drive on further until I found a sign directing me to my rig. At that intersection, I would turn down a track which the drilling contractor had pushed through the forest.

I had two mishaps. One was a flat tyre which happened at daybreak. Changing a wheel is normally a straightforward exercise, however, it took me well over an hour in the freezing cold before I managed to jack up the truck and change the wheel. I was amazed how much more difficult the job had been made by a foot of snow and the freezing conditions.

On the second occasion I found my rig sign and turned onto a rough track. The track had not been ploughed recently so I was finding it hard to follow any wheel tracks. The condition of the track was so poor that I started to question whether I was even on the right road. Eventually, on a particularly bad bit, I slid off the side and got totally stuck.

It was late at night. Outside It was pitch dark, snowing, and minus 30 °F.

I grabbed my flashlight and went outside to investigate. I found that the bottom of the truck plus the front and back wheel on one side were totally buried. It didn't look good. I took my shovel and started to clear away the snow. After ten minutes my hands and feet were so cold I had to get back into the cab to warm them up before having another go.

I worked on and off for ten minutes at a time, slowly making progress.

While I was outside digging, although I was in the middle of nowhere, I could hear the sound of a drilling rig in the distance (sound travels a long way in extremely cold, still, conditions). The rig I was hearing might easily have been five or more miles away and might not even have been along the track I was on.

I thought about using my two-way to call for help, but I wasn't sure anyone would find me if I wasn't where I thought I was. Another worry was that my truck might stall. The fuel line was fitted with a heat tape and the warmth it provided was the only thing enabling the engine to keep idling. If the diesel stopped flowing the engine would stall and would probably not restart.

I knew it was far too dangerous to leave my truck and set off on foot so I had to keep digging. If I couldn't free the truck, or the engine stalled, I might need to build a fire in order to survive. As I shovelled I thought about this and tried to think how I could possibly find any firewood under the snow. Everything about the situation was very frightening.

After two hours of digging, I tried to move the truck and managed to edge it forward a little and then backward a little. I kept rocking forward and back, gaining a few inches each time. After twenty or thity shunts, I got the truck moving and finally managed to get back on the road. I was a very relieved man.

After driving another couple of miles, I finally came upon a rig. I was never so happy to see a drilling rig in my entire life. It turned out that I had been on the right road and had arrived at my destination.

Apart from the scary driving conditions and H_2S, testing wells in Alberta was different from testing wells in Australia in other ways. In Alberta the government would grant a number of oil companies a permit to drill a well on a lease located on a specific acreage. This acreage could be a square mile or more in size and generally correlated in size and shape to a subterranean formation previously identified using seismic data. The government would set a date to auction off the lease, so all the permit wells had to be completed and all the, geological, test, and logging, data from these wells had to be reported back to them before this auction date. At the auction any oil company could bid for ownership of the entire lease, including all the permit wells.

After all the wells were drilled, the oil companies knew the potential of their wells, as did the government. With information coming in from four or five oil companies and four of five different locations, the government had a pretty good idea of the value of the acreage. Any bidders at the auction would have paid a lot of money to have the same information.

The bidding oil companies were keen to have any information they could get their hands on from any of the permit wells. Some companies even employed 'Oil Scouts' to spy on the drilling rigs, hoping they might observe something of interest.

Oil scouting became a highly paid occupation. Nearing the time the wells were being completed, these guys would camp in the woods near a rig site and try to ascertain what was happening. Obviously they were not allowed on site, so their spying had to be done from a distant vantage point. They could usually determine when drilling was completed and maybe, by seeing the service company vehicles on site, work out what else was happening.

On the other hand, oil companies went to great lengths to conceal their well data. By far the most difficult to conceal was the test data. A gas flare or oil flowing into a tank, could generally be observed. However, the Oil Scout was not just interested to see if there was oil or gas, he would also try to guess the potential production rate.

During a test, the potential production rate could be fudged by restricting or choking the flow. If a well could produce one hundred barrels of oil per day through a very small choke, it could usually produce a lot more through a bigger choke. Having a selection of tanks to flow the oil into would also create some confusion. We could do something similar to fudge the potential gas production.

I was involved with two such permit wells.

As the tester, I was called out well in advance of when I was needed. My tools were removed from the back of the truck and assembled on the catwalk. I then drove my truck to the side of the lease and covered it with a tarp to conceal my company's identity.

Both of the permit wells I tested produced gas, not oil. On both occasions we choked back the gas flow so much that there was only a small gas flame at the end of the flare-line, thereby concealing the potential to produce at a much higher flow rate.

It was cloak and dagger stuff!

As the oil company could not run the risk that I might be tempted to sell my information to an Oil Scout, after each test I was not allowed to leave the rig site until the auction had taken place. After I finished testing the second well this meant spending an extra two weeks on site.

One advantage of spending all this extra time on site was that I became a good gin-rummy player. Gin-rummy was the card game of choice in the oil industry. It involved melding a sequence of three or more cards from the same suit or three or more cards with the same value from different suits. It was always played for money, not necessarily high stakes but if you weren't good enough, over a few days you could easily lose a few hundred dollars. With little else to do, it helped pass the time and became somewhat addictive.

Mostly 'service-hands' like myself would play against the oil company rep. He always had time available and knew it wasn't in the service-hands' best interests to win big. If you won one hundred dollars off him, he would not be happy. The trick was not to lose too much and not to win too much. Fifty dollars one way or the other was a great result. One company rep, Charlie, and I would often play for three or four hours at a time, sometimes as much as six hours in one day.

Charlie was like a lot of company reps in Canada. He drank a lot of coffee, enjoying cards and loved country music. He always had Willie Nelson or some other lonesome cowboy serenading us while we played. After six hours of country music every day, I got to know all the singers and all the songs. I enjoyed them, but did think their songs were all pretty similar.

One day Charlie asked, "Hey Roy, do you know what you get if you play a cowboy song backwards?"

"No Charlie, what do you get when you play a cowboy song backwards?" I replied.

"You get your wife back, you get your dog back, you get your house back … "

Very clever Charlie.

One incident which occurred while I was on that rig was a visit from a bear. In the autumn or early spring there were often bears around the perimeter of the site, mummy bears with cubs or daddy bears on their own. The ones I saw were never aggressive, in fact they seemed to shy away from people. However, the reason they were nearby in the first place was because they could smell food and were keen to get into any food waste or food storage.

Because of the bears, the kitchen staff were always careful about the disposal of food waste. This was stored outside in a steel shipping container. It was usually pretty cold so the waste froze solid, didn't smell and wasn't accessible.

However, there was still a strong cooking smell coming from the camp mess and this attracted some bears to explore closer. They tended to stay away when there were people about during the day, but in the dead of night, they occasionally came right into the camp.

A typical rig camp was made up of two groups of modular units set out in parallel, with a walkway in-between joining them together. On one side there were four or five sleeping units for the staff of around thirty to thirty-five people and on the other side the amenities – kitchen, mess room, and food storage.

Early one morning, I had a 'call of nature' and badly needed to go. As it was very cold outside, I put on my slippers and a duffel coat, then set off to make the twenty-foot dash along to the amenity block.

I never made it.

About five paces away, between my door and the amenity towards which I was headed, a rather large black bear was coming my way! I returned to my sleeping quarter a lot quicker than I'd left, pulling the door firmly closed behind me.

Well, the sudden blast of cold air combined with the shock encounter of the bear made my 'need to go' a whole lot more pressing. I quickly grabbed the nearest container I could find and took care of business there and then.

The next morning I tried to conceal my hard hat as I carried it to the amenity block. I gave it and the cold-weather liner a thorough clean but, in the end, decided the liner had to go.

When I mentioned my bear encounter to the boys I didn't include the bit about my use of the hard hat. Knowing their sense of humour, they would surely have found a way to 'take the piss ...'

After finishing two weeks captivity on the rig site I drove back to High Level. For a bit of added excitement, a large moose jumped out of the woods onto the road right in front of me. It was the size of a horse and gave me an awful fright. I was lucky not to run into it.

The oil patch in Canada was certainly a whole different ball game from the Australian scene. I had left the hot sun and bull-dust in exchange for extreme cold and deep snow, and that moose was certainly a lot bigger than any kangaroo I'd ever seen.

CHAPTER 12

The Ice Bath

Inside, the trailer homes were dry as toast so there was always a fire risk. If a fire started and wasn't caught immediately, a trailer could quickly be engulfed in flames.

This actually happened one cold sunny morning early in March. I heard a fire engine come past my trailer and went outside to see what was happening. I saw that a trailer five or six down from mine was totally on fire.

When the fire engine arrived it was travelling too quickly and nearly skidded straight into the burning trailer. As I arrived, the fire chief was frantically trying to back up his engine and calling for his crew and volunteers to help push it away from the flames.

Eventually the fire engine was moved back to a safe distance. The water hoses were then unrolled and the firemen plus myself and other spectators ran with these towards the nearest fire hydrant some two hundred yards away.

We found the hydrant. It had been hit by a snowplough and was frozen solid. No water would be coming from it any time soon.

The next closest hydrant was three hundred yards in the opposite direction. The lengths of hose all needed to be repositioned. This was being done at speed with two men running along, one on either end of a length of hose. Occasionally the front man would go too far so the back man would suddenly stop, causing the front man to fall on his backside. With other hoses, the front man stopped and the back man kept going. There appeared to be people running with hoses in both directions at the same time. It was chaotic.

In spite of the seriousness of the situation, seeing men running in opposite directions and falling over with their hoses while the trailer continued to burn seemed rather comical. It reminded me of an episode from the *Keystone Cops*!

Finally all the hoses were joined together and connected to the second hydrant. This hydrant had been maintained in a serviceable state so, when it was turned on, a flow of water eventually arrived at the fire engine.

The time lapse between calling the fire department, the fire engine's arrival, pushing it back from the flames, connecting the hoses to a serviceable hydrant and delivering a jet of water, coincided almost exactly with the collapse of the trailer roof onto the steel chassis. Ten minutes later the fire would have gone out of its own accord.

Had the owner been there I don't think he would have been overly impressed with the High Level fire department. The fire chief's mission to save the trailer had not been a success.

A month later, when I moved out, although I hadn't set fire to my trailer, I also left the owner with a little surprise.

In order to make the trailers liveable in the extreme cold, porches, extensions, and skirting were added as well as extra insulation. Electric heat tapes were also wrapped around the water pipes and drains to prevent them from freezing.

One day, after I'd taken a bath, I pulled the plug, but the water didn't drain. The bathroom had never felt as though it was properly heated, but that shouldn't have prevented the bath from draining. I usually took a shower and this was the first time I'd taken a bath so maybe the heat tape around the bath drainpipe had failed or had never been fitted. I was needing to go out on a testing job so I wasn't about to crawl under the trailer to investigate. I just left the water in the bath and headed off to my job.

When I returned a few days later, the water was frozen solid. I had obviously been right about the bathroom not being properly heated. I could still use the shower but for the next month I couldn't take a bath. The bath remained full of melting ice and dirty water until I left … a little something for the landlord to take care of before renting out the trailer to the next tenant.

Before it was time for me to leave High Level, I went out to core and test one final well. In order to cut the core, I needed to bring a core barrel and core bit with me. The core barrel was pulled along behind my test truck on a purpose built 'jockey' trailer which carried the two thirty-foot long sections of barrel. I made it out to the rig okay, cut my core, tested another gas discovery and then headed back to town. I must have driven five miles before coming to an intersection, turning a corner, and being surprised not to see the trailer behind me in my mirror. Sometime after leaving the rig, my trailer hitch must have disconnected leaving my core barrel behind.

I stopped my truck and discovered that the hitch hadn't disconnected, it had broken off completely! I drove back and there it was in the middle of the track about two miles from the rig.

Using the hoist on the back of my truck, I managed to lift up the trailer and then attach a chain to fashion a makeshift hitch. I then set off again, gently towing trailer back to town. The incident reminded me a lot of the running repairs I'd occasionally had make in Australia.

After the coring job, my training in High Level was finished and it was time to leave.

Spring was just around the corner and, although the roads were still frozen solid, they would soon start to thaw. In Alberta this was known as Spring Break Up. As the government was keen to avoid expensive road repairs, most big trucks were banned from public roads during this thawing period. Any vehicles wanting to go south would need to get out of town before the road ban started.

I drove my test-truck back to Edmonton a week later and prepared to travel to California.

Working in northern Alberta through a cold winter had certainly been a different experience from working in the Australian oil patch. I'd had the most amazing time but, in the end, decided I was quite happy to leave the

Canadian oil patch to the Canadians. I much preferred working in warmer climes. At least in Canada I was never troubled with any blood-rush from the heat!

I left behind a lot of great memories of hard work, tough oilmen and even tougher Indians.

CHAPTER 13

The Shark Attack

After leaving Edmonton I flew to Los Angeles where I was given some training on how to assemble and operate the various casing tools I would soon be responsible for. All the training took place in the factory where the tools were manufactured. I got to see how the tools were made and then learnt how to service and assemble them myself. It took a month and I finished in April 1967 by which time I had been away over six months. My training was then finished and I was ready to fly back to Australia to start my next adventure … working on my very first drillship.

Upon my return to Brisbane, I had one week at home with my parents and then flew thirteen hundred miles north to Port Moresby, Papua New Guinea (PNG). This country lies one hundred miles off the northern tip of Queensland only a few degree south of the equator. I had never been to PNG before so it was quite a culture change. It is one of the most primitive countries in the world; the least explored, both culturally and geographically. There was even one tribe the, Korowai, who continued to practice cannibalism well into the twentieth century.

At that time there were around two million inhabitants in the country and over eight hundred different languages spoken by the many different tribes, so the only way many tribes could communicate with their neighbours was in Pidgin English.

The Glomar Conception was probably the biggest drillship in the world at the time. It had sailed all the way from America to Papua New Guinea to drill a number of wells for Phillips Petroleum Company. It was a six-thousand ton vessel, over four hundred feet in length and loaded to the hilt with all the latest technology, including the most modern drilling equipment available. (On the rig floor they even had a fancy new mechanical *pipe spinner* which had replaced the spinning chain!) Compared with the size of the land rigs I had worked on, this drillship was something to behold.

The rig had around sixty people on-board. I was one of the two BJ service engineers assigned to work on the rig. My back-to-back relief was Fred, a Canadian from Edmonton, with whom I was to alternate working offshore two weeks at a time. Most of the work we did was cementing and operating casing tools. However, if the drillers were to find something interesting we might also need to core and test the well.

Since everyone on-board was new to the drillship we were all learning how to work with this new 'toy'. Everyone was finding their way and people were quick to offer help if someone needed assistance. We worked together, bonded and became a little community.

There were a lot of great characters on-board including Sid, one of the *roustabouts*. (A roustabout is employed as a deck-hand to look after the ship itself as opposed to roughnecks, who worked on the drill crew.)

Sid loved working the night shift. As the Gulf of Papua is in the tropics, the night-time temperature was nice and warm making it a pleasant time to be outdoors. Also, night-time workers were requested not to make any noise with hammers or paint chippers as this might disturb people trying to sleep, so Sid would just mop the decks and maybe do a bit of painting to keep himself busy.

Sid also had a passion for fishing and often had a fishing line in the water while he was working. He usually caught one or two fish every night. After he'd caught a red snapper or something equally tasty, he would give it to the cook to be included on the evening menu. Thanks to Sid this was something many of us looked forward to and regularly got to enjoy.

As well as fish to catch, there were also lots of sharks and sea snakes around. The sea snakes were particularly impressive. At night, after midnight, you could always see four or five snakes floating past the rig. Some were six to eight feet long and seemed to float with their heads just above the surface. Although they were poisonous, apparently they weren't deadly, however, they certainly didn't look like something you would want to be in the water with.

As much as Sid loved catching fish, his ambition was to catch a big shark. On five or six occasions he thought he'd caught one, but always failed to hang on to his catch. It seemed like every other day he would be telling us a story about the-one-that-got-away because his line or his hook had failed.

That simply wasn't good enough. He got the welder to make him a 'proper' hook and baited this hook with a 'proper' twenty-pound fish. He then attached his hook to a nylon rope and tied the rope to an anchor bollard. Sid threw the line overboard and went back to work.

Well it wasn't long before he had a shark on his line, and a big one it was too. So big, in fact, that he couldn't do anything with it.

He was determined we should all get to see his catch, so he woke up the crane operator and got him to hoist the fourteen-foot shark out of the water. By lassoing the shark's tail and using an *air tugger*, Sid was then able to pull the shark onto a walkway in an area called the *moon pool*. (The moon pool is a twenty-foot square hole through the hull of the ship above which the derrick is located on the main deck.)

A handrail ran around the moon pool walkway on all four sides. Sid operated the air tugger to pull the shark's tail as the crane operator carefully lowered the shark onto a part of the walkway which ran at right angles to the line of the ship. It was wedged in by the handrail and held there with the tugger line still attached. Sid could now prove to us all that he'd caught his shark.

Unfortunately Sid hadn't taken the night watchman into consideration.

Clive was the night watchman. At night, his job was to walk around the ship every two hours and check that there were no fires, spillages, or other dangerous situations. In order to verify that he'd made this regular inspection he had to turn a key in various clocks strategically located around the ship. The inspection tour took him along the lower deck past the moon pool area.

I don't think a shark attack was one of the dangerous situations Clive had expected to encounter on his inspection tour.

Apparently, as he walked by the moon pool a fourteen-foot shark lurched toward him. At least this is what the night-time superintendent 'Red' Reel understood from Clive's frantic ramblings after he'd scurried back to the safety of the accommodation area.

Red took Clive down to the galley for a coffee to let him compose himself.

Listening to Clive's story, it soon occurred to Red that Sid may have been involved. He left the galley and called Sid on the internal phone. "If there is a shark onboard, it had better not be there when I come down to check out Clive's story." Red suggested.

Sid ran back to get the crane operator out of bed a second time. They hoisted up the shark, undid the tugger line, cut the rope with the hook and released the shark back into the sea.

Upon Clive's return to the site, with Red walking well ahead of him, there was no evidence of any shark to be found.

Sid was probably the most popular man on-board. Red had correctly suspected his involvement and was looking after him. Unfortunately, Clive was never going to win a popularity contest. Red suggested that he may have been under stress and had imagined the shark attack.

Clive began to wonder if he'd been hallucinating.

The stress of the event prompted him to resign. The next day he booked a seat on the helicopter and never returned.

As well as being a first class drilling superintendent, Red was one of the best storytellers I've ever met and could spend hours drinking coffee and recounting his oil patch escapades back in Louisiana. If I was around when he was on duty, I always took the time to have a coffee with him and listen to a few more of his tales.

He was one of the most unusual oil men I have met, and the only man I've ever met to have been married three times … to the same woman!

He certainly wouldn't be the first oilman to have found it difficult to combine life on the rigs with a stable marriage, but three times to the same gal? That takes some doing!

After two failed marriages, he must have told his wife one of his best stories ever to get her to agree to a third attempt.

CHAPTER 14

The Broken Back

The Glomar Conception was the site of my second significant oil-field accident. Once again I fell, but rather than just breaking my nose, this time I managed to break my back.

I was getting ready for a big cement job when I discovered that one of the silos wouldn't discharge cement powder. There were six twenty-five-foot-tall silos located inside a watertight hold on the drillship. Two silos contained dry cement powder and the four others held drilling mud additives; barite and bentonite. I needed to find out why the cement silo wouldn't discharge properly.

As the hold containing the silos was only accessible through a single manhole on the main deck, I went in through this manhole and climbed down the ladder.

To get a silo to deliver cement it needed to be aerated and pressurised to around thirty psi using compressed air. This would enable the powder to be blown out of the silo through a discharge line. The discharge line passed through a bulkhead and fed into a small gravity-feed silo in the cement pump room. Anyway, the discharge line was blocked, so there must have been some moisture in the air from one of the compressors. I set off to sort out the problem.

First, making sure that the silo had been depressurised, I removed a section of discharge pipe. Immediately, I discovered that the cement was not all dry and fluffy as it was meant to be. I poked a bar into the line until some dry powder appeared. I then attached a fitting and blew air through the discharge pipe to clean it out. Having successfully done that, I then changed the fitting onto the silo end and blew air back up into the silo. Everything was now clear and appeared to be working correctly.

After I finally finished reassembling the pipework, I prepared to make my exit from the hold. Being a watertight compartment, it's worth mentioning that the hold had no air conditioning and no ventilation. I had been working for three hours in well over 100 °F, and now had a thirty-foot ladder to climb to get back onto the ship's deck.

I never made it.

Somewhere along the climb my old friend 'blood-rush' kicked in. I fainted and fell off the ladder onto the steel floor, once again like a sack of potatoes. This time there was no handy dope bucket or brake handle nearby to ease the impact.

Being unconscious helped, as I fell in a limp state and missed landing across one of the "I" beams upon which the silos are mounted by only a matter of inches. Fortunately my hardhat stayed on so my head was cushioned from crashing onto the deck.

Although I had been working alone, I had made a roustabout aware that I had finished and was about to come out. Pretty soon he realised that I had fallen and went to get help.

The medic, Reg, was called to attend to me. Even though I was unconscious, he was astute enough to realise I might have broken something. He stabilised my neck and back with foam braces and a few of the boys eased me onto a stretcher which had been brought in through the manhole.

Once I was on the stretcher, it couldn't be taken back out through the manhole so, the welder was called to cut an access passage through the bulkhead adjoining the cement room. Although I don't remember any of this, apparently I was taken out through this hole and carried up to the helideck.

There was a helicopter already on the drillship. It was a Bell 206 model, capable of carrying four passengers, three in the backseat and one next to the pilot. The stretcher was longer than the helicopter was wide so, in order to carry it, both doors had to be removed. The stretcher was then loaded across the back seats with one end sticking out each side.

I awoke when they put me on the helicopter. Reg had just given me a painkiller injection but as yet it wasn't having much effect. I was in serious pain.

Anyone who has ever flown in a helicopter will appreciate that when the blades start rotating, the helicopter vibrates. This vibration accelerates as the rotors get up to speed. I was awake and I can confirm that having a broken back on the equivalent of an airborne vibrating table is not fun. The pain was excruciating.

Reg sat up front. He told me afterwards that I only lasted a few minutes and was out cold for the rest of the flight to Port Moresby.

In Port Moresby, the helicopter was met by an ambulance and I was taken to the local hospital. Apparently the ward in the main part of the hospital was full so they took me to an older, more basic, accommodation where I finally regained consciousness. I awoke to find myself lying on an army-style bunk bed in a room with three other patients who were all natives. I remember it was very hot and there was a very pungent smell, although I was in so much pain I couldn't care less.

I think I was only there for a short while before Red, who was onshore at the time, came to find me and insisted that they move me to a 'proper' ward with a proper bed. When I next became aware of what was happening, I was in a hospital bed on a veranda, just outside what appeared to be a modern hospital ward.

I assume that they had taken X-rays and done some other investigations but I wasn't conscious for any of these. The nurses had secured me to my bed in a traction harness, pulling my legs one way and my upper body the other. Whenever I awoke I could hardly move. It was very uncomfortable but I was given plenty of painkillers so most of the time I just slept. As I had to remain in traction all the time, when I was awake I discovered that, in addition to the pain from my broken back, other parts of my body were also sore from the traction harness.

I spent two full weeks in traction and, when I finally got up and was walking again, my back seemed to have made a remarkable recovery. Apart from feeling very weak, my back pain was almost gone.

Although I was slim and fit at the time of the accident, I had managed to lose twelve pounds while in hospital. After flying back to Brisbane for some rest and recuperation, I quickly regained much of the weight I'd lost and, after two weeks, got the all clear to go back to work. I had really missed the drillship. I missed all the guys, all the chat and all the excitement.

Back when I had my fall, four hours after I had left the rig, my relief, Fred, arrived on-board. He had been urgently recalled and was able to go ahead with the cement job without any problem. Apparently, before I fell I had managed to fix the line blockage.

After returning to work on the drillship, one bit of excitement I could have done without occurred when the well took a *kick*. A kick is the term used to describe what can happen when the drill bit penetrates through non-porous rock into a porous rock containing pressurised oil, gas or water. When the pressure confined in this porous rock is higher than the hydrostatic pressure exerted by the column of drilling mud some oil, gas, or water, enters the wellbore, forcing a volume of the mud out of the well. Hence the term *kick*. If it's a *blow out*, then all the mud is being blown out of the well by the high pressure oil or gas before the driller has been able to seal off the top of the well by closing the *blowout preventer*.

For two days after the kick the the drillers worked hard to get the well back under control. The driller immediately closed the blowout preventer to seal off the top of the well. This seal enabled the drillers to choke back the mud flow leaving the well via the *mud return line*, thereby containing the pressure within the well. They increased the weight of the mud by adding tons of barite powder into the mix and then pumped this 'heavy' mud down the drill pipe. While holding some back-pressure they continued to pump this heavy mud as they worked the entrained gas out of the system. This back-pressure also prevented more gas from entering the wellbore from the porous formation.

It was all going as planned. Slowly but surely progress was being made, then the blowout preventer started to leak.

Red, the superintendent, instructed me to go down to the cement pump room and get ready to pump a slurry of fast-setting cement in case the leak became serious. I was to await his instruction and then start mixing and pumping cement as soon as he gave the order. This cement was to be pumped down the drill pipe and placed across the formation where the gas was coming into the well. It would be left there to set and hopefully, prevent any more gas from entering the wellbore. He sent a roughneck along to be my helper.

The roughneck and I waited three hours but no instruction was given. I told my assistant to run back to the galley, grab us some food for us and then return as quickly as possible. When he returned he said that it was really weird, there weren't any other people about. As a precaution, apparently everyone except the two of us and a few drilling crew had been evacuated.

Should there be a *blow out*, the situation would be extremely serious so a partial evacuation had been carried out to minimise any potential loss of life. These people were all safely onboard a supply boat about a mile away from us.

I called the superintendent and suggested that the roughneck and I would also like to be on the supply boat. He needed to decide pretty quickly whether he was going to pump cement or not.

Half an hour later we were instructed to start. The cement slurry was mixed and pumped down the drill pipe. A few hours later it had set and the kick was sealed off. A day later the well was permanently *plugged and abandoned*.

On another occasion we had a proper *blow out* from a shallow rock formation containing a small 'pocket' of gas under high pressure. The driller and his crew left the rig floor immediately and hadn't time to activate the blowout preventer. It was all very dramatic. Everyone ran to the accommodation block to get away from the roar of gas blowing up through the derrick. The alarm was sounded and immediate action was taken to get all non-essential personnel evacuated.

I was told I would need to stay onboard.

The primary blowout preventer controls were located on the rig floor, but there was a back-up control unit in the superintendent's office looking out towards the rig from the accommodation block. Unfortunately, no one had ever activated the blowout preventer from the remote control unit.

There was some confusion, but eventually, after ten or fifteen minutes, someone worked it out and the blowout preventer was activated. Instantly, the well was sealed off, the gas flow stopped, and they had the well back under control. On that occasion we were very lucky that there hadn't been a spark which could have ignited the gas. Had that happened there would have been a huge explosion. It could have been a very serious accident.

Apart from these little 'events', we were all having great fun learning how to drill wells with our fancy new drillship. During the eighteen-month drilling campaign, Phillips Petroleum Company managed to drill four wells. Unfortunately, none of them encountered any commercial quantities of oil or gas. An awful lot of money had been spent, but in the end all the wells were plugged and abandoned.

As a footnote, I bumped into my medic hero Reg a number of years later in Aberdeen, Scotland, where he lived. He remembered me and the accident. Unfortunately his own life had headed in a bad direction and by then he was an alcoholic.

He had been able to deal competently with any medical emergency on the rig, but couldn't work out when it was time to screw the top back on a whisky bottle. Sadly, he died a few months after I'd met him.

CHAPTER 15

The First Promotion

Port Moresby is the capital city of PNG and, at the time I was there, it had around two hundred thousand inhabitants. I was given an apartment where I would live whenever I wasn't offshore or back in Australia on leave.

My eighteen months in Port Moresby was quite an experience. Although I was only supposed to be on the drillship for two weeks at a time, I spent at least two-thirds of my time there, so I only lived in my apartment, on and off, for a total of four months. When I was in town I wasn't on holiday. I usually had to help out at the bulk storage facility BJ had constructed down on the wharf. They had set up three silos, one each for cement, barite and bentonite.

Shipments of these products arrived from Australia by freighter in sacks on pallets. BJ employed a team of men to cut open the bags and dump the material into small silos for transfer into the bigger silos. From there the powder was transferred to silos on a supply boat for delivery to the drillship.

As there was a constant consumption offshore, getting the material into the storage silos was a never-ending job. The manpower BJ employed for this work were all locals. Twelve natives, all around five-foot tall with big feet and woolly heads of hair. They were strong and could work hard.

One of the lead hands was a twenty-year-old man named Tommy. I'm sure that wasn't his real name, but it was the name he would answer to. Tommy constantly chewed betel nut. Apart from giving him bright red gums, this betel nut also gave him the extra energy he needed to work in the heat of the day. I got to know Tommy a little. We could only communicate in Pidgin English but he was a happy chap and I liked him. He worked hard and was always smiling.

One day, from our conversation, I worked out that Tommy was getting married and had asked if I would meet his bride-to-be. I agreed and we arranged to meet three days later.

That evening at the sports club I mentioned my upcoming meeting to a friend.

He said, "I hope you didn't agree!"

I said that I had agreed and the meeting would take place on Sunday.

"Why shouldn't I meet his bride-to-be?" I asked.

"Well, what you're expected to do is give her a 'test run'. Tommy wants you to confirm that she will be able to satisfy his needs," he said.

"Holy crap," I said.

I had no idea I had agreed to this undertaking. This was not a proposition I thought I could accommodate.

The next day I begged off, explaining to Tommy as best I could, that he needed an older, wiser, and more experienced man who could do the job properly.

Two months later he did get married, so if there was a 'test run' I assume it was a success.

At the end of my eighteen-month tour of duty, I had to go to one last job on a 'land rig' which was working in the western part of the country. The well was being drilled twenty miles from the mouth of the Fly River on a drill site constructed on swamp land by the side of a river. To get to the rig, I took a charter plane to Daru and then travelled upstream on a small flat-bottomed barge.

When I arrived, I saw that the entire drill site was built on piles which had been driven into the ground.

A camp, also on stilts, had been set up about fifty yards from the drill site. There were rig hands and local natives everywhere. As well as the people needed to man the rig, at least twenty natives had come along in canoes. Some of them had been put to work carrying sacks of cement and other material, while others were shifting boxes of food and catering supplies from one place to the next. Many of them were naked apart from shorts or a small loincloth. Not a single native was wearing a hard hat or boots. As they weren't working on the rig, safety gear probably wasn't necessary but their lack of clothing did make them look strangely out of place.

Bill, the toolpusher, told me he was happy to provide a job for any native who wanted to do a few hours work in exchange for some food. His rig site was not far away from cannibal country so he was trying to make sure he didn't offend anyone.

Apparently, a week earlier, one afternoon a native had left in his canoe and hadn't returned. He had gone for dinner. The suspicion amongst the others was that, unbeknownst to him, he had gone to be someone else's dinner.

After I had been on-site for five days, the mud logger said they hadn't found anything to test, so I returned to Port Moresby and prepared to move back to Australia.

At the ripe age of twenty-four, I moved back in Roma and was promoted to be the new District Manager. I was put in charge of six service engineers, three trainees, one admin person, three cement trucks, three drillstem testing units, and four core barrels.

Somewhere along the line I had learnt to operate all this equipment and I was now the one training others and giving them their induction information. My new salary was four hundred and seventy-five Australian dollars per month.

Along with my promotion came many new responsibilities. I was responsible for managing a budget and ensuring that all the equipment was in top shape, ready to go to work at a moment's notice. I decided which service engineer and which equipment was sent out to a job and ultimately was the one responsible for the success of every job. It felt like a huge responsibility.

I was very particular about the readiness and appearance of our trucks and equipment. If there wasn't any maintenance to be done, I would always get the boys to put another coat of wax on the cab of a truck. Our units were well maintained and always looked as neat as a pin.

One day I got a heads-up call to say I would need to send a cement truck out to a rig near Windorah, four hundred and fifty miles west of Roma. The job wouldn't be happening for another four to six days but, as rain was forecast, I decided we should take our cement truck out early to avoid having to drive on wet roads. The road beyond Charleville wasn't paved and the last ten miles to the rig would just be a graded track. Getting to the rig before the rain came was going to make the drive a whole lot easier.

Two of us drove out the following day. We parked the cement truck fifty yards from the rig then headed back to Roma in my utility truck. (As the District Manager my pick-up truck had been upgraded to a new 'ute'.) Driving eight hours each way wasn't an issue. Distances in Australia are vast but you got used to long drives and just did them. In fact we often spoke about a place being four, six, or eight hours away as opposed to the actual mileage.

Anyway, a few days after we'd taken out the cement truck, the rain did come, and, it rained for days on end. There was no word from the rig about the upcoming cement job. Eventually, I got a call from the drilling superintendent in head office to say that work at the rig had been suspended. The entire rig site was ten feet under water.

When I asked about our cement truck, he said we could take it back to Roma as it would not be needed anytime soon. However, the only way to get it would be by boat. It was submerged up to the windscreen!

It took a month before the water subsided and a few more weeks before it was dry enough to rebuild the access road.

I then arranged for a large truck pulling a low-loader trailer to go out to recover the cement truck and transport it all the way back to Brisbane. Once there, it took two months to strip the engine and repair all the electrics, before we could drive the truck back to Roma. By the time the boys finished servicing the pumping equipment and applying one final coat of wax to the cab, nearly six months had passed.

I had learnt a very expensive lesson. Because I decided to drive the truck out to the rig before we were officially called out by the oil company, they didn't have to pay any standby charges, usually around two hundred dollars per day, nor did they have any liability for the repair costs.

My attempt to give the customer the best service possible had cost our company dearly. Never again did I mobilise equipment without an official call-out from the customer.

CHAPTER 16

The Last Date

In Roma on a Saturday, rather than spend my afternoon sitting on a barstool, I would head over to Roma Golf Club. Back then this was a typical outback golf course. There was very little grass to be seen anywhere. The tee-boxes were dirt, the fairways were dirt and the greens were 'browns' (oiled sand). From tee to green, every shot was played off a tee peg. When it was really dry the ground became rock hard, so hard in fact that I sometimes carried a claw hammer and nail to make a hole in the ground for the tee.

I could definitely drive the ball a lot further on the rock-hard fairways, but if I missed the green with my second shot the ball could go anywhere.

On the 'browns' a special rake was used to smooth a track to the hole. The idea was to roll a putt along this path. I can assure you this isn't as easy as it sounds. Making a putt on oiled sand was difficult enough, just keeping it on the raked path was often a challenge.

In the springtime some golfers also carried a shotgun in their golf bag. This was not used to take care of a 'sandbagging' opponent, it was used to deal with the crows. Possibly thinking they might be eggs, the crows would swoop down to steal the golf balls. Shots could often be heard around the course giving them short shrift!

In spite of these idiosyncrasies, I enjoyed many Saturday afternoons playing golf and having a few beers with some great blokes. It was good fun.

The other sport I enjoyed occasionally was squash. I had played social squash for many years and considered myself to be a reasonable player. This opinion may well have been helped by my choice of opponent.

One such opponent was my good friend Walter. Walter was one of Australia's pioneer cattlemen. He and his brother Robert had both been successful in a government land ballot back in 1963. Ballot winners were each allocated one of sixteen blocks of land in Arcadia Valley, some fifty miles north of Injune, one hundred miles north of Roma.

When Robert and Walter initially rode their horses onto their Valley properties they travelled through dense, mature bushland covered with twenty-to-twenty-five foot tall trees called *brigalow*. This tree propagates through its root system and, over time, totally infests the land. They both intended to start cattle businesses but when they arrived the land was unusable for ranching or farming.

They and the other ballot pioneers had an enormous task ahead of them. Before they could bring in any cattle they had to clear away as much brigalow as possible, excavate dams, erect fences and construct cattle yards, as well as build houses for themselves.

They cleared a lot of brigalow by hiring a contractor to bring in two D8 Caterpillar tractors. These big machines would drag a heavy, forty-to-fifty-yard long, steel-link chain along the ground. Each tractor was connected to one end of the chain, and as they drove forward some thirty yards apart the chain would pull down the brigalow. The tractor drivers would also use the tractor blades to fell some of the bigger trees. Any taller indigenous trees were left standing to provide shade once the cattle arrived.

Each property needed to clear five thousand acres or more, so it was a big job. After knocking down all the Brigalow, the ground still needed to be raked and cleared. Only then, after the dams and fences were in place, could the first cattle be brought in. It would be a year or two thereafter before any cattle could be sold for a profit, finally generating some cash to pay for the expenditures.

The scale of the task was daunting. Developing each property to support a herd of two thousand cattle took a lot of very hard work. To have a fully functioning cattle property with all the infrastructure in place, finally becoming a viable, profitable, business, took the best part of thirty years.

What impressed me most about these pioneers was how they worked together as a community. Each property was five miles or more away from its neighbour, but if anyone needed assistance, distance wasn't an issue. They were always ready to help one another.

The most dramatic example of this occurred when there was a fire. Occasionally a lightning strike in the hills or down on the valley floor, would set off a fire. Everyone would come to the affected property and work day and night, building fire breaks, back-burning, or do whatever could be done to bring the fire under control.

If a fire ever got out of control, it could sweep across a huge area destroying everything in its path: fields, forests, houses, and animals.

While fighting the fire was mostly a job for the men, the women were also fully involved. They had to keep the properties going. They needed to look after the children and the cattle, as well as provide food and water for the firefighters.

It was tough for everyone, but for these pioneers, the community spirit certainly helped make their life in the bush a very rewarding way to live.

Everyone I met in Arcadia Valley also had a strong sense of responsibility for nature and the environment. They all worked towards sustainability in the way they ran and developed their properties, in harmony with bird life, wildlife and the natural vegetation. 'Arcadia' is a Greek word and 'Arcadia Valley' was named after the European Renaissance arts word for 'unspoilt, harmonious wilderness'. They intended to keep it that way.

When I met Walter, he had been living in Arcadia Valley for more than five years. He occasionally came to Roma to pick up supplies and for some R & R. Not for the want of trying, Walter still hadn't found a wife so he would often make time on his Roma trips to continue his search.

When he came to town we would usually meet up and play a few games of squash. I got to play a lot more than Walter did, so I usually managed to win and he usually got to buy the beer.

On the social side of things, there was often a party or the occasionally dance to attend as well as the annual 'Roma Charity Ball'.

Every year in Melbourne, there was a Miss Australia contest. The winner of this contest would visit many towns around Australia where she would host a charity ball. This ball, when she came to Roma, was the social event of the year.

A few weeks before Miss Australia was due to arrive, I received a phone call from one of the organisers to ask if I would escort her to the ball. "Wow! Hell yes, I would be delighted!"

Later that evening I called Walter to share my good news. He was pleased for me and said that he had also received a call asking if he would escort Miss Australia's chaperone. "Great," I said. "We'll both be going to the ball and we'll be in the same party … it should be a lot of fun!".

As the conversation went on, Walter revealed that he had been the one asked to escort Miss Australia on a previous occasion. While he was very pleased for me, I could tell he was a little disappointed that he had not been offered the job again this time.

Knowing how much I enjoyed a contest, Walter said, "It's a shame we didn't get to decide who would be escorting Miss Australia by way of a sporting competition." As a bit of a tease I said, "Well we could always have a game of squash if it will make you feel better," thinking he would remember his last defeat and decline the offer.

However, Walter didn't decline. In fact I was surprised how quickly he accepted the challenge and was left wondering why I had made the suggestion in the first place. I had suggested a match where I had nothing to win and could only lose the date with Miss Australia I had already been given. On the upside, losing a five-game set had never happened so it wasn't going to be a problem. At least I didn't think it was going to be a problem.

When we played our match the following week, Walter played with total focus and pure passion. He won the first game. I thought possibly I hadn't tried as hard as I might have, but was certainly caught off guard by his determination.

I then won the next two games so normal order was restored. "Win one more game and it will be all over," I said to myself. Walter had a different idea. He lifted his game once again and won the fourth.

Never before had I seen such commitment and determination from Walter as he displayed in the fifth game. He literally bounced off the walls, throwing himself at every shot, eventually winning the game 9 – 6 and the match 3 – 2.

My one and only chance to have a date with Miss Australia, I had now lost, all because I thought Walter couldn't beat me at a game of squash. Not a smart move on my part. I hadn't factored his male pride into my game plan.

Apparently the chance to escort Miss Australia, as opposed to her chaperone, really was something worth fighting for.

The following Saturday, Walter returned to town and together we headed off to the reception at a private home.

We were there to meet Miss Australia and her chaperone. Walter really looked the part, a tall strapping cattleman dressed to the nines in his finest bib and tucker. He was ready to meet his match-winning 'reward'.

When we met the organiser, I had to inform her that there was a slight change of plan. Walter would now escort Miss Australia and I would escort Miss Chaperone. She looked a bit surprised but said okay and headed off to get the girls.

Well, Miss Australia was every bit as impressive and beautiful as you would expect. Miss Chaperone (Walter had assured me that she would be one of the runners up) was not a beautiful young woman. She was an attractive lady in her mid-forties. Great, I was not going to have the night I thought I might have had.

The evening started well. After everyone else was seated, we arrived with our girls on our arms to make a grand entrance. We entered the hall and paraded up to the top table.

All eyes were on Miss Australia and her handsome partner.

Throughout the dinner it was obvious that Miss Australia was well taken with her cattleman escort. Walter was also enamoured, keeping her entertained with all his best stories. One amazing story after another. I'd heard them all before but Miss Australia was enthralled.

Miss 'C' and I didn't seem to have the same rapport, although we did chat a little about this and that.

As the evening progressed, Walter and Miss Australia had a few dances while Miss 'C' and I sat and watched their romance start to blossom.

Eventually, when the girls went to powder their noses, Walter leaned across and asked, "Any chance you could make sure that Miss Chaperone stays here a while longer?"

When the girls returned, Walter suggested to Miss Australia that they go out for a bit of fresh air. As they walked from the hall, many men watched them leave, with knowing looks and maybe a little envy. "Lucky bastard," I heard one mutter. Walter's eligible bachelor status and his ongoing search for a mate were well known around town.

Miss Australia, with her blond hair, wearing a white dress with a white feather boa wrap, held the arm of red-haired Walter in his black tie dinner suit. I'm not sure why, but the scene reminded me of a sly fox leading an innocent rabbit off to his lair.

I stayed inside with Miss 'C' and managed to keep the conversation going for another thirty minutes. When we eventually left the hall, neither of us was surprised to find there was no sign of Walter or Miss Australia.

The next day Walter called to say what a most enjoyable time he'd had at the ball. "Hopefully you found Miss 'C' to be good company as well," he added. He offered no additional information.

With hindsight, I told myself it was probably all for the best. Two months before the ball I had become engaged to marry the girl who would become my own Miss Australia.

However, it would just have been nice for the final entry on my bachelor CV to have read; "Escorted Miss 'A', not Miss 'C', to the Roma Ball."

In the years that followed, Walter went on to escort a few more Miss Australia winners to the Roma Ball. He never did marry one, but eventually he did marry Helen. I think he made a wise choice. She is a star.

Forty years later for a milestone birthday of mine, Walter sent me his old squash racket as a birthday gift. What a great friend he is, helping me to remember the wonderful time he'd had back in our Roma days.

CHAPTER 17

The Angry Emu

On more than one occasion while I lived in Australia I had encounters with some of the country's wonderful wildlife. There are more kangaroos in Australia than there are people. With an estimated twenty-eight million of them bouncing around the outback, accidents between vehicles and kangaroos are not uncommon. Over the years I ran into two kangaroos while driving and once I ran into an emu.

The emu accident happened early one evening when I was driving north in my ute going to see Walter. At that time the road from Injune onwards wasn't paved, and the last fifty miles to his property was not busy. At dusk, when emus and kangaroos are often on the move, they might dart out from the shrub alongside the road, catching drivers by surprise. I was probably driving too fast, so I wasn't able to avoid an emu which suddenly decided to cross the road in front of me.

Most vehicles out west are fitted with 'roo-bars' to protect the front of the vehicle, particularly the radiator, from damage. A big 'roo' can still cause some damage and some have even been known to smash through the front windscreen after they've come up over the bonnet.

Hitting an emu was a little different. An emu has long legs and, as it runs, the main body mass is three feet off the ground. My roo-bar took the legs right out from under the one I hit. He bounced off the windscreen, flipped over the back of my ute and ended up on the road behind me.

There was a splodge of dust on the windscreen where he'd made contact, but no blood.

Out in the bush there is an unwritten rule; 'if you injure an animal, you are supposed to stop and put it out of its misery'. Having stopped the ute some forty yards beyond the point of impact, I sat and looked in my mirror for any sign of life. There wasn't any. I assumed that Mr Emu was unconscious and probably had broken legs and maybe a broken neck.

I would need to go back with my ball-peen hammer and knock him on the head. (I carried such a hammer in my toolbox for this very purpose.) I got out and walked back towards the emu. I could see that his legs were somewhat tangled and that his head was lying at an odd angle. As I approached, however, he opened one eye and fixed me with his gaze. I stood still. "Well, he isn't unconscious, so that will make it more difficult to give him a tap with my hammer."

As I watched a little longer he moved a leg. "Well at least one leg isn't broken."

He then moved the other leg. "How about that, maybe both legs are okay."

He then lifted his head off the ground a bit. "I guess his neck isn't broken either. Maybe he's okay and I don't need to do anything. I think I'll walk back to the ute and see how he gets on from there."

By now Mr Emu was attempting to get back on to his feet but fell down again.

"I'll just keep walking."

He got up again, a little more stable this time.

"I think I'll hurry back to my ute a little faster."

He was now heading in my direction, moving forward and sideways at the same time. I started to run towards my ute.

As he gained more control, the last ten yards was a flat-out foot race between me and Mr Emu. I dove into the ute and quickly pulled the door behind me. Mr Emu was right outside. He gave the top of my ute half a dozen pecks before I managed to start the engine and speed away.

I'm sure Mr Emu had thought, "That bastard, he's hit me with his ute and now he's planning to tap me on the head with his ball-peen hammer! I'll show him!"

Just imagine if Mr Emu had caught me and pecked me on the head. The next people to come along the road would have found me lying there. I bet it would have taken them sometime to work out how my 'accident' could possibly have happened.

Years later, I hit a kangaroo when driving my family along that same stretch of road in a rental car. With no roo-bar on the front of the vehicle, the radiator was damaged and the kangaroo was well and truly dead. No ball-peen hammer required.

On that occasion we needed to wait for a Valley cattleman to come along the road to rescue us. With his help, we pushed my car through a gate on the rather appropriately named "Linga Longa" property and left it there.

After a night's stay with Walter and Helen, Walter drove us back to Roma. He took us back to the car hire company so I could tell them where they could find their car. I paid the two-thousand-dollar insurance excess and then headed to the airport for our flight back to Brisbane.

As my wife pointed out, I should have known better than not to take out full insurance cover when I saw the rental car didn't have a roo-bar. Quite right. I won't be making that mistake again.

CHAPTER 18

The Sales Call

Apart from my other management responsibilities, Jim, the new Region Manager in Brisbane, asked me to start making some sales calls. I needed to make the drive from Roma to Brisbane every few months and this meant that I had to pass through Toowoomba on the way. Jim asked me to meet with a drilling manager who had his office there. He wanted me to make a sales call on Carl.

I had never made a sales call before and had never met Carl. I phoned his office, got to speak to him, and was delighted when he agreed to meet me at 4.30 pm in two days' time. As we spoke I was gaining confidence. Thinking that our meeting would last until the end of his working day at five o'clock, maybe we could go to a pub for a beer and then have a bite to eat? Carl thought this was a great idea and said he was looking forward to meeting me.

Wow! What a response to my very first ever sales call request!

Two days later I arrived at Carl's office well ahead of time and spent a good half hour reviewing my sales material and practising my sales pitch. Armed with brochures and catalogues I entered his office ten minutes early for my 4.30 appointment, determined to do the best I could to get him to use our services.

Carl's office looked just like any other drilling office. He had a cup of coffee on his desk, a bookcase full of catalogues, one from BJ and every other service and supply company in the business, and there were a lot of drilling reports lying about. The photos on his walls were mostly of him standing in front of a drilling rig or next to his company pick-up. Seeing his office gave me the comfortable feeling that Carl was just another, 'regular oilman'. I relaxed and felt ready to make my pitch.

Carl was easy to talk to and after a few social niceties I plunged into my 'sales spiel'. He listened for a while and then suggested that he was aware of all the services BJ had to offer and would, maybe, consider using us sometime in the future. End of conversation.

"That would be great," I said.

"Now let's go for a drink," he said.

By 4.45 we had left his office and ten minutes later we were sitting on bar stools in his favourite pub. I knew it must be his favourite pub because the barman greeted him personally and, before Carl could order a drink, he pulled a bottle out from under the bar, half-filled a glass with Bacardi, added two ice cubes, topped it up with a dash of Coke and set it down in front of him.

Carl asked if I might like the same. Aiming to please I said, "Yes, but make mine a small one."

My drink was served, we clinked glasses and Carl consumed half of his drink in one gulp. A couple of minutes later his glass was empty! Without him having reordered, the barman took a clean glass and prepared another drink just like the first.

"Are you ready for another?" asked Carl. "Not quite yet thanks," I replied. I had only just started my first drink.

Over the next hour, Carl consumed four more of these Bacardi and Cokes. (The barman needed to open a new bottle of Bacardi and placed it back under the bar for speedy access.)

I had managed to get to the bottom of two glasses and was staring blankly at the third. Carl was sober. I was decidedly tipsy. I needed to get out of the pub … I needed to eat.

Earlier in the day I'd been too nervous to eat so hadn't anything in my stomach since my bowl of Weetabix. I mentioned to Carl that I'd made a booking at The Steakhouse not too far away. He finally agreed that we could go eat and offered to drive. He thought I shouldn't be driving and was probably right.

After walking back to his office, Carl drove us to the restaurant. I remember that we both ordered steaks plus a nice bottle of red wine. Once our meal was served, Carl asked the waiter if he would cut my steak for me as I appeared to be incapable of the task.

The dinner was a big success. The food was great and Carl seemed to enjoy himself immensely.

After dinner, Carl, who had consumed most of the wine, said he was meeting four or five friends back at his pub and "Would I care to join them?"

He drove us back to the pub, more drinks were ordered and another full glass of something or other was set down in front of me. I remember trying to join in the conversation. Everyone was having a great time! Lots of laughs and lots more drinks. My first sales call was obviously a big success.

I bumped against a number of people and chairs on the way to the toilet for the third time in fifteen minutes and then, holding onto the top of the urinal while doing my business, thought, "I have got to get out of here!" I had no idea where I was or where I wanted to go, I just had to get out of the pub.

Somehow I managed to find the back door and headed down the street, anywhere, as long as it was away from more drink. I happened upon a motel and must have convinced the landlady to let me have a room. "Please take whatever you need from my wallet, just show me to a room," I think I said. It was only 8.30 pm!

The next morning I awoke with a big hangover, feeling very ill. I couldn't believe that I'd managed to get so drunk while trying hard not to.

I left the motel, eventually found my car, and headed for Brisbane, arriving safely an hour and a half later.

I went straight to Jim's office in Albert Street. He usually worked on a Saturday morning and was still there when I arrived.

I was greeted with a big grin. "Well," he said, "sounds like you had a good time!"

He'd had a call from Carl, a bit worried about what might have happened to me when I scarpered from the pub. "But absolutely," Carl had said, "one of the best sales calls he'd ever had!" Couldn't wait for me to call on him again next time I was in town.

Well it's not often you get a customer … potential customer … calling to ask when you are coming to make another sales call, but Carl did. I put him off as long as I could but eventually I needed to go back to Brisbane and agreed to see him once more.

The second sales call followed pretty much along the same lines as the first. On that occasion we went straight from his office to the pub without me telling him anything about our products and services.

We had a lot of drinks and another nice meal, but this time I didn't go back to his pub after dinner. I had taken a passenger with me from Roma and had arranged for him to pick me up from the restaurant. My friend drove my car back to Brisbane, stopping only occasionally for me to be sick by the side of the road.

Carl did eventually give us a few jobs. I often spoke with him on the phone, but when I stopped offering to visit him for another 'sales call', the work eventually dried up.

If all sales calls were going to be like selling to Carl, I concluded that I was never going to make it as a salesman. If I was to succeed in the oil patch, it would need to be in management or some other job.

CHAPTER 19

The Region Manager

My job as District Manager seemed to be going really well. The service engineers were all cooperative and the business was ticking over.

One service engineer, Mark, was very enthusiastic and loved the job he was doing. He enjoyed working for BJ and was very happy to work with me as his boss. All the guys would do any jobs I asked of them, however, it didn't matter how difficult or menial the task was, Mark would always be the first to offer his service. He was also very capable so it was great having someone like that on the team.

Mark was a classic oilman. He worked hard and played hard. He never went crazy with drink but he did enjoy a good party and always had a romance on the go. Those characteristics were typical of many oilmen I've met around the world and, like a lot of oilmen, Mark loved talking about the various rigs he had been on and all the different problems he'd had to deal with. Go to any oil-town bar and you will hear them, drilling their oil wells as they drink their beers.

Mark even had a favourite cement truck, the same one we used on the Eromanga job. He christened his truck *Proud Mary* after the *Credence* song. Whenever I hear this tune I always think of Mark, 'rollin down the highway'.

One time back in Roma, Mark and I both needed to find new accommodation so when Richie, one of our cementers, got transferred to Perth with his family, Mark and I got together to rent his house. It was quite a nice house by Roma standards on a good-sized plot of land. It had a big back lawn with around a dozen fruit trees and ornamental shrubs which Richie's wife, Betty, had nurtured for many years. We promised to take good care of both the house and the garden while they were away.

While we did promise to look after everything, watering those shrubs and cutting the grass soon lost its appeal. However, a solution of sorts presented itself when Mark arrived home with a young nanny goat.

When coming back from a job Mark happened upon a family of goats crossing the road in front of him. He stopped his truck and managed to get out quickly enough to catch one of the youngsters.

Billy-Jo was provided with an old crate for shelter and a large tub of drinking water in the back yard. We attached her to a lead so she could graze over a circle of grass. The idea was to move her around so she could access some new grass each day. The mowing problem was solved! However, Billy-Jo wanted more than just grass and one night she managed to pull free and got stuck into the shrubs. When we looked out the next morning, every one of the trees and shrubs had been trimmed up as far as she could reach. Some of the smaller ones were completely stripped of their leaves and looked to be beyond recovery. Hopefully some of the bigger trees would recover before Betty returned. She was not going to be happy.

Apart from that little mishap, Billy-Jo was good company and quickly became domesticated. Once she got used to the idea of living in our back yard she would happily take food from anyone who cared to offer her something. A daily habit she rather enjoyed was to come towards the kitchen window so we could toss her a piece of toast at breakfast time.

When she wasn't eating, which she seemed to do most of the time, she liked to pretend she was a mountain goat. She entertained herself by climbing on top of her crate and making fancy leaps back to the ground.

At one of the occasional parties at our house, some lad thought he would see if Billy-Jo also enjoyed a beer. Apparently she did, and while we weren't watching he managed to get her a little drunk. Eventually she started to stumble about and headed off to lie down in her crate. The next morning she didn't even manage to come over for her toast. She spent the entire day inside her crate nursing her hangover. I guess a goat hangover is much the same as the hangovers we humans get. Nothing works better than a good rest and drinking lots of water.

Billy-Jo stayed with us until we moved out of the house, after which we found her a new home on a property just outside Roma. We made sure her new owner knew her preference for brown toast and left her there to live happily ever after.

At work, things settled into a routine. As the months went by, work was always steady but never busy. There were more cementing, testing and coring jobs to do and one or two more interesting experiences along the way.

One new experience happened when I took a trainee out to test a well on a rig site infested with mice. There were hundreds of mice everywhere. They were just running about on the ground, heading in different directions. The plague appeared to be localised although, around the same time, I seem to remember Walter having a plague of mice at his cattle station one hundred miles away. That probably meant that the number of mice running about the countryside could well have been in the millions.

John, the company rep, had a small caravan on-site where he would work and sleep. I went to his caravan to speak with him about the testing job.

There must have been fifty mice inside the van. They were on the floor, on the counter top, on his bunk, everywhere. I brushed a couple off the bench before sitting down and John swept a few more off the table so we could lay out a tool drawing. John had been staying in the van on and off for around a week and had simply stopped noticing them. He said that the mice never caused him any problem, but it must have felt like living inside the set of an *Indiana Jones* movie.

The next day, after the test had been completed, I was quite happy to leave John and his mice behind. My trainee Adam, didn't like mice at all and couldn't get away from the place fast enough.

Four months after the Roma Ball, towards the end of my second year as manager in Roma, I went to Brisbane to marry my 'Miss A'.

I had met Neva, my wife-to-be, in Brisbane when she was still at Queensland University finishing off her PhD. The previous year her research assistant had married my brother Steven and we'd met at their wedding. We got on famously and within a few months decided to get married.

Walter was my best man at the wedding and he made a great speech, telling everyone that I was the kind of guy my new wife would be proud of. He did owe me one, so it was a nice way to be paid back.

I was a proud man. Even my dad was impressed. He thought my new bride was the cleverest and most charming person I could possibly have married. I'm not entirely sure he didn't think that she could have done better than to marry his second eldest son. Fortunately, he didn't voice that opinion. However, back when we got engaged another concerned adult had taken my fiancée aside to make that very point. She pointed out to Neva that, while I was a District Manager I was actually just a glorified truck driver and she should really be expecting to marry a young professional. Thankfully, she didn't take any notice and, as they say, the rest is history.

A few days after the wedding, Neva and I headed back to Roma to start our life together. It was a wonderful time. Mostly we were just getting on with life and learning how to live with one another. While I went off to work every day she kept herself busy writing up her PhD.

The biggest change to my life happened in the evenings. I discovered that my new wife was a great cook and liked preparing different meals. Having a nice dinner to come home to was a big improvement over cooking a meal for myself every night.

Neva was also happy to have dinner guests.

Most of the BJ boys were on their own so an invitation to dine with us was a welcome treat. On one occasion Neva decided she would have a fondue for desert where the boys could cook their own pieces of fruit in a hot chocolate sauce. The fondue was spiced with a generous portion of rum which hadn't all vaporised. This was a big success, particularly for Johnny who was three weeks into his month without alcohol. He really enjoyed it, especially once he'd convinced himself he wasn't breaking his non-drinking pledge.

We continued living in Roma for the next seven months, then our stay came to a sudden end when Ken, (who had returned to replace Jim as the regional manager in Brisbane) was recalled by head office and transferred home to California.

I was surprised, but very chuffed, to be offered his job as Region Manager. Two weeks later we packed up our few belongings and moved to Brisbane.

Out of the twelve Region Managers BJ had working in different parts of the world, at the age of twenty-six I walked into my new office in Albert Street to become their youngest one ever.

So began the next leg of my journey.

CHAPTER 20

The 53 Points

After having lived in Roma for four years, I was sorry to leave. For my first job in the oil patch I don't think I could have picked a better place to have worked and lived. My last two years as District Manager had been both interesting and exciting. The BJ people I worked with, Smitty, Ben, Cliff, Adam, Russell, Mark, Stan, Richie, Johnny, Rob, Bill, Jon and Lowell (Thruppy), were all great guys. Unfortunately, over the years I lost contact with many of them, but I do hope they were all successful and continued to have as much fun in their careers as we did when we worked together.

When I became the new Region Manager in Brisbane in 1972, together with a staff of three, I oversaw BJ's business interests in Australia, New Zealand, Timor, Papua New Guinea and Tonga. This was the company's largest region geographically but one of its smallest business units by revenue. For the next eighteen months I tried hard to find more business opportunities.

Ironically, my main job as Region Manager was making sales calls. This wasn't something I particularly enjoyed doing, but I discovered that all customers weren't like Carl. I had expected the worst, but it actually wasn't that bad. I even had two clients who preferred having a game of squash rather than going out for lunch.

Once every month I would fly to Sydney, Melbourne and Perth, and occasionally Adelaide, to visit the oil company offices there. There were a few hot spots of drilling activity around Australia but our competitor, Halliburton, had secured the lion's share of the available work. Most oil companies I went to see had Halliburton on a long-term contract and couldn't see any reason to change over to a different service company. My best chance for getting business was with oil companies starting up new drilling ventures.

I had one big disappointment when we lost a contract on a semi-submersible drilling rig working in Western Australia. We had our cement unit on-board the rig and had been providing the cementing services for twelve months. Everything had been going well, then a piece of our equipment failed during a cement job and it cost the oil company a lot of money. It was a one-off but it shouldn't have happened.

We lost the service contract to Halliburton. Eventually Halliburton's manager also convinced the oil company to remove our cement unit and replace it with one of theirs. This was a big setback. Losing the service contract was bad enough, but having the cement unit removed from the rig would make it doubly hard to win another contract when the rig moved on to work for another oil company.

In an effort to expand our business in Western Australia, I had also installed a bulk storage facility at

Point Samson to supply cement for the job. Now this facility was no longer required.

Russell had been in charge of setting up and running the bulk plant. He had installed two large bulk storage silos and a compressor near a jetty, and mounted a couple of small transport silos on two rail carriages. The cement would be taken out to the end of the jetty on a narrow-track jetty-train and then transferred pneumatically into silos on a supply boat. This arrangement for loading the supply boats seemed to work pretty well, although it usually required three or four train trips down the jetty to fully load the boat.

What didn't work so well was getting the cement powder out of the cement bags into the storage silos in the first place. Russell took delivery of five hundred bags of cement at a time and needed to empty these one by one into a purpose-built hopper. From there the powder could be transferred into his storage silos. Carrying and cutting the cement bags in the heat of the day was not a job he could do himself so he needed to hire two or three men to help with this work.

There weren't many men around however, and those that were didn't want the type of work Russell had to offer. Finding men often involved visiting pubs and coercing a few 'locals' to stop drinking beer for a few hours. After they'd done the job once, they weren't interested in ever doing it again so, getting manpower became a bigger problem each time a new delivery arrived. Because of this manpower problem, after five months, operating the bulk plant became nearly impossible. When I called to tell

Russell the bulk plant was no longer required he was not disappointed.

Closing down the facility made his wife happy as well. There was so little for the two of them to do in Point Samson they were both bored to tears. Once Russell demobilised the bulk plant they couldn't get out of town quick enough.

The oil price had been very low for a number of years but towards the end of 1973 it suddenly increased dramatically. In many countries this was having a big impact on drilling activity. In most regions where BJ was active business was booming and these regions urgently needed more men and more equipment. This boom wasn't happening in Australia as yet.

Commercially BJ Australia was surviving and had always made a small profit but, one day, head office in California called me to advise that the Australian operation was being shut down. They had decided that the service engineers and assets could be more profitably deployed elsewhere.

I was disappointed that my job as Region Manager was coming to an end, however, there was still one big job to do. I had just secured a contract to provide cementing services on a well to be drilled in Tonga (probably the only well ever to be drilled there). The Tonga job was still going ahead.

The drilling rig, a cement truck and all the service tools were loaded onto a freighter in Brisbane. A few weeks later, everything was offloaded in Tonga. Once the rig was on location, the drilling contractor anticipated the well would take forty-to-fifty days to drill.

I assigned our service engineer, Thruppy, to the job and he flew over to Tonga once drilling commenced. He was only there to do the cementing, so would only need to work one day a week.

Thruppy was pretty good at making use of his spare time when he wasn't working. Wherever he went, he liked making friends and particularly enjoyed making friends of the opposite sex. He was a very sociable chap and loved to party.

As far as crew changes went, it was company policy that we would try to get someone relieved from an ongoing job after two weeks, unless the job was nearly finished, in which case they might be asked to stay another seven-to-ten days to finish it off. After four weeks there was no question, a relief man would be sent.

On this occasion the rule was broken.

I'd heard from the drilling contractor that the job was going pretty much as planned. After three weeks I managed to get a call through to Thruppy and suggested that I fly his relief man out in two days' time. There was only one connecting flight to Tonga each week and if we didn't crew change then it couldn't happen for another nine days.

Thruppy said that no relief was required. He was sure the job would finish within the week. He expected he would be flying home on the first available flight thereafter.

Seven days passed and the drilling contractor called to say there had been a delay and they were not expecting to finish for another ten days. I made arrangements for a relief man to go to Tonga and called Thruppy to tell him this was happening.

"Don't send the relief. He's not required, the job's nearly done and I'll be fine to stay to the end."

"Well, what about if I fly your wife over to keep you company for your last week?" I asked.

I received the clearest possible response. "Under no circumstances. I repeat. Under no circumstances send my wife …!"

Finally, the penny dropped. I guess some assignments just weren't as tough as I thought they were.

As soon as I had started winding down the business in Australia some of the service engineers were given overseas contracts. Two of the Australian boys, Cliff and Adam, were now living in Penang, Malaysia, working in an oil field in Northern Sumatra, Indonesia. They were working 'back-to-back', week on, week off.

At the outset this arrangement worked very well, then it went through an awkward patch. At the start of the job, Cliff had moved up to Penang together with his wife Beryl and Adam had moved up as a bachelor on single status. By the end of their assignment, Adam was married to Beryl and Cliff had changed his name to Mohamed and was married to a local Malaysian girl. After the reshuffle everything seemed to be working fine again.

Before closing down the Australian operation I agreed to take an assignment as the District Engineer in Aberdeen, Scotland. I was planning to move there with

Neva at the end of August 1974. On our way to Scotland we would first go to Texas where I would be given the engineering training I would need to have in order to do the job.

First, I had to tidy up some loose ends from my thirteen years in Australia. One loose end was twenty days of accumulated holidays with BJ. I needed to take them or lose them so, for the last few months, I took one or two days off every week. I used these days to work on my golf game.

I hadn't been playing much golf so my handicap had eased out to sixteen. Playing a couple of times a week I soon started to improve. So much so that when I played in the Saturday Stableford at Indooroopilly, now the St Lucia course, off my sixteen handicap, I came in with fifty-three Stableford points. I had shot one under par gross, my best round ever.

A funny thing happened when I came into the clubhouse. I'd played in the second-to-last group of the day and, back then, the day's prizewinners were always presented with their gift vouchers immediately after the last group completed their round.

One chap had finished his round some three hours earlier and had scored a remarkable forty-six points, ten under his handicap. After his game, he stayed in the bar celebrating what would surely be his first big win. Many beers were consumed during the time he'd been waiting.

Anyway, he was well oiled when his buddy came over to inform him that he had not won, but had come second. "Someone has just come in with fifty-three points," he said. "You are second by a seven point difference." "Yeah that would be right, and I suppose he can walk on water as well?" came the reply.

He was sure they were pulling his leg and wasn't buying the story. Shortly thereafter, the prizewinners were announced in reverse order. His name was called out for second place.

"You're all in this together," he shouted. "You're all a mob of bastards. Quit messing with me and give me my first prize!"

Even after my name was called and I was given the first-place voucher, he still wasn't convinced. "How the hell can you score fifty-three points, its …ing impossible!" he said. He stood there in disbelief. He looked down at his second-place voucher and then back up at me a few times. I wasn't sure whether he was going to laugh or cry. It was as if I'd ruined his day. I suspect I probably had.

Playing in the same competition the following week off my new, eight handicap, by chance I was lucky enough to be paired with the handicap convener. I took eleven more shots than the previous week. Under the circumstances I thought my thirty-four points that day was a pretty good effort.

CHAPTER 21

The Golfing Career

Over the years, through painful experience, I've found that listening to a golfer talk about their golf game doesn't hold much interest.

There is, however, one golf story worth telling – not about my golf game, but about my Dad's. This happened back when I was eighteen years old and still living at home. Dad was a big man, six foot four inches tall and weighing two hundred and thirty pounds. He was not a golfer. In fact, he was not a sportsman of any sort. He was a hard-headed Dutchman.

One day, after my Mum had spoken to him about his lack of participation in his boys' sporting activities, Dad came into my bedroom and asked what my plans were for the weekend. I said that I was intending to play a round of golf at Keperra, where I was a junior member. Dad suggested it would be nice if he and my younger brother Steven could join me.

Having never had Dad express an interest in my golf, I was absolutely delighted.

Dad had never swung a golf club or set foot on a golf course in his life. However, I didn't think of that, I quickly called the club and arranged for the three of us to play together.

On Sunday morning, we left the house ready for our game. Steven and I were wearing golf attire and Dad was dressed to go on a geological field trip, hiking boots and all. I had a half-set of golf clubs for myself and had given Steven and Dad five hand-me-downs in a well-worn pencil bag for them to share.

Off we went to Keperra. Along the way Dad asked, "How do you play golf?" Suddenly I realised, that apart from knowing the object was to get a very small ball into a very small hole some distance away, Dad didn't have a 'scooby' … no idea whatsoever … about how to play golf.

I became anxious about how this was going to work out.

We arrived at Keperra about twenty minutes before our tee time. I spent this time trying to show him how to hold a golf club and how to make a basic swing.

We hadn't made much progress before the starter, who resided in a little hut right next to the first tee-box, called us to the tee.

I decided to get Steven to drive-off first and, thankfully, he hit his ball with his first swing. It landed in the rough off the right side of the fairway, around one hundred and fifty yards away.

Next it was Dad's turn. I gave him a ball and a tee. When he pushed the tee into the ground and managed to get the ball to balance on top he gave me a big smile, as if to say, "How hard can this game be?"

Steven handed him the second-hand driver and he was ready to go.

Having completely forgotten my instruction about holding and swinging a club, Dad gripped the driver much as he would have gripped his rock pick.

He then took a swing at the ball. A lump of sod, a few inches long, was removed from the tee-box approximately one foot behind the ball. The ball never moved.

Unperturbed, Dad wound-up and took another swing. Another piece of turf was airborne but, once again, the ball never moved.

A little surprised, he swung a few more times in rapid succession. More turf was airborne and, on the last attempt, contact was made with the ball. It took off low and left, coming to rest seventy yards away, just off the fairway.

I avoided looking at the starter. As quickly as possible I gathered up Dad's divots and patched up the tee box as best I could.

Dad left the tee and was walking purposefully towards his ball. He still had the driver in his hand. He had named this the '*houte klomp*', Dutch for wooden shoe.

I still had to tee-off, so I called out, telling Dad to wait and stand clear. Thankfully, I hit a nice drive. We were off.

When I caught up with Dad, I told him he had the wrong club. He should now be using one of the three irons in the set. I took away his driver and gave him a seven iron. (Again, for ease of reference, he immediately named this club the '*vishaak*', Dutch for fish hook.)

Dad said he could see his ball so I went to help Steven find his.

During our drive to Keperra, the one piece of information I'd given Dad about the rules of golf, was that he must never touch or move the ball once it had been 'put in play'. He was now remembering my instruction.

Had I realised Dad's swing was impeded by a staked tree I would have told him to move it. However he didn't know about the free-lift rule.

He was a big man and such a small tree wouldn't present a problem. As he took his stance, he gently pushed it to one side with his size-fourteen boot. He took two deliberate swings and then reverted to the perpetual motion technique. Eventually, contact was made and his ball went another fifty yards up the fairway.

Suddenly I heard a huge commotion. I looked back to see the starter running down the fairway. He had left his little hut and was yelling out at Dad as he ran towards him. Dad knew he'd done something wrong.

Realising that his handling of the tree might have been a bit harsh, he carefully straightened it back upright and signalled to the starter that everything was okay.

Once we found Steven's ball, he played his second shot and we then walked forward.

Meanwhile, Dad had kept moving, he was 'in the zone'. He marched past my drive and kept going towards his ball. He was enjoying himself.

As I came to each place where Dad had stopped to play another shot, I carried out as much repair work as I could. Steven and I then waited at my ball. We couldn't play until the foursome ahead cleared the green.

People on the green weren't a problem for Dad. Even though he was less than one hundred yards away, he was attempting to play his next shot. One man was still putting. His three playing partners were looking back in disbelief.

On the third swing of his swing sequence Dad made contact with the ball and hit a great shot. The ball took off and sailed straight over the green, some fifty feet above their heads, clattering into the trees beyond.

The foursome ducked. The last player quickly holed out, then they all dashed off to the next tee.

A little too late, I called out telling Dad not to move.

Steven and I played our shots and walked forward.

I gave Dad a proper lecture about hitting his ball when people were still in-range on the green.

"I didn't know they were in-range," he replied, "I had no idea I could hit the ball that far."

Fair enough I suppose. His longest shot ever had only gone seventy yards.

Dad's ball was lost so I gave him a replacement.

After we finished putting, Steven gave Dad the putter and suggested that he 'have a go'. Dad gave the ball a good smack and it hit Steven's foot. Enough putting I thought … off to the next tee.

It went on like that for another eight holes. By the time we eventually finished the front nine, I decided that we'd all had enough. It had simply been the most harrowing experience I'd ever had on a golf course.

On our way home, Dad said how much he'd enjoyed his game. "We should do it again sometime," he said. My head was still spinning. "I think we should have a few sessions at the driving range first," I suggested.

I was back playing at Keperra the following week and was in a group with three members. As we were walking along, one asked if I'd been there the previous week. "Did you hear what happened?" he asked. Not knowing what he was referring to, he started to tell me about some giant of a man with two boys who damn near destroyed the front nine! I pretended to have no knowledge.

Dad played his second, and last, game of golf a few weeks later. A sales rep had called on him and asked if he was a golfer, to which Dad replied, "I played with my boys two weeks ago."

An invitation was extended and that Sunday Dad headed off to play Royal Queensland. Once again, he left home dressed in his field gear. He didn't take anything with him, no golf clubs, no shoes, and no balls. He hadn't realised it was normal practice to supply these himself.

Mum said afterwards that Dad was not happy when he came home. I didn't get any details, but his day had not gone well. Apparently he and his host had been asked to leave the golf course and told never to return.

That was the end of Dad's golfing career. For the three of us who had experienced playing with him, it was a brief, but well remembered, career.

I felt sorry for the unfortunate drill bit salesman. I just hope Dad bought a few drill bits from the man.

CHAPTER 22

The Dung Beetle

Everyone has a story about a coincidence. My amazing coincidence happened thirty years after I'd left Australia when my good friend from Arcadia Valley, was about to celebrate his sixty-fifth birthday. I wanted to get Walter something special, after all, he'd sent me his squash racket for a special birthday of mine.

My wife was aware of my search and one day when she was in Edinburgh shopping, she called to say that she'd found the perfect gift. A solid silver dung-beetle rolling a ball of dung, and, it was on sale! (My guess is there wasn't a huge demand for silver dung beetles in Edinburgh. If she hadn't bought it, it would still be there today.)

Walter had been involved as a pioneer with the Queensland trial to introduce dung beetles onto Australian cattle properties, so for him this was the perfect gift.

Basically the dung beetles do a great job of rolling up and burying cattle dung. This fertilises the soil and helps keep down the fly population. Today, many years after they were first introduced, there are millions of beetles on properties everywhere and they are making a huge difference to both the amount of dung lying around and to the fly population. The overall productivity has improved and with fewer flies, the cattle properties have become nicer places for both people and animals to live.

Neva purchased the beetle then, on our next trip, we carried it with us from Aberdeen to Arcadia Valley. As expected, when we gave it to Walter he thought this was a very special and unique gift.

At the time, Walter had Brian, a cattleman from Zimbabwe, working with him. When Walter showed Brian the sculpture he recognised it straight away as a piece by Patrick Mavros. Walter checked and sure enough, he was correct.

"How did you know?" asked Walter.

"Well, when I was living in Zimbabwe, I used to supply the silver ore which Patrick used for making his sculptures and that piece is typical of his work," Brian replied.

Fancy that. While living in Zimbabwe, Brian supplied the silver to Patrick, who sculptured it into a dung beetle. Patrick then sent this sculpture to Edinburgh to be sold. Neva purchased it and we carried it to Australia. We gave it to Walter in Arcadia Valley, where Brian, who had supplied the silver to Patrick for the sculpture in the first place, was now working.

Now that's what I call a coincidence!

Another 'coincidence' I sometimes wonder about happened ten years later. Walter's son, Rowan, became friends with the son of the same Miss Australia Walter had taken to the Roma Ball we attended all those years ago. When traveling around Europe, they and their girlfriends came to stay at our place in the UK.

That was also a coincidence … or, had Walter somehow managed to find a really clever way to make sure that I was never going to forget the match I'd lost and the date he'd had with Miss Australia?

Surely winning a squash match couldn't have meant that much to him … or could it?

Book 2 - Aberdeen Days

CHAPTER 23

The Beautiful City

While I was going through the motions of closing down the Australian office, BJ's management offered me the option of three different overseas postings. I could move to Edmonton to work with the tool design group, I could move to Singapore to work as a service engineer, or I could go to Aberdeen to work as the district engineer. Although I wasn't qualified for the job, I decided my best choice was a move to Aberdeen.

I accepted a two-year assignment and was thinking I would extend this for an additional two years if the job worked out and Neva and I enjoyed living there. We were keen to see the UK and explore Europe so Aberdeen seemed like an ideal posting for some interesting holiday travel.

Neva and I left Australia when I was twenty-nine. We packed a few of our possessions to send to Aberdeen, then sold our car and our Brisbane house. We were making a complete break with Australia and looking forward to the challenge of starting the next chapter of our lives in Scotland.

Before going to Scotland, I was told that I would need to spend some time in America. Once in Aberdeen, as the District Engineer, I would be responsible for designing cement jobs for North Sea wells. In order to prepare myself for this job, I needed to go to Arlington and then Houston, Texas, where I would be put through a crash course in engineering. Mostly, my new job would involve selecting the correct additives to add to the cement powder. Every cement job differs depending on the volume of cement needing to be pumped and the temperature at the depth it was to be placed. You certainly didn't want the cement to set too soon, but also, you didn't want to wait any longer than necessary for the cement to harden. When the cost of an offshore drilling operation was two hundred thousand dollars a day or more, time spent '*waiting on cement*' needed to be kept to a minimum. On the other hand, if the cement set before it was in place, it could cost many days of rig time to sort out the problem.

I spent most of my time in Arlington. After work, we occasionally went to the Six Flags Over Texas amusement park or to a Texas Rangers baseball game. Back when I was living in Canada, I had played a lot of baseball, so I understood the game and particularly enjoyed going to those events.

When Neva and I travelled to America, our Australian suitcases were looking pretty shabby. As the summer sales were on, we decided we would take the opportunity to upgrade. We eventually purchased a five-piece set of luggage at half price in Dallas. We hadn't intended to buy five pieces but the salesman was so persuasive and the price was so good we couldn't resist. To show us how durable the Hartman luggage was, the salesman took a three-pronged fork, slammed it down hard and ripped it along the side of one suitcase. I couldn't believe it! The prongs were sharp but yet there wasn't even the slightest mark on the suitcase. I was very impressed.

We took our beautiful new luggage back to our motel and threw out the old suitcases. We now looked like two very-well-to-do travellers.

The next weekend we invited acquaintances from Dallas to join us for lunch at a superb Mexican restaurant near our motel. After lunch, I was proud to show them our new luggage. Tom said we had bought a top brand. I thought I would let him see just how tough this stuff was.

I went to the kitchen drawer and took out a steak knife. I raised the knife, brought it down hard, and ripped it along the side of the case. Everyone was aghast as we stood looking at the cut mark across the side of our new suitcase. I stood looking at it in disbelief. Tom and Dulany couldn't believe it either. Tom finally broke the silence. He said, "Jesus, Roy, you're hard on luggage!"

Neva quietly started to cry.

I couldn't work out how the salesman had done it, or why I did it what I did. It was an act on impulse I've never been allowed to forget.

After six weeks, I finished my training in Arlington and went to Houston to attend an in-house training seminar with other senior staff members. At the time, there had just been a major shooting incident in America so there was a lot of news coverage about handguns and gun control.

The next morning I was telling the others how crazy I thought the gun laws were. "How can you reduce the number of gun deaths if you don't regulate the sale of guns?" I asked. "You don't know how it is over here, we need handguns to protect ourselves," came the reply. I didn't ask how they thought owning a handgun would provide protection if someone else decided to shoot them, but I did ask, "Okay, how many of you would think of owning a gun?" Turns out, I was the only one in the room who was unarmed!

Everyone else either had a gun in their briefcase, their car glove box or back in their hotel room. These were just ordinary sales, engineering and management guys, yet they all felt the need to own a handgun to protect themselves. No wonder they have a problem. With millions of guns around, it maybe explains how thirty thousand gun deaths can happen every year.

As we continued our pre-meeting chat, one of the sales guys said that he and his colleague had been to a really rough bar the night before. "How was it different?" I asked. He replied "We knew it was a rough place when, upon entering the front door, we were searched for guns and knives. When they found that we didn't have any, they gave us some!"

Everyone had a good laugh … nothing better than a good gun joke to start the day.

Once I completed my training in America, we flew to London as scheduled. Upon our arrival, I went to meet George, my new Region Manager, who had his office in Guildford, near London.

I told George about the arrangements I'd made for travelling six hundred miles north to Aberdeen. Before leaving Australia I had ordered a new car for collection in London. The plan was to pick it up that day and then drive to Scotland the following day. George said, "Don't plan on picking up any new car today, this is the UK not Australia. There is no chance it will be ready for collection on the day you've arranged."

He was amazed when I called the dealer and was advised that my car had arrived from Germany that morning and would be ready for collection at 2.00 pm. George still wasn't convinced. I got a lift over to Park Lane and drove my spanking new car back to his office at 4.00 pm. (Apparently the way BMW did things in London was the same as the way they did business in Australia.)

On our drive north we had intended to overnight in Edinburgh but there wasn't any accommodation available. It was not yet the end of August so the Edinburgh Festival was still in full swing and all the hotels were fully booked. We eventually found a place to stay forty miles further north at Ballathie House Hotel. What a wonderful spot for our first night in Scotland. The hotel is situated in the Perthshire countryside on the banks of the River Tay. It was all very Scottish and very beautiful. The hotel is now owned by a former Aberdeen oilman and is every bit as wonderful today as it was the first time we stayed.

The next day we headed north, into the Highlands, then drove east along Royal Deeside towards Aberdeen. It was a lovely drive through more beautiful countryside.

When we arrived in Aberdeen on 1 September 1974, it was still a quiet north east Scotland fishing port about to be overwhelmed by the oil industry. We discovered we had come to a very beautiful city. The sun was shining and the granite buildings were all looking their sparkling best. All the houses, churches, banks and public buildings looked magnificent. The city was clean and tidy and the parks we saw were beautifully kept. Even the ring-road had magnificent roses growing along the central divider.

The city councillors obviously placed a high priority on their gardens and public spaces. They were all beautifully presented. This effort was recognised nationally making Aberdeen a frequent winner of the Britain in Bloom competition. I'm sure all Aberdonians and the many visitors to the 'granite city' appreciated this effort as much as we did.

Within the city, the councillors also prohibited anyone from altering the original granite buildings with any out-of-character modifications, including extensions or even modern window fittings. What great foresight. The buildings all looked as magnificent as the day they were built.

What a shame that years later, the present councillors didn't continue to cherish these buildings. Instead, they let a TV company randomly stick satellite dishes on the walls of hundreds of granite homes. I remember how magnificent one sweep of terrace houses looked. Today, the same drive up Rosemount Viaduct would make you weep.

BJ had rented a flat for us which was ready to move into the day we arrived. We quickly got settled in and, the following day, I headed off to work while Neva went off to look for something intellectually stimulating to fill her time.

Within our first six months we saw a lot of the local culture. We went to a few Highland Games in various small towns near Aberdeen, a fish market display down by the harbour, Saint Andrew's day celebrations at the Marcliffe Hotel, and then got to experience our very first Hogmanay. We had never seen a New Year's celebration like it. Essentially, it was two days of drinking, eating and 'first-footing'. The 'first-footing' involved visiting friends in their home for the first time in the New Year for a drink and a bite to eat. We met other people there and instantly became friends with strangers we'd never met before. In Scotland Hogmanay is good fun and an important part of the Scottish culture.

At the end of January, we also attended our first Burns Supper, celebrating the life of the renowned Scottish poet, Robbie Burns. Some Burns poems were read and some clever speeches were made. However, my lasting memory of the evening was working out how much whisky to pour on my haggis to make it edible. The evening eventually came to an end after a set of Scottish music was played.

Aberdeen felt like a really nice place to live.

CHAPTER 24

The Blue Whale

By 1975, Aberdeen was booming and a large number of oil companies, drilling contractors and oil service companies from all around the world were setting up offices in town. Housing, office, and warehouse accommodation was all scarce and every company was short of staff.

As BJ's District Engineer, time passed quickly and I was kept busy designing cement jobs for some of the most expensive wells being drilled anywhere in the world. I enjoyed being an engineer, but it was a bit repetitive, so after nine months when I was asked if I would like to move back into management, I jumped at the chance. By then I realised that managing a business was the job I enjoyed most.

The Aberdeen District Manager's job I was given was a completely different kettle of fish from the management jobs I'd had back in Australia. Here I was responsible for over forty people and there was no shortage of work. There was, however, a shortage of qualified service engineers and equipment.

One big problem I had was that I could never say no when there was work on offer. Sometimes I accepted work from clients even when I didn't have the foggiest idea how I would source the manpower or the equipment.

One example of this reckless behaviour involved my office manager Albert and my replacement district engineer, David, who, unlike myself, had a proper engineering degree. David accompanied me to a meeting with an oil company client to discuss a grouting job we had tendered for.

The grouting operation involved mixing a cement slurry with a purpose-built cement-mixing unit and then pumping this slurry into the annular spaces around 'piles'. These piles were to be driven some forty feet into the seabed through 'sleeves' attached to the outside of each of the *jacket* legs. (A 'jacket' is the huge substructure upon which the platform is mounted. It sits on the seabed and extends up approximately one hundred feet above sea level.) In all, there were over forty piles to be driven and cemented. Once completed, the cement bond between the pile and the sleeve would secure the platform leg to the pile, thereby anchoring the jacket to the ocean floor.

Depending on the weather, the operation was expected to take three to four weeks to complete.

Technically the job wasn't that challenging. The equipment required was not complicated and the skills needed to operate the equipment were pretty straightforward, however, depending on the progress made when driving the piles, the job might go on around the clock so a team of three cementers and five helpers needed to be on-site.

At our meeting with the client, we were advised that our tender had been successful. We were given the job and told that it was expected to commence in approximately six weeks time. David knew we didn't have either the men or most of the equipment needed so he assumed that I would, regrettably, decline the contract. He was dumbstruck when I said, "That will be fine, just give us a call a few days before we need to mobilise and we'll be ready to go."

David was aghast! He had come from an oil company background and couldn't believe that this was how the service industry worked. First get the job, then go back to the office and work out how to do it. Oil companies spent weeks or months planning things in advance. They must have assumed that the service industry was also as well organised. Often, however, this was not the case.

When the call-out from the oil company came, it was nearly two weeks earlier than anticipated. By then I had managed to source enough equipment from other districts, Stavanger and Great Yarmouth, to get the job started.

What I didn't have was enough people to send offshore.

A couple of the cementers I intended to use were still offshore on other jobs. They would need to finish those assignments and then have some time off before I could send them out again. I didn't have a single qualified cementer available and only two trainees I could send. I needed to find six more people, including three qualified cementers, to make up my crew of eight by Saturday afternoon and it was now Friday evening.

I called Albert, my office manager, explained the problem and arranged to meet him at the office first thing in the morning.

There was one glimmer of hope. A guy named Joe had come in to see me about changing companies. He had just resigned from working as a cementer for a competitor. I'd met him on Wednesday and had confirmed that he was indeed qualified but was waiting for a reply from two references he had given me before I could make him an offer.

By the Saturday morning, even though I still hadn't heard back from his referees, I gave Albert his Dundee contact number and told him to 'sign him up'! "Call Joe, tell him he's got the job and get him to come to Aberdeen to go to work this afternoon," were my instructions.

Albert got Joe on the phone. "Joe, Roy says that you've got the job and he needs you to come to Aberdeen right away. We need you for a grouting job … you will be going out on the 'Friedenstein' to the 'Blue Whale' this afternoon.

The Friedenstein was the supply boat being loaded up with all the equipment for the job. It would make its way out to the Blue Whale, which was a construction barge moored alongside the platform. The grouting work would be done from onboard this barge.

When Joe took the call, he was still hung-over from his Friday night out. Albert finished talking and waited for a response. There was no response. "Are you there?" asked Albert. After another long silence, finally came a response, "Who are you, and what's all this shit about a Blue Whale?" asked Joe.

Albert managed to say, "I'll call you back". He came into my office laughing so hard he couldn't speak.

Eventually, he managed to tell me about the call and Joe's response. Albert said that I would need to call him back as he didn't think he could keep his composure to speak with him again.

I called Joe. "Joe this is Roy from BJ. You've got the job we spoke about on Wednesday and I need you to come to Aberdeen right away," I said.

"I don't have any offshore gear with me," replied Joe.

"What size boots do you wear? I'll have them here, together with hard hat and coveralls, when you arrive," I said.

"I can't drive because I've been drinking," he said.

"I'll arrange a taxi," I said.

"I don't have any cash," he said.

"I'll get the taxi to bring you all the way to Aberdeen and I'll pay for it," I said.

Eventually Joe couldn't think of anything else which prevented him from coming, so he came. He arrived after lunch, filled out an employment form, was given a briefing about the job, handed his kit and boarded the Friedenstein at 4.00 pm.

Once we knew Joe was coming we had three 'hands' sorted … now we just needed to find five more.

My first port of call was the youth hostel on Queens Road. Word had reached Australia and New Zealand that there was a possibility of finding work in Aberdeen, so there was a steady stream of backpackers coming through town. Most of these guys were fit and able and were always in need of funds to finance their next excursion.

After some very brief interviews, I found three capable lads who were all keen to go to work. I got their boot and coverall sizes and arranged for them to be brought to my office for a briefing. Meantime, Albert had convinced another two trainees who had just come ashore to forgo their time off and head straight back to work, assuring them it would only be for one week.

Although we only had one qualified cementer in the group, we now had a crew of eight. After getting the new-hires to sign on and giving them a briefing on the 'do's and don'ts' offshore, they were all ready to go.

Everyone boarded the Friedenstein and at dinnertime that evening introduced themselves to one another as they headed out to sea. It was the first time any of them had met Joe. Joe told them that he had just signed on with BJ as well, and, that he was their boss!

A day later they arrived at the new platform and pulled up alongside the Blue Whale. Once all the equipment was transferred across they spent the next few days getting everything set up and 'taking on cement' into the silos. Joe then put his helpers through a few dry-runs with the equipment so he was sure they knew what to do.

As I had anticipated when I received the early call-out, the job was not ready to start. It worked out that Joe and his team of helpers had only just started the first grouting job before the two trainees were changed out for two qualified cementers, seven days later. The job was now properly staffed and went ahead without a hitch.

Actually, there were one or two small hitches. Mark, from Australia, was one of the other cementers I had sent out to the job. At one stage he told one of the new boys to turn on a wash-down hose. Rather than opening the ball-valve slowly, the lad turned it fully open in one move. Mark was holding the hose under his arm when the sudden pressure surge lifted him off the cement mixing unit and flung him down on the deck. He got a nasty crack to the back of his head. The next thing he knew he was on a helicopter headed for the nearest hospital in Lerwick, Shetland. He needed a few stitches but fortunately it wasn't a serious injury. After two days in hospital for observation, Mark was allowed to return to the Blue Whale.

Mark's accident would never have happened had the lad been properly trained before going offshore. Mark had been lucky and I got a sharp reminder about my responsibility for proper staff training.

One of the new boys also managed to connect a potable water supply hose to a cement silo. Instead of getting the cement powder they were supposed to be receiving from the supply boat, the silo took in one hundred gallons of water before the mistake was noticed.

Turns out it was not an easy mistake to have made. The lad had to physically change a fitting off the cement hose onto a water hose in order to attach the wrong line.

With water in the silo, the cement set solid, taking the silo out of action. Fortunately, it happened towards the end of the job so the boys were able to finish the job using the cement in the remaining silos.

Apart from those two incidents, the grouting job was a big success and ended up being a very profitable contract for the company.

Once it finished all the equipment was demobilised back to Aberdeen. There wasn't any problem getting our equipment back, however, getting a silo half full of set cement offloaded required a heavy-lift crane. The silo was lifted onto a low-loader and delivered back to our fabricator's workshop.

I had asked the fabricator if they could do anything with the silo. I thought they might know how to clean it out, or if not, maybe they could salvage some of the steel.

The fabricator said they did not want the job, but one of their staff was keen to make some extra money and offered to clean it out for us. The guy intended to do the work in his spare time. He offered to remove all the cement for one thousand pounds.

It sounded like a great deal to me.

It didn't go well for him. He had no appreciation of how difficult it would be to remove cement which was rock hard. He needed to get inside the silo through the manhole and work away with a small jack-hammer.

As the silo was lying on its side, in the beginning he had to hold the jack-hammer in front of himself, pushing it against the cement. It was very hard work and it took him hours just to make a little headway. All the broken cement then had to be taken out through the manhole, loaded onto a small truck and transported to a landfill site.

For three weeks he worked on the job every evening and all weekend. His wife would bring his meals to the silo and, in order for his kids to get to see their dad, she would bring them along as well. The kids would look in through the manhole to see how dad was getting on.

When he was half-way through the job, the silo over balanced and rolled twenty yards down a gentle slope. Fortunately, he managed to scamper out when it started to move, but the position in which the silo came to rest meant that the cement was now above him. In order to continue his work he needed to hire a tractor to roll the silo back a bit.

Eventually, having spent well over one hundred hours inside the silo, all the cement had been removed. The fabricator fitted new aeration slides inside and pressure-tested the silo. They then applied a fresh coat of paint on the outside.

Two months after the grouting job had finished, the silo was ready for use again.

The man had done a great job. When he added up the cost of his tool rental and paying for the cement removal, by the time he finished I'll bet he felt he really had earned his one thousand pounds. If anyone else was ever needing a silo to be cleaned out, I very much doubt he would have been offering to take on the job.

CHAPTER 25

The Staff Shortage

After the success of the grouting job, I decided the company should sponsor a thank-you night out for the boys. I invited the grouting crew to bring their wives or girlfriends and invited the rest of our staff to join the party. That Saturday, I hired a bus to take us all to the small village of Tarves just outside Aberdeen. We ended up with around fifty people at the Aberdeen Arms for dinner and a 'free bar'.

The dinner was most enjoyable. Then, as soon as the meal finished the boys got stuck into the free drink. A free bar wasn't a concept many of the local lads had come across before. They went wild!

By 10.00 pm they were all having a jolly good time and many of them were stumbling about. Graeme, one of my newly qualified local cementers, was really enjoying himself. He went outside for a breath of fresh air, dumped the flowering plants out of the ornamental wheelbarrow he'd found at the front door and wheeled it back into the lounge. He reloaded the barrow with a drunk colleague and, to a chorus of hysterical laughter from the rest of the boys, did a few laps around the dance floor before dumping the lad outside on top of the plants.

Things were getting out of hand … it was time to go home.

Fortunately our bus for the return trip arrived early so I shut down the bar and, after a bit of a struggle, managed to get everyone on-board.

Along the way home the bus made a pit stop so the boys could relieve themselves.

My friend Russell, who was in Aberdeen on assignment from Australia at the time, decided he'd seen enough. He scampered off the bus and didn't return. I worried what might have happened to him as the rest of us headed back to Aberdeen.

The next day Russell called to say he was having such a difficult time dealing with the amorous attention of one rather intoxicated lady that he decided it was safer to leave the bus in the-middle-of-nowhere and walk the last few miles.

Back at work on Monday morning I got the full post-mortem. All the boys had a great night. "Best night ever!" they said.

I, on the other hand, decided that having a free bar in Scotland possibly wasn't the best idea I'd ever had.

The success of the first grouting job led to other contracts. The biggest of these was on a platform made of cement, known as a Condeep. The particular structure we were on had three legs which were six hundred feet tall and sixty feet in diameter. These legs were encircled and supported by a base made up of nineteen silos. The base silos were also sixty feet in diameter and around ninety feet tall. The bottom of the structure covered an area of approximately seventy thousand square feet, the size of a one-and-a-half football pitches. It was a huge platform.

The platform had been built in Norway and was towed out to location on the UK side of the North Sea by six tugboats. It was then sunk, slowly, until the base came to rest on the seabed. Because of their shape, when all these twenty-two domes made contact with the seabed there was a point-loading on the bottom of each dome.

The object of the grouting exercise was to displace the seawater trapped between each of the domes within the outer circumference of the base and replace this water with a soft cement mixture. This effectively provided each dome with a larger area of contact. Imagine an egg carton with the spaces filled in so that the bottom is flat.

The grouting job was straightforward enough, it just took a long time to mix the volume of cement slurry needed to fill the gaps.

One interesting aspect of this job was the way in which the grout was directed to each of the voids in turn. This was done via a manifold and around eighty flow lines, two inlet and two outlet lines coming from each void. The lines had been installed when the base of the platform was being built and a manifold was placed inside one of the three legs, near the bottom. One of us needed to be near the manifold whenever cement was being pumped, so we took it in turns to climb six hundred feet down inside the leg to 'man' the manifold. Just below where we sat, there was only one foot of cement between the inside of the leg and the seabed itself. To be sitting there, on your own, for three hours at a time, just six feet off the seabed felt very strange indeed.

For some reason, the thought of climbing up and down the six hundred foot ladder didn't bother me. The ladder was staggered in ten-foot sections so I couldn't have fallen far, however, in hindsight, it probably wasn't a smartest thing for me to have done. At least I didn't participate in the time-trials the rest of the boys were having. They were trying to see who could manage the six-hundred-foot ascent in the fastest time. As I recall, Jim won in a time of around one minute and twenty seconds.

When the cement mixing commenced, the water being displaced from the void was pumped back to the surface and a void was deemed to have been filled once cement-returns arrived back through the outlet line. Typically, it took a full day to completely fill one section, so the job went on day and night for twenty days.

I was on this job for three weeks. We were so short of staff at the time that I had no option but to leave Albert in charge of the office and go out to the job myself. The day I went offshore was 17 July 1976. I remember this date because it was exactly two days after my first daughter was born. I had left Neva and baby Janna in the care of the NHS and headed out to the North Sea.

As there wasn't anyone available to relieve me, in the end I was there for the entire job. Only after the last void was cemented was I finally able to come home.

Our staff shortages went on for at least three years so we needed a steady supply of expats. We got Mark and

Russell over from Australia and a few cementers from Canada, but mostly the expats came from America.

In order to reduce our need for expats, right from the day I started as District Manager I set up a training programme for locals. We were training them up as quickly as we possibly could. Eventually we would have a number of top-notch Scottish cementers but, in the meantime, we continued to need any qualified expat we could get hold of.

Because our remuneration package was so generous, I couldn't understand why there weren't a lot of foreign cementers lining up to come to work in the North Sea. However, I found out for myself what it meant to leave your family behind when my Dad became ill. It was hard not being at home at the time and difficult to give much support from ten thousand miles away. When Dad died a short while later, I understood one of the main reasons why many cementers were reluctant to move away from their home town.

CHAPTER 26

The Superstitious Sister

The expats who did come to Aberdeen were chosen by head office in Houston. I have no idea how some of these people were selected.

One man arrived from Louisiana and I needed him to go out to relieve another cementer as soon as possible. The plan was for him to overlap with the cementer on the rig for a few days in order to become acquainted with the cementing set-up and then perform any cementing duties once he was left on his own. Although cement jobs are much the same in every oil field, because the cementing set-up on each rig differs, I wouldn't send a cementer out to a rig he wasn't familiar with without an overlap.

The new man was a qualified cementer so I knew he could do the work. When I discussed the job with him, he confirmed that he had the necessary experience, but had only ever worked on land rigs and swamp barges. He had never worked offshore, and informed me that he had no intention of starting his offshore career in the North Sea! He said he was ready to go to any land rig whenever he was needed.

I didn't have any work on land rigs.

I desperately needed a cementer and was really annoyed that he'd been sent all this way and wasn't going to be of any use. Because he wasn't even prepared to go offshore, I couldn't use him at all.

I was not impressed. When I called head office in Houston the manager told me he had assumed the cementer would be okay to work offshore but hadn't confirmed this with him. I suggested that, in future, it might be a good idea to check that people were actually prepared to do the job they were coming to do.

I called our travel agent and told them the cementer would be coming in to book his flight home and gave them a purchase-order number to cover the cost of his ticket. He was to leave Aberdeen as soon as possible.

I didn't find out until the travel agent's bill arrived a few days later that he had booked himself a first-class seat all the way back to somewhere in Louisiana. He realised that I hadn't specified economy class on the purchase order and had deliberately taken advantage. I had already been annoyed that he'd been sent to Aberdeen but thought it probably wasn't his fault. Now that I saw he had taken advantage, I was pretty angry.

Another lesson learnt. I never again gave out a purchase-order without specifying the class of travel.

Some of the other expats who came to Aberdeen to work could do the job but, boy, were they ever unusual people. I remember Ken and his wife, whose name I can't recall, arriving to meet me. One of our staff had met them on arrival at Aberdeen airport and brought them to my office. Before coming to Aberdeen, Ken had been living in Malta while working on assignment in North Africa. His new wife was from Malta, where he met her at a club he'd frequented.

Ken seemed a nice quiet sort of guy but his wife was a real bombshell. She wore a low-cut red dress with a split up to her thigh. She had what looked like a small cut scar on one cheek and something similar on her arm. I was curious if she'd been in a knife skirmish but decided not to ask.

I welcomed them to Aberdeen and explained to Ken that I really needed him to go offshore as soon as possible. Ken said he was okay with this, however, he had arranged for his seventeen-year-old son to come from Texas for three weeks during his summer holiday. "Not a problem," I said. "I will arrange for someone to meet him at the airport." Ken's wife then added that she had arranged for her sister from Malta to come and stay for a couple of weeks as well. "Also not a problem," I said. "Give me their arrival details and I'll arrange for both of them to be picked up and brought to the flat."

Ken agreed to go offshore the next day.

The company had rented a furnished flat which was ready for them to move into. I gave them some funds, and then made arrangements for them to be given a quick tour of Aberdeen and taken to the local shop to pick up supplies.

Before leaving my office Ken asked, "Could you also look after this while I'm away? I'm not happy to leave it in the flat." Ken handed me a handgun. "Holy crap! I'm pretty sure you're not supposed to have one of these in this country," I said.

At that particular moment I couldn't think what else to do, so I took the gun and locked it in my desk drawer.

I asked if they had any more questions. Ken's new bride then asked, "If Ken dies when he's on the job, am I entitled to compensation?" That certainly wasn't a question I was expecting. In Ken's presence, I assured her that would be the case, although I had no idea who might actually be entitled to make a claim should any misadventure occur.

As promised, Ken went offshore the following day, did his three-day overlap then stayed on for a further two weeks.

Two days after Ken left town, one of our staff met and collected his son Jake, then the following day collected Ken's wife's sister, Maria. Once they were all in the flat I pretty much forgot about them. As always, I was really busy and fully occupied with other matters.

Jake, Maria and Ken's wife were in the flat for six days when I got a call from Jake. "Holy smoke, I'm so sorry," I said. "I forgot to check how you were getting on. You must be needing some more cash for food … I'll come right over." "Yes," Jake replied. "We do need some more money, but the reason I'm calling is to say that Maria is in hospital."

"Oh my god! What happened? Don't tell me, I'll be right there!" I said, and raced from the office.

I arrived at the flat ten minutes later. The door was answered by Ken's wife, wearing nothing but a bra and panties. Jake, who I'd never met, had obviously just thrown on a shirt and pants, but much to my surprise, his face was completely black.

I stood at the door wondering what question to ask first. I went with, "Maria, how is Maria, what happened?"

Well, it appears that Maria was a very superstitious girl and her fun-loving sister had decided to play a little prank on her. Using a burnt cork, she had blackened Jake's face and then cut a hole in a bed sheet and pulled it over his head. Next, Jake went into Maria's bedroom and woke her up with a loud, "BOO"!

Maria awoke, passed out, and couldn't be revived.

Jake panicked and called 999. Within ten minutes the ambulance arrived and off she went to Foresterhill Hospital. Apparently Maria had come around before the ambulance got there but the medic assumed ... I'm not sure why ... that there must have been drugs involved so had insisted she be taken to hospital for a check-up.

Just before I arrived on the scene, Maria had phoned from the hospital to say that she had been given the all-clear.

I drove up to the hospital with Ken's wife, who was now fully dressed, to bring Maria back home. Why Ken's wife had been undressed in the first place I have no idea. The flat was heated to around 30 °C, so maybe it was just too hot inside to wear clothes. I don't know and didn't ask.

Anyway, I am certain this was one summer vacation Jake will remember for the rest of his life. I can only imagine what they'd been getting up to the previous six nights.

Back at my office, I was continuously troubled by the fact that I had a gun locked up in my desk. The first thing I did every morning was to check the drawer and make sure it was still there. Even though there weren't any bullets, I was pleased that Ken hadn't left it at the flat. No telling what pranks his wife may have come up with if she'd had a gun available.

When Ken returned onshore I immediately gave him back his gun, thankful that it was no longer my problem.

Ken and his wife only stayed in Aberdeen for a few months. He said his wife hadn't settled so they needed to move back to live in Malta. I thought it was probably the right decision, but I was sorry to see him go. Ken turned out to be an excellent cementer. He was easy to manage and did a good job offshore. The customers liked him and, according to his relief, he kept his cement unit in excellent shape.

After he left I thought I wouldn't mind getting him back if he was ever looking for an assignment on single status. From what I'd seen, I thought that could be a distinct possibility.

CHAPTER 27

The Escort Service

After I had been the District Manager for two years, a new salesman arrived from America to work out of the Aberdeen office. Troy wasn't assigned to work with me, he answered to the Region Manager, George, in London. His job was to focus on equipment sales. He was posted to Aberdeen to deal with oil companies and drilling contractors who were building platforms and drilling rigs for the North Sea. These new builds would need to have a full spread of cementing equipment on-board. High priority was placed on getting BJ's equipment installed, particularly on platforms, as the contract for cementing services was usually negotiated together with the equipment sale. There were often forty to sixty wells to drill from a platform so a service contract could run for many years. It was an important selling opportunity.

Troy had one of those jobs where there really wasn't any specific work to do from one day to the next, or even one week to the next. He needed to find out which oil companies and drilling contractors were building rigs and platforms and then secure the opportunity to tender for a sale. Mostly this just required him to 'network' and develop relationships with potential clients.

Troy wasn't in the office very much and probably didn't need to be. When he did come in however, he was always relaxed and happy. He was easy to get on with and a pleasant man to be around. He would have a chat with me, drink a cup of coffee, make a few phone calls and then leave again.

I always asked how he was getting on and he was always pleased with his progress. I had enough on my plate without being overly concerned about what he was doing. However, when I found out through a client that he was offering an escort service, I thought I'd better take a little more notice.

When I asked him about his enterprise he explained that the 'facility' was only there to help him get close to some potential clients.

I didn't like the sound of his sales approach and was sure it wouldn't be approved of. I called George and told him about Troy's little 'business on the side'. George wasn't impressed. He called Troy and suggested he make plans to 'escort' himself and his family on a trip back to the States. His assignment in Aberdeen had just come to an end.

I had one other 'ladies of the night' event but I didn't do much about this one. When we were getting ready for one of our grouting contracts we needed to set up a cement bulk plant at Leith Harbour near Edinburgh. There was a big rush to get this facility working as the job was about to start.

We sent two men down to rig up the silos. Unfortunately it was the middle of August and, once again, the festival was in full swing. There were no hotel rooms to be had anywhere. The offshore construction company with whom we were working was based in Leith. When they offered to find rooms for our boys I accepted gratefully.

Whenever I spoke with our men about how the job was going, I also checked if they were still okay with their accommodation. "No need to change to a better hotel when one becomes available," they said.

Apparently, many of the rooms in the house they were in were being used by ladies of the night. No need to ask any more questions ...I was just pleased to have a happy workforce.

As District Manager, meeting and socialising with drilling engineers and drilling managers was an important part of my job. My first priority was always to get the jobs done properly so there weren't any problems and I wouldn't need to spend time ironing them out. Also, the profitability of the business depended on making sure our customers were happy with our service.

I knew a lot of the drilling engineers and a few drilling managers. However, there were over twenty oil companies in Aberdeen so there were at least twenty drilling managers and maybe a couple of hundred drilling engineers. I couldn't possibly get to know them all. We did most of our work with five or six companies so most of my contact was with those clients. I would usually meet the engineers in their offices and occasionally have lunch with them.

BP was one of our regular clients and we were working on one of the rigs they had under contract. I knew the engineers involved with our rig but I'd never met the drilling manager, John.

When John attended an oil event on a trip to Houston he happened to meet my International manager, Roland. Roland said, "You will know Roy, our District Manager in Aberdeen." John replied to say he didn't know me and that we'd never met.

The next day I got a call from Roland asking why I had never called on John, suggesting that I wasn't taking care of business by looking after an important customer.

A week later I called John and asked if I could meet with him. "What do you want to meet about?" asked John. I couldn't tell him I only wanted to see him so I could tell Roland that we'd met, but I did think to say, "I think it's important that you know who I am in case we ever have to deal with a problem together." He replied that he didn't think a meeting was necessary. He knew I was the local manager and if he had a problem he would call me, or my boss in Houston if he felt the need. No meeting required.

Anyway, Roland was planning a trip to the UK and was coming to Aberdeen, together with George from London. When I said that I still hadn't met John he wasn't impressed. He said he would set up a meeting and arrange for me to be introduced to him. Roland arrived two weeks later and confirmed that he had a meeting with John scheduled for 4.00pm. When I picked him and George up from the airport at lunchtime, Roland asked if I knew the way to John's office. I said I had spoken to him at BP's Aberdeen office in Dyce and pointed this office out to him as we left the airport. Roland then said, "No wonder you haven't met him, I have his address in Dundee."

I'd never been to BP's Dundee office, so I felt a bit silly for not knowing John actually had his office there. From the airport to the Dundee address would be a two-hour drive. It was one o'clock, so I suggested that we set off immediately to make sure we got there on time.

Having made a brief stop in Montrose for afternoon tea, we arrived in Dundee in plenty of time for our 4.00pm meeting. I had some difficulty finding the BP office so I stopped to ask a man for directions. "You're looking for Shed Sixteen," I was told as he pointed to a number of storage sheds along the wharf.

My immediate thought was, "This does not look like a place where I would expect to find a drilling manager". When we got to Shed Sixteen I asked the warehouseman where we could find John. He replied, "John has his office in Aberdeen, just across from the airport … Do you want to know the way to Aberdeen?"

Roland called John to apologise for not being at our meeting and tried to reschedule, but John couldn't see us the next day so the meeting wasn't going to happen. Roland was not happy.

I drove Roland and George back to their hotel in Aberdeen. It was a long drive without much chat.

I did finally get to meet John at an oil event. I introduced myself and asked if he would like to have lunch so we could become better acquainted. He said he was pleased to meet me but didn't want to have lunch and that was that.

I think Roland saw my inability to build a relationship with John as a major shortcoming. He thought I needed to socialise with him to be a proper District Manager. I'm sure he also thought I was a jolly nuisance for wanting to employ an operation's assistant and always calling him to ask for more cementers.

I never did have a great relationship with Roland and that day certainly didn't make it any better.

He never once mentioned that the Aberdeen District was a well-run operation and one of the most profitable districts in the company.

CHAPTER 28

The Broken Strimmer

Our in-house training programme for locals was a successful initiative and pretty soon we had more Scottish cementers.

The programme was directed by David, our District Engineer. He kept track of every trainee. He monitored all their work experience and then worked out what training they needed to have next. On one occasion David spotted a trainee coming into the office and took him aside to discuss his progress. The lad had just come back onshore so David spent half an hour with him outlining the next phase of his training.

The lad was delighted to have such interest shown in his career and was very enthusiastic about what lay ahead.

After their session David said, "I think Roy wants to see you while you're here." David brought him into my office and started to tell me about the progress the lad had made and how keen and capable he was.

What David didn't know was that I had arranged for him to come ashore as he had been caught with marijuana on the rig. He would have known that he had violated our zero-tolerance policy so wouldn't be surprised to find out that he was being 'let go'. I already had his final pay cheque prepared and just needed to hand it over before showing him out the door.

"Bloody marvellous!" said David with a hint of sarcasm as he left my office.

In spite of these few setbacks, after Jim and Graeme had become our first qualified locals, the training programme continued to bear fruit. In addition to their North Sea training, they had been sent to a dedicated training facility in Arlington, Texas. They were the first to work offshore as local cementers and when they did a good job, it was a lot easier for others to follow. Within three years, as more locals were trained up we were able to reduce our dependency on expats to around half the total cementers on our staff. Having qualified Scots made life a whole lot easier. They were all from Aberdeen so there weren't any problems with housing, schooling, or unsettled wives. There was also a big cost saving as I could employ three local cementers for the cost of one expat. The net effect of this cost reduction meant that, for a while, Aberdeen became the most profitable district within the company worldwide.

Even though the business was a big success, for me it was proving to be both the busiest and most trying time ever in my working life.

All the hard work and long hours were taking a toll on both myself and my family. I had one stretch over a six-month period where I worked every single day. Not necessarily all day, but I spent some time at work or working from home every day including Saturdays and Sundays.

Being that busy was very stressful. This stress would occasionally spill over into my home life. Neva was studying at university and we had a young daughter. No one was getting the time and attention they needed.

I started to feel unwell and had developed a rash and a nervous twitch. When I finally took the time to go see a GP he suggested I was only a few months away from having a total nervous breakdown.

I knew I wasn't well, but I certainly hadn't expected that. I couldn't believe it was happening but, when I thought about it, I realised the doctor was probably right.

One day around this busy time I had arranged to play golf on Saturday afternoon. I needed to finish some gardening chores in the morning and then intended to head over to Murcar Golf Club around lunchtime.

It didn't work out that way. What did happen gave me a strong indication that I was indeed getting very stressed.

In Aberdeen we lived in a house with a big garden. The garden was both a joy and a chore. Cutting the grass and trimming the edges could take over five hours and during the summer, this needed to be done every two weeks. It was always hard to find enough time to look after it properly.

When B&Q advertised a wonderful new invention called a "strimmer", I thought this could really speed up my gardening. I immediately went out to buy one and was looking forward to using it the following day. I thought if I could get all the edges and some of the mowing done, then I could play golf and finish the rest of the work in the evening.

I unpacked the new strimmer, fitted the shroud on the bottom and off I went. I strimmed a few feet and then the strimmer-line broke.

"I'll just remove the spindle, feed through some more line, reassemble, and start again," I thought to myself.

Fifteen minutes later I started again. I strimmed another few feet, then the line broke again.

Remove the spindle, feed through more line, reassemble, and off I went a third time.

Three more feet and a third breakage. I could now do the repair job in seven minutes.

A few more feet, and another breakage … another repair … and then another breakage.

I looked back and saw that I had managed to strim around thirty feet in one and a half hours. I still had a couple of hundred feet to do.

I realised I wasn't going to make my golf game and totally lost it.

I grabbed hold of the strimmer swung it around my head and flung it as far as I could. I then fetched it and did another hammer-throw back up the lawn. The strimmer looked no different so I took it onto the driveway and smashed it up and down as hard as I could. The spindle was in pieces and the shroud was broken but still attached.

I tried to force it back into its box but it wouldn't go. I took it back out and smashed the shroud on the driveway until it was 'no-more'. Now it fitted back into the box. I threw the box into my car and headed back to town, back to the B&Q store.

Carrying the box under my arm, I marched into the store straight back to the department from where I had collected the strimmer the previous day.

The same sales girl was in attendance. I handed her the box and told her that the strimmer was the "most useless piece of crap" I'd ever had the misfortune to purchase! I had come back in person just to tell them how angry I was. I gave her the box and turned to leave.

She said she could tell that I was unhappy and said calmly, "I can see that you are not happy with our product. Come with me and I will get you your money back." "I don't want my money back, I just want you to know what a total piece of garbage this strimmer is!" I replied.

She insisted, "You must get a refund. I'll take you to the returns counter and take care of it myself."

A few minutes later I was given my refund and rather sheepishly left the store.

Back at the store, I know someone will have opened the box and pulled out the pulverised strimmer. I'm not sure how they would have described the malfunction on their returned-goods report but I'm sure it would have made interesting reading. I just hope the nice sales girl didn't lose her job for giving me the refund.

Apparently, Neva had seen the 'death of the strimmer' take place on our driveway from the upstairs conservatory and when I returned, she asked if I was still planing to play golf that afternoon.

Sometime later, I heard that B&Q had been supplied with a batch of faulty strimmer-line. I figured that I must have got some line from that batch. However, I still needed a strimmer so eventually I purchased a new one from a different store and it worked perfectly.

On another occasion things didn't work out well when I purchased a bright yellow ride-on mower. I was sure this would reduce my mowing time dramatically. The mower was delivered in a crate, hoisted off the back of a truck and set down on my driveway. After attaching the wheels and the grass-catcher it was ready to go.

There was a warning tag on the oil fill cap reminding me to 'Check the Oil', which I did, (after all, I had once worked as a motorman, so I knew about these things ….). There were traces of oil on the dipstick but it was obviously needing more. Anticipating that I might need to top-up the oil, I had a can of oil ready and waiting.

What I hadn't anticipated was that all the oil had been been drained out of the engine sump before it had been shipped from the factory. Putting a warning tag on the oil cap telling me to check the oil implies that it might be low on oil. The tag certainly didn't convey the message that all the oil had been drained and there was no oil at all in the sump. Surely no one would do that? It just didn't make sense.

Anyway, I decided to run the mower up the lawn one time and then re-check the oil level so I would have a proper reading on the amount required.

Unfortunately, the mower wasn't designed for my lawn. I have more moss than grass so with my weight on-board the mower was just too heavy. After making a twenty yard pass, that strip of lawn looked more like it had been shaved rather than cut and the grass-catcher was completely full.

I left the mower idling and went to empty the grass-catcher. Two minutes later, by the time I was heading back to the mower, there was a cloud of black smoke coming from the engine exhaust.

I ran back, arriving just in time to witness a death-seizure as the engine choked to a stop. That engine was never going to run again.

I phoned B&Q and explained my problem to a very calm Duty Manager.

He confirmed that he would pass the oil-level-warning-tag problem back to the manufacturer and gave me the phone number for a repair company. "Is there anything else I can help you with this afternoon?" he asked as I hung up the phone.

This all happened in May, just as my grass was needing it's first cut. I got the mower back in September, just as my grass stopped growing. After spending four hundred and fifty pounds for a new engine I now had nearly fifteen hundred pounds invested in my ride-on.

When I tried it the second time, once again it proved to be the wrong tool for the job. Even on the highest setting the lawn still looked like I was shaving, not cutting, the grass and the grass-catcher was again full within twenty yards. At that rate I'd need to dig a twenty-by-twenty-foot storage pit just to hold the cuttings.

I'd fallen out of love with my mower and decided to give it away as a Christmas secret-Santa gift. I made out a gift voucher for the mower and one lucky friend got a big surprise on Christmas Day.

My yellow mower spent the rest of its days cutting grass in the adjoining Aberdeen suburb.

After I'd gone to see the doctor, I called George in London to tell him about my impending nervous breakdown and pressed him once again to provide me with more help. A couple of months later when help finally came, rather than sending the Assistant Operations Manager I had been asking for, George sent in another District Manager to oversee what I was doing. I was more than a little annoyed. The day I found out I came home and, for the first time since starting work with BJ thirteen years earlier, I questioned whether I should change my job.

Just a couple of months before my 'help' arrived, there had been another incident which showed just how crazy things had become. I had a call from our bulk-plant manager, Bert, to say that he was having a big problem getting the cement to transfer from one of the storage silos onto a supply boat. It must have been late June or early July because it was the middle of the night and yet it was broad daylight when I arrived at the quayside.

I couldn't believe what I saw. The supply boat being loaded was covered with cement powder. The crew were all outside washing and scrubbing, trying to remove cement from every surface. The captain of the vessel was very angry. He was no longer speaking to Bert and, when I arrived, he promptly gave me a piece of his mind as well!

Apparently, the bulk delivery hose had blocked. Bert disconnected the hose from the boat then fed in compressed air until the blockage finally dislodged, blowing out all the cement. The open end of the hose had been tied down, but the sudden burst of pressure when the blockage released flung it around like a snake covering everything in a huge cloud of cement.

When Bert reconnected the line and tried again, the hose blocked a second time. He was about to go through his procedure for clearing out the line when the captain called a halt. That was when I got the phone call. Fortunately my experience on the Glomar Conception enabled me to sort the problem. An hour later the supply boat was fully loaded and ready to set sail.

While I was away attending to that problem, my wife received a call from one of our cementers offshore. He was having some difficulties and asked to speak with me. When Neva said she didn't know when I would return he explained the problem to her and asked, "What do you think Roy would tell me to do if he was there?"

That was how crazy things had become.

CHAPTER 29

The New Job

After giving it a lot of thought, I made up my mind to find another job. I quit BJ then thought, "What have I done? I'm thirty-five years old, unemployed, in Aberdeen, with no big salary, no housing allowance, no company car, no annual leave back to Australia, with a young child, and a wife at university. This is not good."

I thought about all the great times I'd had and all the great people I'd had the pleasure to work with. I couldn't think how I could possibly have a better time working with another company, yet, I was sure I'd made the right decision. I had been having more frequent disagreements with my manager and this was adding to my stress level. When neither George or Roland tried to get me to stay I knew I'd made the right decision. It was time to move on.

Fortunately the oil industry in Aberdeen was still, 'a-blowin' and a'goin'. The shortage of people hadn't changed. Although I thought my experience and skills limited any future employment to competitors of BJ, I couldn't see myself working for one of the companies I'd been competing against. I just had to believe in myself and look further afield.

It didn't take long before I found Lynes, another American oil service company which had just made a start in the North Sea. I had been aware of this company while working in Canada, where they offered drillstem testing services in competition to BJ. They also manufactured a range of down-hole *inflatable packers* and down-hole pressure and temperature recording instruments, *'gauges'* (An inflatable packer is a sealing element which could be assembled into a string of casing to provide an annular seal between the casing and the wellbore. Often one or more of these packers be installed and inflated between the casing and a wellbore section to augment the seal achieved with the cement bond. They were used in applications where a good annular seal was critical.) Selling these packers and providing instrumentation services with their gauges was the market they were targeting in the North Sea.

Lynes had already rented a workshop in Aberdeen and had located two Canadian service engineers there. Soon after I got in touch with them they offered me a job to develop the North Sea business for them. I accepted their offer and headed off to Houston and Calgary for some training. A month later I returned home to tackle the new challenge.

Once I started making some sales I needed to hire additional people. I was pleased that Graeme and Jim from BJ were keen to join Lynes as service engineers and that Albert agreed to join the company as the Region Sales Manager.

I also hired a few trainees including two very capable brothers, Steven and Philip. Whenever I was looking to hire people for work in the oil service industry I usually tried to hire them from either a farming or armed-services background. I always found that these people had the qualities needed. They were reliable, were prepared to work hard, could follow instruction, could think for themselves and could get out of bed in the morning, all traits needed in the oil service industry. Both Steven and Philip proved to be excellent trainees and both went on to become first class service engineers.

Philip was only seventeen when he started with us and you couldn't have found a keener worker. Whatever I asked him to do, he would keep doing it until I told him to stop or until someone turned out the lights.

After his six-week trial period I decided to offer him a permanent job. He accepted the salary I offered and became a member of staff. At the end of the month, when he got his pay cheque, he noticed that it was more than he had been expecting. He checked with our accountant to see if there had been a mistake. "No," she said, "the amount is correct."

Philip had misunderstood my salary offer to be an annual amount, not the monthly amount. Instead of getting six thousand pounds per year he was getting six hundred pounds per month. In his mind he had just received a twenty percent salary increase before he'd even started. It took weeks to get the smile off his face.

I still see Philip occasionally as we both curl in the same curling club and occasionally play on the same team. He is still the same as he was all those years ago. When I yell, 'sweep', he gets stuck in and doesn't stop until he hears my 'stop' command. From a very early age he must have been very well trained.

Right from the start, the Lynes business was a success. Albert and I were kept busy meeting all the oil company engineers to promote the business. The majority of the work was selling and installing inflatable-packers.

At that time in Aberdeen there were a lot of excellent drilling engineers. Oil companies had brought them here from Europe, Australia, Canada and America. The American engineers outnumbered the others by at least two to one and most of them were great to work with. Some were sophisticated, but some were 'good ol' boys' with some very unusual habits.

I remember one sales call I made with Albert when we called in to see an American drilling engineer in his office. Albert was getting into his sales presentation when our client casually reached over to grab a jar from the side of his desk. The jar was half full of a foul looking dark brown sludge. He picked up the jar and discharged a huge flow of liquid into the jar. I knew that it was from his chewing tobacco but Albert had never seen this before. He went as white as a sheet. I thought he was going to pass out.

I quickly ended the meeting and helped Albert to get up to leave.

Outside Albert wanted to be sick and was virtually dry-retching. It took some time for him to regain his composure. He couldn't get the image out of his head and became nauseous again and again just thinking about the man and his brown jar.

From then on, whenever Albert called on an American engineer, he would first check to make sure there weren't any suspect containers before starting his conversation. He worried that he would be physically ill right there in the man's office if he saw him grab for a jar to have a good spit.

The Lynes pressure and temperature instrumentation gauges had been developed in-house and incorporated the latest state-of-the-art electronics for recording downhole data. These services attracted a lot of customer interest. The problem was that the gauges were not reliable.

There were two other manufacturing companies developing tools similar to the ones Lynes were using and three other competitors offering pressure gauge services in the North Sea. Lynes didn't have the market to themselves. We were getting a share of the work but the frequent tool failures were limiting our ability to build market share.

Using state-of-the-art technology certainly had its problems. I remember one occasion when our repair technician, Bruce, came into my office holding the innards of a gauge which had recently failed. Bruce looked a bit professorial and had a flare for dramatics. At the time, Albert and I had been reviewing what might be done to get better results with our instruments. It appeared that we could get them to work perfectly well in the workshop, but the handling and downhole environment was occasionally just too much for them.

Anyway, in his hand, Bruce held a circuit board with wires and a few components dangling off one side. He started rattling on about one component after another, none of which made any sense to either of us, and then announced, "These bits are never going to work again, we're going from one disaster to another! We're all doomed! I quit!"

Why all this should strike us as being funny I have no idea, but it did and we both just laughed as Bruce stood there with a bewildered look on his face. We weren't doomed, Bruce didn't quit, and eventually we would get more reliable components.

In spite of the gauge problems, the inflatable packer business continued growing so I decided we needed to open an office in Stavanger to service the Norwegian market. I met and hired a man who is possibly the most wonderful Norwegian in Norway. Helge, a Norwegian with a sense of humour. This is a rarity, but Helge could see the funny side of every situation. He fit seamlessly into our team and we got on like a house on fire. Helge was also a salesman from the same school as myself. "Sell it first, then work out how to deliver the goods later."

On one occasion this didn't work out too well. One of the new instrumentation systems Lynes was introducing could monitor the wellhead pressure from a number of wellheads and report back this information in real time to an onshore control centre. Jess, the development engineer from the Houston office, sent over some information about the kit and with that Helge went out and found an oil company client. This client wanted to have twenty wellheads monitored.

Helge relayed the requirement back to Jess and suggested he come to Norway to demonstrate the system and provide the client with all the technical information. After much persuasion Jess came. He brought with him a pressure-sensor and a readout box. He didn't bring any technical data or any other information on how the system would actually work. Nothing! Helge and I said we couldn't give our client a presentation without more detail. We needed something more professional.

That evening Jess went back to his hotel room and drew a picture of a table with a box sitting on top and a number of lines coming from the box to some short pipes which represented the sensors. He now had his engineering drawing for the customer.

Neither Helge nor I were brave enough to present this to a team of professional engineers so we decided, for the time being, we would put the sale on hold.

For years thereafter, whenever we needed a technical presentation, Helge would quickly draw a table with a box and say, "Right, we're ready to go!"

Helge's sense of humour could also be mischievous. When he was in Aberdeen attending the oil show, we parked our car at Baker Oil Tools across from the exhibition centre. Helge had his briefcase with him but decided at the last minute that he wouldn't be needing this, so he asked the gate guard if he could leave it in his booth rather than walk back to his car. The guard, an elderly gentleman, was reluctant to take care of the briefcase for safety reasons. This oil show was taking place at a time when there was a lot of trouble in Northern Ireland so he was being cautious. He explained this to Helge but Helge convinced him it would be okay since they were both working for the same company. Lynes was owned by Baker.

We got on the shuttle bus and sat at the back for the short ride across to the exhibition entrance. As we left the carpark, Helge turned to the guard, scrunched up his face and stuck two fingers in his ears. By the sudden look of horror on his face, there was no doubt the guard had also never come across a Norwegian with a sense of humour.

CHAPTER 30

The First Hiccups

After I left BJ, the interim manager, who had supposedly come to help me, stayed to run the business for six months, and then, Billy-Dean arrived. Billy-Dean had previously been BJ's manager in Singapore at the same time I was their Region Manager in Brisbane. We'd never met but I did know he had a reputation for enjoying a drink or two. When he transferred to Aberdeen, George, who had by then moved his Region Office from London to Aberdeen, decided that the company should have a social function to introduce both himself and Billy-Dean to their clients and the Aberdeen oil industry. As it was coming up to Halloween, the plan was to invite around eighty couples to a costume party at the Beach Ballroom.

Being aware that Billy-Dean might get a bit obstreperous once he'd had a few 'bevies', a minder was appointed to keep an eye on him. His role for the evening was to make sure that Billy-Dean left the party as soon as there was any indication he was becoming difficult.

On the night many of the guests came in costume, including Billy-Dean, who came dressed as Friar Tuck.

After being served a fine meal there was a lot of free drink and a lively dance band to keep everyone entertained. The evening went well and everyone was having a great time.

Around 11.30 pm the minder saw the signs that Billy-Dean needed to go home. Billy-Dean was reluctant to leave but the minder called a taxi and eventually persuaded him to leave the building. When they came down the steps outside the Beach Ballroom, there were a number of cabs waiting to collect guests so the minder went off to search for the cab he had booked.

No sooner had he left when Billy-Dean decided to step into a cab parked directly in front of him.

After asking his name, the cab driver informed Billy-Dean that the cab was not his and asked him to leave. Billy-Dean informed the cab driver that he was the boss of the event and instructed him to take him home. He was not leaving.

"That's not how it works," said the cab driver. He got out, opened the door for Billy-Dean and, once again, politely asked him to get out. Billy-Dean came flying out of the cab like a bull out of a chute. He tackled the cab driver and proceeded to show him who was the boss.

As more guests started to pour out of the Ballroom they were greeted by the sight of 'Friar Tuck' in his full length robe rolling across the sidewalk trying to knock spots off the Aberdeen cabbie.

Meantime, having found Billy-Dean's cab, the minder returned to see his worst nightmare unfolding in front of a gathering crowd. He managed to stop the fight and quickly whisked Friar Tuck away to his cab before returning to placate the assaulted cab driver.

They say no publicity is bad publicity, and although I wasn't there, judging by the number of people who called to tell me about the event, the evening and Billy-Dean were certainly well remembered. Everyone who had witnessed the scrap thought it was the best possible ending for a Halloween party!

It was not, however, the smooth ending George might have hoped for.

As I settled in to my new job with Lynes, life was pretty good. I was a lot less stressed than I'd previously been and had far more independence. For the most part I was left to manage the business as I saw best. I enjoyed this responsibility and enjoyed the satisfaction of once again building up a profitable business.

Whenever I did need help or advice from Houston, my manager always tried his best to support me but, as had been the case with BJ, he wasn't always on the mark.

On one occasion I called to explain that I couldn't proceed with a tender submission because it didn't comply with the anti-competition rules in The Treaty of Rome. My boss in Houston passed the problem over to his sales manager. I couldn't believe it when the guy called back the next day to assure me that the submission would be okay. He had studied a map of Europe and found that Rome was in Italy … our tender was not for Italy, it was for work in the North Sea, so there wasn't a problem.

Meanwhile, over in Norway, Helge was making good progress developing the business for Lynes' on that side of the North Sea. In addition to inflatable packer sales and instrumentation services Helge was looking after one additional Lynes product line.

Back in Houston, Lynes also had a construction division dedicated to 'super-size' products. These were designed to be used during the construction phase when an offshore platform was being installed. When the platform sub-structure *'jacket'*, was being secured to the seabed, in order to place the cement where it was required, large inflatable packers were used to provided a seal around the pile. Also, in conjunction with this packer a large *rotating sleeve* was used to open and close a flow port above the packer.

Unfortunately, the actuation tool for the rotating sleeve didn't always work as well as it should. Helge had one client who had installed these tools and was having difficulty getting the equipment to work properly. The job on the platform was ongoing at the time, so they urgently needed help.

Helge called the manager of Lynes Construction Division, also named George, and he flew over from Houston. However, instead of going to the oil company's office to meet with their engineer, George gave Helge a few suggestions on how he might be able to help them himself. He then caught the next plane back home. He didn't fly directly back to Houston, first he made an overnight stop in London to give himself some much needed R & R before flying home the next day.

Helge did his best to help and eventually managed to provide the assistance needed. Needless to say, neither Helge nor the Norwegian engineers were impressed.

My own experience with the Construction Division was also disappointing. They didn't want me to deal direct with any of their UK customers, so I was not even made aware of the Aberdeen companies to whom they had supplied products. When Albert and I were making the rounds to introduce ourselves, I was therefore surprised to visit one engineer who had a large technical drawing of a Lynes inflatable packer and rotating sleeve hanging on his office wall. When I saw these I thought, "Great, Dick is already a customer, introducing him to my products will be easy."

This was not the case. When I asked Dick about the blueprints, he said he kept them on his wall to reminded himself how much trouble the products had given him and how angry he was with the lack of support he'd received from Lynes. Wow! When I called this report back in to George his suggestion was to keep well away from Dick as he was giving him a lot of trouble.

I couldn't believe that one of our division managers could treat a customer like that. Suddenly I felt a little less certain that everything about my new employer was as great I thought it would be.

Albert eventually managed to help Dick sort out his problem, which Dick greatly appreciated, and the two of us then carried on with our task of meeting potential customers and building the business.

CHAPTER 31

The Special Person

One of the nice things about working with Lynes was getting to take a few more holidays. We had always intended to see more of Europe and now we finally had the chance. We planned our first holiday to France. My mother had come from Australia and, as she was staying with us for the summer, we intended to take her with us.

The holiday started with an overnight train trip from Aberdeen to London. From London I intended to drive to Dover and then catch the ferry across to France.

The trip didn't start very smoothly. I drove my car onto the train in Aberdeen and then went off to find the four sleeper bunks I had booked. The sleeper car didn't exist. British Rail had missed off one train carriage and that carriage happened to be the one with our bunks. The conductor apologised and gave us a compartment where we could sit for the nine-hour trip to London. He said we would be the only four people in the six seat compartment, however, other people were also missing their bunks so two more people came in to join us. Outside the compartment there were even more people sitting on the floor in the passageway. The train was heavily overbooked.

After arriving in London at 7.00am I got the car off-loaded and headed towards Dover. Having not had any sleep, I was not very alert and didn't get very far before I bumped into the back of a Volkswagen. The VW had a proper dent in the back but it was still drivable so they were okay. On my car the accident had pushed the front fender against the wheel preventing it from turning. Fortunately my car was a French-made Citroën with adjustable suspension. I raised the car up high enough to free up the wheel and then drove to Dover with the car looking as though it was riding on stilts.

Once we'd made the ferry crossing we arrived in Calais, France. I stopped at the first Citroën garage I could find and got a mechanic to panel-beat the fender. Once this was done, and the fender was no longer rubbing against the wheel, I was able to lower the suspension back down to the normal driving position. With a slightly crumpled right wing I set off on our drive south.

We had a long drive ahead of us. We were going to Narbonne on the Mediterranean coast, some 650 miles away, where I had hired a canal boat for a week of boating on the Canal du Midi.

After a ten-hour drive we finally arrived at the marina. Our beautiful canal boat was ready and waiting. We loaded up our luggage and other supplies plus the two bicycles I had ordered. I had rented the bicycles so we could cycle to a nearby town every day to shop for fresh croissants and supplies. We were then given a brief instruction on boat handling and boat safety before setting off at five miles per hour. As we headed off in a westerly direction towards Carcassonne, we were all excited about what lay ahead.

The Canal du Midi was constructed back in the seventeenth century. At the time, it became the biggest construction project anywhere in the world. The canal is one hundred and fifty miles long and connects the Mediterranean to Toulouse where it joins the Garonne River, providing a continuous waterway link through France between the Mediterranean and the Atlantic Ocean. Once the canal was constructed, trees were planted all the way along both sides. These trees were intended to provide shade for the horses as they pulled the barges along. For many years I suspect they were never tall enough to provide this shade but, three hundred years later, they were now fully grown and tall enough not only to shade the path but also to shade a good portion of the canal as well. We certainly were enjoying the benefit of this tree-planting foresight.

As we cruised along, every so often there were locks to go through. Most of these we needed to operate ourselves.

Our passage through these locks went very smoothly except on one occasion when it didn't. On that occasion Neva and I got out of the barge to operate the winches while Mum stayed on-board to slacken off the mooring lines as the boat slowly went down. Unfortunately, Mum didn't manage to ease off one mooring line in time and, when I looked around, the back of our barge was hanging at a peculiar angle.

I quickly ran back and managed to release the line allowing the back of the barge to suddenly fall free. Inside everything which wasn't secured flew across the floor, including Mum and three-year-old Janna. Fortunately there were no injuries, however, there was some spillage and a broken glass so it took a little while to tidy up the mess before setting off again.

Two days later we arrived at a big set of locks just five miles from Carcassonne. These locks could only be operated by the resident lock-keeper. Unfortunately he wasn't there. It was July 14 so that would be as far as we could go until he returned from his Independence Day celebrations.

As we needed more provisions, Neva and I decided to cycle to Carcassonne leaving Mum to look after the barge. We had a child seat on one of the bikes and Janna insisted on riding with her mum. This only lasted until Neva hit a tree root and very nearly propelled her out of the seat. Janna refused to go any further with her mum and refused to get back in the child seat. I cycled the rest of the way to Carcassonne and back carrying her in one arm as I pedalled along. By the end of the trip my arm was pretty tired, but, on the upside, we were able to use the child seat to carry the groceries.

Three hours later, when we finally got back to the barge, we discovered that my mother was seasick. I had moored the barge too close to the lock and the current had been causing it to bob about the entire time we were away.

Once back on-board I moved the barge one hundred yards downstream and dropped anchor for the night. We all needed a good rest.

The return trip to Narbonne was also eventful. I steered the barge too close to an overhanging tree and managed to sweep one of the bikes off the top. I tried trawling up and down with the anchor but never found it.

Five miles from home, as we were passing through a lock, we ran out of fuel and needed to be towed out of the lock. I then had to call the hire company who came to tow us the rest of the way back to the marina.

It had been a memorable boat trip, through a beautiful part of France on a magnificent canal, now recognised as a World Heritage Site. We all enjoyed our boating holiday immensely even though it didn't end as smoothly as it might have. We all made it back in one piece but, with one lost bike and no fuel it wasn't a very classy finish to the trip.

Part two of the holiday was sure to be more relaxing. The plan was to meet up with two other families on the west coast of France where we were booked to stay in house-tents near a beach.

When I worked out the time it would take to drive two hundred and fifty miles to our campsite it was longer than I expected.

I needed to buy some lunch before we headed off, so I stopped the car and headed into the nearest shop, leaving all the car windows open to keep it as cool as possible. After lunching in the car, we buckled up to set off again. When I tried to close the window they wouldn't move. Apparently the electrics had failed. I then discovered that the lights weren't working either. This meant that we had to drive with the windows open and get to where we were going before nightfall. I checked the distance again and realised I would need to drive pretty fast to have any chance of making it.

Off we went, driving as fast as I could. For five hours no one could speak or hear for the noise of the wind.

When we finally arrived just before dusk, we all looked like we had been trapped inside a wind tunnel. Mum had a bad headache, Janna was crying, Neva complained that her ears were ringing and I was exhausted.

After putting Janna to bed I drank a few large glasses of wine and felt much better.

The week in the lovely tent was great. The kids had lots of fun on the beach and the adults had lots of nice French food and wine. However, it was 36 °C outside and the tent was not air-conditioned, so not everyone was happy. I hadn't noticed, but apparently it is very difficult to sleep when it's that hot.

When we left to drive home the plan was to make the nine-hour drive from near Bordeaux to Calais in one day. The distance shouldn't have been a problem but in Rouen, partway along the drive, the cars electrics failed totally and, halfway around a roundabout, the car stopped dead.

Fortunately, Rouen had a Citroën garage so once again I was able to get a mechanic to come inspect the car. He opened the bonnet and started checking the fuse box. Every so often he gave me a signal to try the starter. At one stage he raised his hand. I thought this was another signal to try the starter, which I did. This time it worked. His glasses came sailing through the air as he flew out backwards from under the bonnet. There was a rapid flow of French words together with lots of arm waving and hand gesticulation. Apparently I'd got the signal wrong. On that occasion he was warning me not to try the starter until he was out from under the bonnet.

Anyway the electrics were sorted. If we were still going to catch the ferry we needed to get to Calais as quickly as possible.

Just minutes before the scheduled sailing time we finally arrived at the terminal. As we approached the ferry we could see all our friends standing on the back deck looking out to see if we would make it. They all gave a big cheer as we raced down the wharf and sped up the loading ramp. We were the last car on-board. The ramp was lifted and away we went.

Once back in the UK we spent a night in a hotel, then the next day drove north, arriving home safely on Sunday night. It was so nice to be back in my own bed. After a great holiday adventure, I had the most wonderful night's sleep before heading off to work on Monday morning.

The following year my mother came over to stay for the full year. By then, having finished her medical studies, Neva was an intern doing her 'house-jobs', working and living at the hospital much of the time. That year Mum helped to run the family and would often prepare dinner for the four of us. Our meal would be loaded into a cardboard box and I would drive us up to the hospital so we could have a meal together in Neva's small bedroom. That way Neva got to see Janna. This mealtime would usually end abruptly when Neva's bleeper went off. Mum, Janna and I would then head home so I could put Janna to bed and prepare for the next day. Occasionally Neva was also on call all weekend, so the meal service would then happen on Friday, Saturday and Sunday as well. It was a busy and hectic time.

Friends commented that it must be difficult for us. I don't think we ever stood back and said, 'this is too hard', or 'we can't live like this'. It was life, and at the time it was what we had to do. We wouldn't have chosen for it to be so difficult but, in hindsight, dealing with these challenges certainly added colour to our lives. Without these testing times our journey would have been a lot less interesting and probably a lot less fulfilling.

A year later, our second daughter, Elise, was born and Neva started her working career post-university. With a lot of help from others we managed to keep all the balls in the air. We had taken Sheila on to be a nanny. She helped look after Janna and now stayed on to help with the new addition to our family.

Mum usually returned each summer and, once again, would run the household and help look after the kids. She was also a keen gardener so that was an extra bonus, although she drew the line at strimming, grass cutting, and hedge trimming. I don't think we could have made it without her. She was a very special person.

CHAPTER 32

The New Venture

As time went on, although Lynes' business kept growing, we continued to have reliability problems with our electronic gauges and were losing service jobs to competitors whose gauges worked better than ours. The competitors simply had more robust tools and were having fewer failures. I was concerned that the improvements Lynes was making were not happening fast enough, so I kept looking to see if I could find a solution.

I had become aware that Geophysical Research Corporation (GRC), an American company in Tulsa, Oklahoma, had developed downhole gauges similar to the ones Lynes were using. GRC were a manufacturing company as opposed to a service provider. I called Dick, their manager to ask if I could trial some of his tools.

Dick was very keen to supply me with tools as Lynes was potentially a big customer. A few weeks later, four of his tools arrived and I was able to use these on a job straight away. They worked perfectly and it was obvious that their gauges were better than ours.

I thought it would be a good idea to buy half a dozen GRC tools to replace the ones Bruce could no longer repair. We were a service company and needed to provide the best service possible. I didn't think it mattered what brand of tools we used as long as they worked. I was confident that the GRC tools would enable us to keep our market share while the Lynes engineers continued working to improve their tools, so I called my manager in Houston to let him know what I wanted to do.

The GRC tools only cost twenty-five thousand dollars each, but my manager said he didn't want me to purchase them. He said if I needed more tools I could only purchase them from Lynes. He insisted that I soldier on with our own-brand gauges and assured me that more reliable tools would soon be available. I thought it was a poor business decision not to buy tools from GRC in the interim.

During this time two things happened. Firstly, I'd met Leigh who had his own service company (Lasalle), providing a variety of products and services to the industry and he had made a casual approach to me about joining his company. Secondly, after advising Dick that I couldn't buy his tools for Lynes he asked if I was interested in buying them for my own use, suggesting that I could set up my own company. That was certainly not a possibility I had considered.

I had never given any thought to starting a company, but after speaking to Leigh about Dick's suggestion, he thought it was a great idea. He encouraged me to strike out on my own and suggested that we set up a new company with himself as my partner.

I knew nothing about starting a business but Leigh did and said he could help to sort out the funding. Leigh already had a venture-capital provider involved with his Lasalle company so he arranged for us to speak with them about funding the new start-up.

Once I reconfirmed with Dick that he would sell us the tools we needed, everything happened very quickly. Within six weeks of having the idea, we had secured the venture capital funding and registered a new company. I called Dick and he backed up the offer to sell us his tools with attractive finance terms. We were ready to go.

Making the decision to leave Lynes was not easy but it wasn't nearly as traumatic as leaving BJ. My main disappointment was leaving behind a lot of good friends and a team of people I really enjoyed working with.

Starting my own company turned out to be a lot easier than I expected. Many people get to see a golden opportunity in their lives and think, 'I could do that', however only a small percentage ever do. I was lucky to have met Leigh and to have the right combination of circumstances which made it so easy. Still, it was a big decision and I was proud that I had the courage to give it a try. I was thirty-eight years old and had a lot to look forward to.

Leigh and I named our new company Lasalle Pressure Data Services, effectively making it a sister company to Leigh's other Lasalle company. His company was already successful and had a good reputation. Being seen as a part of an established group was most helpful as customers regarded the new company to be an extension of Leigh's Lasalle business and, in fact, forty percent of it was.

Within the Lasalle office, Leigh arranged for me to have a private office, secretarial and admin support and a separate phone line coming in via his receptionist.

My first day at work for the new company was interesting. There was a desk, a phone, some foolscap pads and very little else. The first thing I did was to make a list of anything and everything I could think of that needed to be done. It was a pretty long list but the item at the top of the list was to find and hire someone who knew the business. I made a few calls and within a week had interviewed and hired Sandy. Sandy was working for one of the bigger competitors at the time and saw the opportunity to work for a start-up, where he would have a lot more responsibility, as a challenge.

Sandy started work two weeks later and moved in to sit on the opposite side of the desk from me. Over the next month we ordered the tools we needed and did all the other things that needed doing. We prepared price lists, sales literature, and sourced all the equipment to service and support our new tools.

Within the first six weeks, even before the tools arrived, Sandy managed to employ two service engineers. It all seemed very easy, but I suspect it wasn't. Sandy knew what he was doing and did an excellent job.

After we received our new tools, Sandy convinced a client to give us a job. I thought everything would be okay but, as it was the first job in my first business, it was hard not to feel a little anxious. Fortunately the job went without a hitch and the tools worked perfectly. Over the next two months Sandy managed to convince other companies to give us a try and those jobs were also successful. We were off and running.

We had only been in business for around six months when Sandy and I were out making a sales call on a client who had an urgent requirement to measure and record the wellhead pressure on a subsea wellhead. I said, "No problem, we can do that." He gave us a service-order and we headed back to the office. Sandy asked, "How are we going to do it?" I replied, "I'm not sure, but he wants to mobilise the equipment tomorrow afternoon if possible, so we have twenty-four hours to get something ready to go. Surely you can put something together by then?"

Sandy sat down and sketched out a design for a *subsea carrier* suitable for accommodating two gauges. His design also incorporated an attachment whereby a diver could connect the gauges to a wellhead on the seabed. Using a lot of persuasion, he managed to get a fabricator to build it overnight. Sandy stayed with them throughout the night and kept them on-track with the construction. When he brought it back to our workshop the next afternoon Sandy gave it a quick spray-paint and installed two of our tools. The assembly was loaded-out on the supply boat that evening just as had been requested.

The new gauge carrier was lowered onto the seabed and a diver made the connection to the wellhead. After thirty days the diver went back down. The tools were recovered and the recorded data was downloaded. The gauges had worked perfectly. In the meantime another set of tools had been sent out to replace the first lot and the job carried on. The next set of gauges also worked perfectly. We continued to rotate a new set of gauges offshore every month. By the time the job eventually finished it had gone on for seven months.

That one job gave our new company a big income boost and it meant that Lasalle Pressure Data Services was never to experience any significant financial difficulties. By the end of our first year in business we had made a healthy profit. Leigh and I were able to repay the loans we'd given to the company and it still had a solid balance sheet going forward.

It was a brilliant start for our new company, but, in the oil patch, things can change very quickly.

CHAPTER 33

The Space Shuttle

Working alongside the rest of the Lasalle Group was great. In addition to getting to work alongside Leegh's strong team of people, I got to go to the promotional events Leigh held for his clients. These were always first-class occasions. During our time together Leigh arranged two themed events in Newburgh at the Udny Arms Hotel. The first was a Spanish evening. We all wore Spanish costume and, as the guests arrived, Leigh and I met them at the front door. I would offer them a glass of sangria and then introduce them to the other guests at their table. After refilling my own glass four or five times during the reception process, by the time the first tapas arrived, I was ready to party.

Leigh had booked a troupe of Spanish dancers to entertain us for the evening. After dinner they took to the stage and, as two men played guitars, the two girls did a lot of flamenco dancing and played their castanets. They were very good and it was most enjoyable. Towards the end of their set they called for a volunteer from the audience. I decided to give it a try, I was fuelled up with sangria and just knew I would be a great flamenco dancer. I danced with such enthusiasm I put my foot right through the stage floor!

The evening was a big success. I'd had a ball, however, the next morning I was still suffering and my head felt like it was just one castanet rattle away from an explosion.

Six months later, the Greek evening Leigh organised was also a success, but didn't end quite as he'd expected. Leigh had contacted an agent to help find a suitable entertainer for the evening. When the lady entertainer arrived, Leigh met her and asked about her act. "Well first I come out and do some belly dancing then I have a snake which I pull out of this tall basket. I dance with the snake around my neck then slide it down my arms, gently encouraging it to move down my body. I do this for around ten minutes then I start to strip. Once I have removed all my clothes I run the snake..." "Stop!" shouted Leigh. "You do not take off any clothes and you do not run that snake anywhere!"

Apparently there had been a slight misunderstanding with the booking agent. Leigh instructed her to modify her act.

Anyway, after dinner she came out and did her belly dance … so far so good. Next she reached into her tall basket and pulled out a four-foot long snake.

What Leigh hadn't anticipated was that there might be someone in the room with a snake-phobia. When the snake appeared one of our best clients, a 6' 4" tall man named Billy-John, leapt from his chair and bolted from the room. He pushed aside anyone who happened to block his path bumping into tables and spilling wine and coffee along the way. His wife instantly realised what had happened and dashed out after him. Before Leigh could help wrestle the snake back into its basket they were in their car headed back to Aberdeen.

The event was spoken about for days afterwards and those without a snake-phobia deemed it to have been a big success. Even Billy-John, while getting 'a lot of stick' from his colleagues, managed to see the funny side.

After Billy-John had left, unfortunately, the snake didn't reappear. I was really enjoying the show and felt a little disappointed I didn't get to see the dancer do her snake-floss finale.

For me the most memorable promotion Leigh organised was a dinner in the company of Prince Charles and Lady Diana. Early in their marriage towards the end of 1985, they had agreed to host a charity dinner at Haddo House, an estate some thirty miles to the north of Aberdeen. Leigh booked a table for ten. There were only eight tables of guests so it was a small event and everyone was going to get the chance to meet both Prince Charles and Lady Diana.

After we arrived in the reception room, we were given a location to stand and told to form a circle with our guests. It was all well organised. Before going into dinner Charles and Diana would 'circulate' and come to meet each group of guests in turn. We were instructed to wait for one of them to come to us. After visiting a couple of other groups, Diana came over and introduced herself to Leigh and myself.

I immediately started a conversation. Diana had been out to visit one of the North Sea platforms the previous day and a report together with photos of this visit had been in the local Press and Journal that morning. I asked her about her visit. She said, "Well it was a lot different from what I had expected. I thought it would be very industrial and smelling of oil and grease. However, everything was spotlessly clean and everyone smelt of aftershave." Apparently the crew had been scrubbing the rig for days in advance of her visit and, just before she arrived, each roughneck had been doused in Old Spice.

When Diana was about to move on to the next group, Leigh realised that she hadn't been introduced to one of our guests, a client's wife who was very excited to be at the event and was desperately keen to say hello to Diana. Leigh put his arm around her and turned Diana in the direction of our guest. Within a second Leigh's arm was grasped by a bodyguard who, until then, he hadn't even noticed. The bodyguard firmly removed Leigh's arm from Diana's back. No words were spoken but the message was clear, 'you do not touch'.

Anyway, our guest got to say hello, then Diana moved on. She really was a most charming and beautiful lady. What impressed me most was her total self-assurance. After only being with us a few minutes everyone was relaxed and had been made to feel very special.

When Charles came to our group, once again I got the first opportunity to speak with him. "Prince Charles," I said. "I'm surprised that you have been gazumped." He looked at me somewhat bemused: actually, he already looked bemused when he arrived, so maybe slightly more bemused.

"What do you mean?" he replied.

"Well, I thought that you would have been the first prince to get a ride into space on the space shuttle but I see a Saudi prince got to be the first 'prince in space'. He went up in the last shuttle." I said.

Charles actually laughed but didn't reply other than to say, "Oh well...!"

He then had a brief chat with Leigh, said hello to the rest of our group and moved on.

It had been an outstanding evening and we all really enjoyed getting to meet two very special 'Royals'.

Two months later I wondered if Prince Charles had recalled my conversation with him. The very next shuttle to go up was the one which exploded on 28 January 1986.

CHAPTER 34

The Two Disasters

While Leigh was really good at organising promotional events, Simon, Bob and I didn't always get it right. The three of us had started the 'Oil Capital Classic', a one-day golf event followed by a dinner/prize-giving in the evening. In the first few years we ended up with around one hundred golfers, and together with wives and partners, approximately one hundred and fifty people for the evening event which included entertainment.

In the beginning, both the golf and the dinner were held at Deeside Golf Club. Usually Bob and I organised the golf and Simon organised the dinner and the entertainment.

One year Simon booked Bob Carolgees, with his glove-puppet *Spit the Dog* as our entertainment. Bob arrived at Deeside about an hour before he was due to take the stage so he hadn't left much time to review his act with Simon. After the dinner and prize-giving were finished Bob came out to perform.

Within minutes it was obvious that we had the wrong entertainment for a crowd of oilmen and their wives. I'm not sure what age or social group Bob's target audience would have been, but this one wasn't it. He sang a couple of songs and told a few silly jokes but no one was responding. His act simply wasn't working. He soldiered on for twenty minutes into his forty-minute set and then, when it was all nearly too painful to bear, he decided he should start telling some off-colour jokes to see if that worked. One or two got some laughs and one got a big response, but probably not the response he was expecting.

He told the one about parking his bicycle and used my secretary's cleavage as a point of reference. The joke got only a murmur of laughter so he decided it was time to give up. He took out his trusty glove-puppet and started singing his closing finale, the famous Elvis song, *Old Shep,* to his appreciative Spit.

As he started his song, my secretary, who had thought about the joke for a while, decided she had been seriously offended. She stood up, walked over to Bob, picked up a pint glass of beer and poured it over his head. Bob tried to defend himself, but both he and Spit got a proper soaking.

Some of the audience gasped, some laughed, a few even applauded.

Bob was undeterred. He went on to finish his serenade to what now looked like nothing more than a very wet sock.

When he was done, Bob took off his puppet, dashed over to my secretary and bowled her off her chair onto the floor. He quickly helped her back to her feet and then raised her arms in the air as if this was all a part of his act.

I must say it was quite a spectacular finish, even if he hadn't planned it that way. After enduring thirty minutes of cringe, at least the audience got to experience a memorable ending. He got a polite round of applause as he and Spit left the room.

In spite of these occasional hiccups, the Oil Capital Classic survived and carried on to become the biggest oil industry golf event in Aberdeen. It was very popular and the three of us continued to run it for eighteen years.

There were a lot of oil industry entertainment events in those early days, but one day we all got a harsh reminder that the industry wasn't all fun and games. In November 1986, one of the 'big toys' suddenly went very badly wrong. A Chinook helicopter, making the one-hundred-mile flight from the Brent Charlie oil platform in the North Sea to Sumburgh airport in the Shetland Islands crashed two and a half miles from the airport. The twin rotors lost synchronisation when a bearing failed. This allowed the rotors to collide with one another causing the helicopter to fall from the sky, killing forty-five of the forty-eight people onboard. The Chinook crash sent a shiver through the spine of all those thousands of oilmen who worked offshore and needed to make a regular commute. Many of the flights out to the platforms were quite long and, for nine months of the year, the weather could make flying both uncomfortable and dangerous. The realisation that the Chinooks might be unsafe or unsuitable for the task gave everyone pause for thought.

After the accident, all the Chinooks were grounded. A major investigation was held and it was decided that twin-rotor helicopters should be permanently withdrawn from service in the North Sea. The conclusion was that single-rotor helicopters were safer to operate and better suited for the job of transferring workers out to the rigs and back.

The risks involved with helicopter flights were obvious to everyone. Something that wasn't so obviously a risk happened two years later when the Piper Alpha platform exploded. This was by far the biggest disaster in the history of the North Sea. The total destruction of a huge production platform with a loss of one hundred and sixty-seven oil workers on the platform and two people on a rescue vessel.

The incident made the news around the world and had a huge impact on Aberdeen and everyone in the oil industry for many years thereafter. The scale of the disaster made me appreciate how lucky I was not to be working offshore and reminded me how fortunate I'd been that the *blowout* mishap on the drillship back in the Gulf of Papua hadn't been more serious.

On the Piper Alpha, which was producing one hundred and twenty thousand barrels of oil and thirty three-million cubic feet of gas every day, a series of mistakes led to the explosion. When some highly volatile condensate leaked and exploded, it set off a series of further explosions, ultimately leading to the destruction of the entire platform. Of the two hundred and twenty-six people on-board only sixty-one survived. When the Cullen Inquiry Report was finally published two years later, it determined that the platform operator was guilty of having inadequate maintenance and safety procedures. At that time the resulting 1.4 billion dollar insurance claim became the biggest ever for a man-made disaster.

From that day onwards, the industry's focus on safety and safe working practice was scaled up many fold. No worker could go offshore without having successfully completed the helicopter evacuation and offshore survival courses. All workers needed to be fully trained on safe working practices and anyone undertaking operations such as welding and gas cutting required special permits. Overnight, the industry became a safer place and accident and incident statistics started to show a marked improvement. All the service companies were required to comply with the new regulations and everyone did so willingly. No one ever wanted to see another Piper disaster. If a change of culture was needed then everyone was ready to get on board.

Even in our small company, we introduced additional safety training and followed the industry guideline for sending people on helicopter and rig evacuation courses.

No one ever again hired a backpacker from the youth hostel with a view to sending him offshore the same day.

CHAPTER 35

The New Partner

After two successful years in the electronic gauge business, suddenly the oil price fell, drilling activity was down and there was a lot less work available. Our financial backers, Investors in Industry, became a little concerned about our ability to survive a prolonged slump. As well as providing funding for my company they were also funding another small company in the same business. As the main competition for both our companies came from two large American service companies, our backer believed we would have a far better chance of survival and success if our two small companies were joined together. They suggested that we consider merging.

The idea of joining together of our companies to form one larger, stronger, company made a lot of sense.

A few days later I met with Kevin, the owner of Apex Reservoir Services, and after just one meeting we agreed in principle to a merger. We immediately started looking at financials and thinking about how the new company would be structured. His company and mine were almost identical and appeared to fit together with no staff reductions and very few overlaps. The intention was that

Leigh would be bought out leaving Kevin and myself as the majority shareholders in the new entity. Leigh would realise a significant capital gain and, because Lasalle Pressure Data was the larger of the two businesses, I was to have the bigger equity share.

After a few more meetings, terms were agreed and the formal merging process began. Apex's financial controller, Jeremy, suggested the new company name. It was to be called 'Exal', Ex: 'a' – for Apex, and 'l' – for Lasalle.

Prior to our meetings, Kevin and I had known of one another but hadn't met. We had both worked hard to make a success of our companies and had both enjoyed this challenge. Along the way we also enjoyed the prerogative to make independent decisions. I didn't think we would have any problems working together, however, after the merger we would need to adjust. Instead of working independently, the two of us would need to work together as a team.

Kevin's big strength was his self-confidence and personality. He was outgoing and adventurous, well liked and had great banter. His slightly larger-than-life persona was one of his biggest assets. He even augmented this with his choice of company car, a second-hand Aston Martin. I knew his customers liked doing business with him and that he worked hard to make sure that they got exactly what they paid for. As he had personally been responsible for Apex's success, I thought he would make a perfect business partner.

Once Exal got started, I was very happy to have Kevin lead the sales effort and run the day-to-day operations. I would become the Executive Chairman, responsible for overall governance and business development. This arrangement would enable me to focus on growth initiatives such as international expansion and new products. Sandy was appointed operations manager and Jeremy became the financial manager. We appeared to be a strong and capable team. The new Exal seemed poised to be a big success.

Once the new company was established Kevin immediately took over as the MD.

However, not long after we started working together, it became obvious that Kevin not only wanted to be seen as 'the man in charge', he also felt he needed the freedom to make decisions on his own.

Kevin started managing the business as if the merger had actually been a takeover. His approach seemed to imply that Apex had simply been enlarged and renamed Exal. After only a few months, I could see that we were not working together as I thought we should be.

Unfortunately, I found this very frustrating. Having previously been responsible for building a large part of the company, I couldn't accept the role I now had. I was finding it hard to contribute to the decision making and difficult to deal with Kevin's independent approach. Within six months I found it nearly impossible to exert any influence without edging towards confrontation.

Fortunately the oil price was going up again so business was good. We became very busy and needed more tools and service engineers to accommodate the jobs on offer. Kevin wanted to seize this growth opportunity with a rapid expansion. (At the time a lot of local entrepreneurs were being very successful and Kevin was eager to join this club.) Our financial partners and I were less bullish. We wanted steady rather than explosive growth. We were both more cautious than Kevin and didn't want to be financially overexposed should there be another oil price dip or activity slowdown. Also, the tools we were using were continuously improving as new electronic technology emerged. I was concerned not to end up owning too many tools which would shortly be superseded. Having the financial wherewithal to buy tools with the latest technology to replace obsolete tools was important.

On one occasion, after Kevin had to turn down a job because we didn't have sufficient tools available, he decided to order a number of new gauges which weren't in our budget and hadn't been discussed or approved.

When I next met our financial partners, they pulled me up for not sticking to the capital spending limits we had agreed to at the previous board meeting. They also asked me about an equity stake Kevin had secured for himself with a third-party supplier, commenting, "It doesn't look as though everyone is committed to pulling on the same end of the rope." The need for spending approval and the need to avoid any potential conflict of interest simply hadn't registered with him.

The upshot was that the merger wasn't working the way I had envisioned. Kevin and I were not working together. We hadn't fallen out, but I saw that things could easily head that way and, were we to have a major disagreement, I knew that it could seriously erode the value of the business. If I couldn't change the way things were going there was no point waiting for this to happen.

Being Chairman became more difficult and less enjoyable.

I discussed my concern with our financial partner and they asked if I would consider selling the business. It was in excellent shape and there would certainly be a keen buyer out there somewhere. I hadn't thought about selling but agreed it was worth looking at.

Our financial partners made some phone calls and, within a few weeks, I was contacted by Expro asking about the possibility of acquiring Exal. By then I'd given it a lot more thought and felt that selling the company was a really good idea. I invited them to a meeting.

After receiving the phone call, I spoke with Kevin and he was also interested to see what might be on offer.

Expro did make an offer to buy Exal. After a couple of months, negotiations were successfully concluded and, Expro acquired Exal.

For Expro, this was their first ever acquisition. They were already a successful company with operations throughout the North Sea and beyond. The addition of the Exal immediately helped to spur on this growth even further.

When Expro took over, Kevin was given full control of the Exal business component. I joined the company as a director with responsibility for bringing to market some of the new technologies Expro had developed, or were developing. This should have been a nice assignment, however, I soon discovered that other Expro managers had laid claim to these opportunities and I would need to step on their toes. This wasn't of interest to me.

I was 42 years old. In under five years I had started a company, built up the business, merged with Kevin's company and then sold out to Expro. The capital gain I realised was more than I had earned in wages in my entire working career. Even after paying the capital gains tax it was still a great result.

I decided that the way forward was to get back into business for myself. I really wanted to be back managing a company of my own and trying to build up another business. I decided to resign from Expro and started looking for the next opportunity.

Some time after leaving Expro, I met Kevin at an oil function. He asked, "Why did we ever decide to sell out? We had such a great future ahead of us." I didn't know how to reply. There was no question that Kevin was passionate about the business. Our skill sets certainly complemented one another and I'm sure Exal would have gone on to be worth many times more than what we'd sold it for, had we just carried on for another three or four years. Had he been a little less possessive, or had I been more assertive, together we would surely have built a bigger company. However, having to stand aside and watch him make all the decisions just hadn't worked for me.

We seriously undersold Exal, but we managed to avoid a battle between the two directors and avoided the possibility of a company melt-down.

C'est la vie …

When I left Expro I was no longer involved with Kevin, but when I started my next company, I discovered he hadn't gone away.

CHAPTER 36

The £1,000,000 Lawsuit

After leaving Expro, the question was, what to do next?

As often happens, some of the people you work with are also looking for a way to strike out on their own. A few months after I'd left the company, two Expro people approached me about backing them to start their own business venture. Keith had become a part of Expro when Kevin and I sold them our company. He and Jim, another Expro employee, were now wanting to start a *downhole-sampling* business of their own.

Downhole-sampling involves the use of a special tool to capture a fluid or gas sample from a well. A purpose-built sampling tool would be lowered into a well until it was positioned adjacent to the reservoir. The tool would then be activated and a sample of oil or gas would enter its storage chamber. This sample would be locked in and, once recovered from the well, transferred out of the chamber into a cylinder for transport back onshore.

Together with a colleague, Mark, Keith had previously started a sampling business with Apex, (Kevin's company) as a partner. The two of them had developed a new mercury-free sampling device and had just started offering services with their new sampling tools when, via the Exal acquisition, control of their business was sold to Expro.

Expro was already offering sampling services, but its tools employed the use of mercury. When the Norwegian Petroleum Directorate banned the use of mercury offshore, it wasn't long thereafter before the UK industry banned its use in the UK sector of the North Sea as well.

When this ban came into effect, Expro was able to continue offering sampling services with the new mercury-free tools they had just acquired.

At the time Expro made its acquisition, it also insisted on acquiring Keith's and Mark's individual shareholdings. Keith stayed on to become an Expro employee and run the sampling business for them, while Mark choose to leave and start up another business venture of his own.

With Mark away, Keith needed the help of another experienced person. His friend Jim, who was also working for Expro as a service engineer with the electronic gauges, had previously been a sampling service engineer so Keith arranged for Jim to move over to work in his group.

After joining Expro, Keith wanted to develop yet another, even more superior, sampling device. The idea he had in mind would not use mercury and, from the moment a sample was taken downhole, would store it at reservoir pressure or above. The concept had been around for a number of years and was known as *single-phase sampling*.

Oil companies were aware that the analysis of a sample at pressure lower than its pressure in the reservoir could be misleading. It was a known fact that the drop in pressure when oil or gas flowed from the well could allow some chemical characteristics to change. By obtaining accurate chemical analysis of the *in situ* product, engineers could determine what changes might occur during this flow from the well. This information could be critical for designing the optimum offshore facilities for future production.

Keith believed that a viable business could be built around a sampling service which recovered samples in pristine condition. If a workable tool was made available, he was convinced that oil companies would be interested. At the time, no one had designed a tool which could do the job, so Keith approached his manager, Kevin, with a funding request to develop this 'third-generation' sampling tool.

When Kevin refused the funding request, Keith and Jim decided they wanted to find a way to build the tool themselves and set up a single-phase sampling service of their own. Keith put together a business plan and then contacted me.

As well as getting revenue from taking downhole samples, Keith's business plan showed revenue coming in from renting out high pressure sample cylinders, providing storage facilities for cylinders containing samples, and analysing these samples in a lab. The business model looked very interesting and commercially robust.

I liked Keith's business plan and had the financial wherewithal to back the start-up. Although I'd never worked in the sampling business and had no idea how they would design and build their new tool, I really liked both

Keith and Jim and had every confidence they knew what they were doing. After just a few meetings, once everything was agreed, Keith and Jim both resigned from Expro.

The name Oilphase came about on Newmachar golf course. I was playing with two good friends and mentioned to them that I was getting involved in a new business. I wanted to register a company the following day, so I asked them to help me to come up with a name over the course of our eighteen holes. One friend suggested it be called 'Roy's Phase-two', with reference to Shell which had just opened its 'Phase-Four' office block in Aberdeen. I liked the 'phase' idea, as the thinking behind the new business was to keep a sample of oil or gas in its original state or 'phase'. After kicking around a few other 'phase' ideas, by the time we finished the round, I had settled on Oilphase.

I called Keith with my name suggestion and he agreed. Oilphase related perfectly to what the business was about. It would be a great name for the new company.

A month after Keith and Jim had resigned, Oilphase Sampling Services Ltd was set up in October 1989.

Having been through one start-up, I was very relaxed about the second one. Keith was the manager, Jim and another new employee, Johnny, were his assistants. As opposed to Exal, where I worked for the company, on this occasion it was not the intention that I would work for the business. I became the non-executive chairman.

Once the company got started, Keith and Jim's first task would be to design and build their innovative sampling tool. Only then could they start offering sampling service to customers.

Developing the new tool would be the tricky part.

Designing a single-phase sampler proved to be very difficult. The first idea Keith had was based on a mechanical action. After prototype was built, unfortunately, when it was tested in typical wellbore conditions, the prototype failed. It would only work at very low pressure. With a lot of help from consulting engineers and a new member of staff, a new hydraulic design was conceived. It then took a few more months of engineering and prototype testing before Keith finally had a working tool suitable for North Sea applications.

While the tool development was ongoing, an office/warehouse was rented and a facility was built for the storage of cylinders. The support equipment that would be needed to transfer samples into storage cylinders offshore was also built and a few hundred oil and gas storage cylinders were ordered.

Once the tool development got underway, Keith employed Graham, with whom he had previously worked at Schlumberger, the world's largest provider of technical services to the oil industry. Graham had previously been Keith's boss and was an exceptionally capable and professional individual. He brought with him a lot of sampling experience and was a big help designing the new tool. He and Keith worked really well together.

It took Keith, Jim and Graham seven months before their new tool was finally ready.

When the first job came, Keith coerced Graham to update his offshore survival course and go out to do one more sampling job. The first single-phase sampling job in the world took place in the North Sea for Amerada Hess in April 1990. The sampling tool worked perfectly. The transfer bench for transferring the sample out of the tool's chamber into a storage/transport cylinder also worked, but had a minor design fault which prevented Graham from releasing pressure from the line once the transfer had been completed. Graham could only do this by disconnecting the line mechanically. For his effort, his face got covered with a light spray of crude. The rig crew standing nearby immediately christened him 'Oil-face', the name by which he was known for the remainder of his time on the rig.

Once the equipment arrived back in Aberdeen, the problem with the transfer unit was sorted and thereafter everything worked perfectly. The success of that Amerada Hess job soon led to more job opportunities with them and other clients. Initially, all the jobs were in the North Sea but eventually there were overseas jobs as well. The first international job was on a multi-well project in Venezuela as a subcontractor to Schlumberger. Those jobs were also successful, as were the jobs in Chad, Africa, where Oilphase also subcontracted to Schlumberger on a campaign which lasted nearly six months. During the Africa job, Oilphase and Schlumberger developed a strong working relationship and Oilphase subsequently subcontracted on a lot of other jobs with them.

The sampling tool proved to be an excellent piece of engineering and continued to achieve close to one hundred percent success. The industry recognised the merit of this single-phase sampler and awarded Oilphase the Technology Award at the Scottish Offshore Achievement Awards in 1990. We were all very happy.

Unfortunately not everyone was happy. When Keith and Jim resigned from Expro the year before, Kevin was rightfully annoyed to lose two capable employees. When he saw that Oilphase had successfully developed a single-phase sampling tool and realised that their business concept was a success, he wanted Expro to enter the market as a competitor. Having previously rejected the idea, Expro's management now agreed to fund the development of its own single-phase sampling tool.

While they were working on this, someone thought it would be a good move to file a lawsuit against Keith, Jim and myself. The 'breach of implied term of contract' action claimed that, when we were employed by Expro, we should have disclosed the single-phase sampling concept and tool design to them. This was a bit of a non-starter as the concept was already in the public domain and Keith and Jim, together with Graham, hadn't yet worked out how to make their tool.

Although Keith had spoken with Kevin about developing a tool, a working design didn't exist until sometime after he'd left Expro.

The lawsuit came as a nasty surprise to all of us. The day Neva answered the front door and was served with a £1,000,000 lawsuit certainly wasn't the best start to a day she'd ever had. Keith and his wife Mary had a similar experience.

The 'breach of an implied term of contract' lawsuit didn't appear to make sense. Keith and I felt that the motivation behind the action was simply to make life difficult for us and Oilphase. At first I was tempted just to ignore it, hoping it would go away. However, my solicitor, Gordon, sat me down and told me it was a very serious matter. I needed to make sure that I got specialist legal advice. It was not just going to go away.

For me, I felt very disappointed to think that Kevin and I had sold a great company to Expro at a bargain price and yet he and Expro's management felt a need to scupper my next business venture. I could have understood and expected this action had Keith, Jim, or I defaulted on warranties or non-compete agreements, but that wasn't the case and wasn't what the lawsuit was about.

For some time after the lawsuit had been served, Oilphase went through a lean spell of business. The lawsuit may have made some impact, or it may just have been the market conditions at the time. For whatever reason, business was slow and Keith decided that he needed to reduce his operating overheads. As Graham and Jim were doing similar jobs, Keith felt he couldn't afford to keep them both. Jim and Graham were both great workers, but Graham had more experience and more of the skills Keith needed to build the business. Keith decided that Jim would need to leave. It was one of the most difficult decisions he ever had to make.

After Jim left, Keith and Graham carried on building the company and fighting the lawsuit.

One lucky break came when the Atomic Energy Commission contacted Keith about a job at Sellafield. They needed to collect perfect subterranean water samples. The first job was successful and eventually this led to an additional two hundred and fifty jobs over the next five years. The great thing about the Atomic Energy Commission work was that Oilphase had this all to itself. No competitors had a sampler as good as theirs at the time and, when they eventually did have one, Oilphase was established as the preferred service provider. Most competitors probably didn't know this opportunity for non-oilfield work even existed.

A one million pound lawsuit can certainly make life difficult. It did two things which had a big impact. Firstly, it was a serious situation, so Keith had to spend a lot of time dealing with lawyers and collecting material to prepare our defence. Secondly, the bank took the view that Oilphase was now a higher risk account. Although Douglas, our bank manager, gave as much support as possible, he had to consider the possibility that the lawsuit would be successful and that Oilphase could fail. It was difficult for him to persuade head office to provide any funding above the value of their receivables account. This limited access to funds certainly impacted on Keith's ability to grow the business.

The action by Expro's management to sue the directors of Oilphase was extreme and I didn't think it was normal for a company of their size to react so aggressively against such a small competitor. I concluded that it must have really annoyed someone when Keith and Jim asked me to back their new business.

In spite of the difficulties, Oilphase continued to succeed and in 1992 this success was recognised when the company won the 'Overall Small Company Performance Award'.

Keith and I regularly spoke with one another and we normally had a board meeting once a month. The job of being chairman was a most wonderful experience. Everything was always discussed openly and after considering all the points of view, we never once failed to agree. Everyone expressed their opinion, no one ever got upset, and Keith and Graham always stuck with the decisions that had been agreed. It was all 'too easy' and so different from my time at Exal.

Meanwhile, the lawsuit continued and Oilphase carried on.

CHAPTER 37

The Dream Merchant

Apart from my occasional visit to the Oilphase premises, the only time I met many of the Oilphase team was at the annual BBQ or Christmas party. Keith always made sure these events were special occasions. Everyone looked forward to them and they were always well attended.

One Christmas party was more memorable than most. Ian, who Keith had recently employed, worked in sales and had a rather flamboyant girlfriend at the time. I had not met her before, but she was at the party and ready to enjoy herself. I would often dance with some of the wives and eventually took to the floor with this tall, slim girl in a miniskirt. She had a long silk scarf which she immediately lassoed around my neck. A short while later her next move was totally unexpected. She started 'twisting' and as she went lower, she used her scarf to encourage me to do the same. Once I got as low as I was going to get she promptly stood back up. She swung one leg up into the air and brought it down to rest on my shoulder. I was forced to remain in my crouched position while she danced away quite merrily on one leg, using her scarf and my neck, to keep her balance. It only lasted a few seconds, but it was long enough for me to feel most uncomfortable.

By this time everyone else stopped dancing and stood back to enjoy the show. I was trying not to look at any of them, but I couldn't look straight ahead either. It was a tricky situation.

As our dance carried on she tried a few more exotic moves, but I was on high alert and managed to avoid any other 'mounting' moves she might have been considering.

Eventually, mercifully, the music stopped and I calmly led my 'dancing queen' back over to Ian. All the boys had big smiles on their faces and everyone gave us a nice round of applause.

I found out later that everyone, except me, knew she was likely to do some crazy dance moves. When it finally happened and I was the victim, it was the perfect result. It made their night.

From then on I approached dancing with other people's partners with a lot more caution. I would watch a few dances first, just to make sure I wasn't about to get out of my depth with someone else's party animal.

Ian stayed on with Oilphase for a number of years, then decided to leave the industry and start up a business for himself. I'll be damned if he didn't set himself up as a dream expert! I'll bet he got the idea for this new career that night when he correctly interpreted the nightmare I was going through on the dance floor.

CHAPTER 38

The Bit Business

Once Keith had Oilphase up and running, I didn't need to spend a lot of time with the company. Our phone calls and board meetings kept me up to speed and well informed. Apart from the fact that Keith needed to spend far too much of his time dealing with the lawsuit, the business was ticking along reasonably well.

Not being an employee of Oilphase left me with a lot of free time, in fact too much free time. I still felt a need to work and was keen to find something where I would be fully involved. I wanted to have my own company again.

I was so keen to find something that I jumped at the very first opportunity that came along. 'Opportunity' probably isn't the right word, as the diamond drill bit business I was introduced to became a potential nightmare.

I met Danny at a golf event some nine months after he had started Brit Bit Limited, known as British Bits or BBL. He had decided to start the drill bit company after meeting a drill bit designer, Neil, who was an inventor and had designed a novel concept for a PDC (*polycrystalline diamond compact*) drill bit. His novel idea wasn't about the actual use of the man-made diamond cutters, as there were a lot of companies manufacturing drill bits using these PDCs. Neil's invention was about keeping the cutters sharp. PDC cutters on a drill bit work in a similar way to the cutting tip on a lathe tool. When a piece of steel is being machined on a lathe, there needs to be a constant flow of cooling fluid to dissipate the heat away from the tip of the cutter. Heat, caused by friction, is the main cause of cutter wear. Properly cooled with a constant flow of fluid, diamond cutters will remain sharp for a long time. In a similar manner, when a drill bit drills, each of the fifty to sixty cutters on the bit need to be cooled effectively. Obviously, the less they wear, the sharper they are and the faster the bit drills. Neil's invention had to do with a more effective passage of the drilling fluid across the face of the cutters thereby flushing away the rock cuttings as quickly as possible and dissipating any heat as quickly as possible.

Neil agreed to licence his invention to Danny and he then started BBL on the back of this licence.

Using Neil's design concept, two prototype drill bits were built. One was run for Shell and the other for BP. In both cases the prototypes appeared to have drilled faster than the drill bits they had used to drill a similar rock section in a previous, nearby well. Neil's invention seemed to work. The prototype bits had drilled faster but they hadn't drilled further. Apparently the new design was clever, but for some reason the drill bits weren't as robust as they needed to be. Some of the cutters had been dislodged, putting extra loading on the remaining cutters, eventually causing them to fail. The reason for this wasn't immediately obvious but the final outcome was that the two drill bits hadn't drilled as far as they should have.

A focus on building faster drill bits has been an industry obsession from the time the very first wells were being drilled. The speed at which a bit drills down to the next horizon impacts directly on the daily operation cost and the total well construction cost, therefore, choosing the best drill bit was always a key decision. Selecting the correct drill bit to drill a particular rock type is crucial. Just as a ripsaw and a cross-cut saw have different applications when cutting wood, so it is with drill bits and different rock types. As well as the rock type, factors such as the directional drilling requirement, the total distance the bit might need to drill and the type of drilling fluid being used also have a bearing on drill bit selection.

When I thought about becoming an investor, I assumed that the biggest challenge had been to design a faster drill bit to drill one type of rock, and this appeared to have been achieved. The possibility of BBL becoming a successful business on the strength of this achievement looked very interesting. The engineers just needed to work out how to make the drill bit more robust.

After giving it no more that a few days' thought, I told Danny that I was the new investor he was looking for.

In July 1990, I invested in the company and became the executive chairman. By that time a small but adequate production facility had been set up and a small number of drill bits had been produced, Only six of these had been sold. The six additional bit-runs confirmed that the 'faster' design concept was working, but they also confirmed that more engineering work was needed, and some better manufacturing techniques were required, to improve the durability of the product.

Dennis was Danny's sales manager, a marketing man who had joined Danny at the time of the start-up. Although he had been employed as the sales manager, Dennis unfortunately didn't have the geological qualification or drill bit selling experience needed to correctly engineer drill bit applications. The drill bits that had been sold prior to my arrival had been 'engineered' by Neil. In order to sell more drill bits we needed to have a full-time sales applications engineer. This wasn't a job Neil wanted and it wasn't a job Dennis could do, so I would need to hire someone qualified for the job.

I set about trying to find a sales engineer with the experience needed and got lucky. I found Chris, a salesman who was working with a big competitor. He knew his stuff, had a geology qualification and was an excellent salesman. Chris was keen to join a new company where he would have a bigger role in the sales department.

Making a drill bit sale isn't straightforward. Before I joined BBL, I knew very little about how this business actually worked. However, I found out very quickly just how hard it was to sell a drill bit to an oil company if you didn't have any track record. It was a 'catch-22' situation: no bit runs, no track record, no track record, no new sales. Chris proved to be such a competent salesman that, in spite of BBL's lack of track record, he managed to find a few more customers interested in giving our product a try.

The business model is also a little unusual. Oil company engineers always took a selection of drill bits onto the rig.

These drill bits were supplied on consignment by various manufacturers such as BBL. Before the engineer on the rig chose his next drill bit, he would discuss his selection with the engineer onshore who had arranged the consignment in the first place. Choosing which drill bit was to be run usually depended on how far it was to the next casing point and how much directional drilling was required. If our drill bit was selected, only then, after it had performed successfully, could we raise an invoice. If it wasn't selected it would be returned for restocking, free of charge.

Running a business on a free consignment basis required a lot of stock and a lot of perseverance. Sometimes a drill bit made three or four trips offshore before it was eventually used and sold. By then a full year could have passed with no financial return from our investment. It was a tough business model. However, Chris took control of the sales effort and he was very good, both at getting our drill bits onto the rig in the first place and then making sure that we were at the top of the list to be selected. Without his skill and sales ability, BBL would have been dead and buried within the first year.

Managing our inventory for this business model was a challenge. Managing our cash flow was an even bigger challenge.

Chris had one additional issue he could have done without. He and Dennis weren't quite 'on the same page'. Dennis carried on with his marketing effort and left Chris to do the selling.

On one occasion Dennis was so keen for a drilling engineer with BP to see our new drill bit design, that he hired a van and took two drill bits over to his office.

Unfortunately the van had previously been used to transport fish. It was a hot day and when Dennis opened the back door, the engineer was engulfed by the overpowering smell of dead fish. He gagged and wouldn't come any closer than ten feet.

Dennis got full marks for trying. A year later when Chris managed to sell the engineer a drill bit, he had remembered Dennis's visit, so his marketing effort had not been in vain.

One successful initiative Dennis instigated was to get our drill bits into the Nigerian market. Dennis found a distributor in Nigeria and arranged for the managing director to come to Aberdeen to see our drill bits. He was impressed and bought a dozen bits from us at a discount. At the time this was a huge sale and the income was most welcome.

The distributor was planning to sell these drill bits to oil companies drilling in Nigeria. In order to do this they needed someone who could sell them. Dennis offered to take the job himself. I didn't think he was best qualified but Dennis liked the thought of an overseas posting so I didn't interfere. His move did offer a solution to the difficult relationship he and Chris had in Aberdeen. Two months later, Dennis and his wife moved to Nigeria and I promoted Chris to be the new sales manager.

It ended up being a win-win situation. I now had an excellent sales manager and one less salary to pay every month.

My next challenge was to find and employ an experienced drill bit design engineer to support and enhance the work Neil was doing. Fortunately, thanks to Chris's recommendation, I found Mike. Mike was a fully qualified and experienced drill bit designer and had previously worked together with Chris in the same drill bit company. After telling Mike about our clever drill bit design and explaining what we were trying to do, he decided to join our team. He relished the opportunity to become the lead engineer in a new company.

Within weeks of his arrival, I discovered that we had found an outstanding engineer, capable of sorting out engineering problems and keen to help the production team produce a better product.

Mike very quickly became the backbone of our product line.

At last there were a few good things happening with BBL. Back at Oilphase, Keith was still fighting the lawsuit.

CHAPTER 39

The Silly Boy

During my first six months with BBL, although there were some encouraging results, overall business was disappointing. We'd had two or three more excellent drill bit runs, but amongst the good runs there had also been some poor ones. If we wanted to increase bit sales, it was obvious that the product still needed further development.

As is the case with many privately owned start-up companies, cash flow and funding often become a big problem. In the early days, BBL was living hand-to-mouth. Somehow the company needed to sell drill bits to generate the cash needed to develop the product and build more drill bits.

It wasn't long before we simply ran out of cash. If the company was to continue in business it would be necessary to make a cash-call on the shareholders. I had the funds available from my Exal sale and was willing to make the 'call'. Danny held over sixty percent of the equity, so he had a much bigger payment to make. He also made the 'call'.

I knew that Danny had equity in another private company as some of this was held by our bank as collateral for our overdraft. I assumed he had access to other funds as well and had used these to make his cash-call. I didn't give it any further thought.

Six months after we put in the additional funds, I received a call from our bank asking me to come over for a meeting. "When would you like me to come?" I asked. "Right now," came the reply.

At the time, I was awaiting confirmation that our overdraft facility had been approved for renewal and I assumed this was what the meeting would be about. I asked Morton, our accountant, what could possibly be wrong with the information we had submitted. "Absolutely nothing is wrong," Morton replied. "All the information we sent them is correct. Nothing is overstated." "Well you had better join me for the bank meeting, they appear to be very concerned about something," I said.

When we arrived, we were met by a secretary at the front door and immediately escorted through to an office where the senior manager, his assistant, and another secretary were all waiting for us. The feeling I got upon entering the room was not good. There was no offer of cups of tea or any welcoming chit-chat. Morton and I took our seats and I immediately launched into a presentation, defending our overdraft submission. The senior manager stopped me. "Your overdraft submission is not a problem," he said. "The problem is the collateral for your guarantee."

I hadn't given any guarantee, but was aware that Danny had used the shareholding he held in another private company as collateral when the business was initially set up. I couldn't believe that these shares were not valuable enough to cover the amount required, as the company in question was doing very well at the time. "I don't question their value," said the manager, "The problem is that they have been sold. New share certificates were issued replacing the ones we are holding, and those have been sold. The paper we hold as collateral is worthless!"

Morton and I sat there trying to take in what we were being told. No collateral, no guarantee, no overdraft, and no BBL.

I had made it clear from the outset that I wasn't giving any guarantee and had no intention of now changing my mind and replacing Danny's guarantee with one of my own. Sitting there, at that point in time, in spite of the previous cash-call, the company was effectively worthless. Without an overdraft facility, BBL couldn't continue in business. I waited to be told that the bank was no longer going to provide any funding and that I should go back to my office to wind up the company.

That didn't happen.

The managers had obviously considered their options and, now they were satisfied that neither Morton nor I had been a party to the deception, they were prepared to find a solution. (This was the same bank I had been involved with at Exal, so maybe that helped.) The solution was not good for Danny. The bank would continue its support, provided I held a controlling interest in the company and that Danny could not benefit from any future value of his shareholding. If he was not prepared to sell or relinquish his shareholding, the bank would not provide any further funding and the business would be wound up. They said they were not planning to take legal action, but made it clear that they could and, in the future, should other information come to light, might reconsider their decision to continue providing BBL with any funding.

As soon as I got back at my office I called Danny. He knew immediately why we were meeting and said he was so relieved that the matter was now out in the open. What he had done, in order to make the cash-call, was to declare the share scripts held by the bank to have been lost. When he received replacement scripts, he sold these to raise the necessary funds.

Danny hadn't considered the possibility that the bank auditors would check BBL's quarantees but, when they did, they discovered the scripts they held were no longer valid. Danny was counting on BBL doing well enough, quickly enough, for him to be released from the guarantee before there was ever an issue.

"Well it looks like you have really screwed up," I said. "You sold your valuable shares and have now lost all the money you have invested in BBL. You have no chance of getting any return should the company become a success in the future."

Danny started to realise the magnitude of his action.

Looking at it from my side, I was very lucky that Danny hadn't told me about his share sale before I'd gone to the bank. Had I known, and had the bank manager thought I was a party to Danny's action, he would never have continued his support. I also realised that Danny's action very nearly cost me the investment I had made in BBL as well. However, the outcome whereby the bank insisted that I acquire Danny's equity and then continued providing the overdraft facility BBL needed, without any guarantee, turned out to be a good result. A good result for me, but not for Danny.

Danny had made a bad decision when freeing up his capital to make the cash-call. He had managed to make the payment but was now left without any holding in either company. It was a real shame. He had worked hard and taken a lot of risk to build the value in his first venture and then invested everything in BBL. Now he had lost the lot.

Ironically, had the bank manager decided to shut down BBL, the bank, Danny, myself, and our suppliers would have all lost money. Because the bank manager continued to give his support, and the company went on to become a success, the only one to lose out was Danny.

Danny was not a bad person, he had just been a silly boy and made one really bad decision.

Danny continue to work as production manager, but after a while this proved to be untenable. After six months he left the company and left Aberdeen.

The bank manager was true to his word. He continued providing BBL with an overdraft facility without any guarantee and I was able to carry on with the business.

After the shareholding was restructured, I moved from being the executive chairman to become the full-time managing director.

I reflected afterwards that there will have been many cases where directors have come unstuck after getting caught with their fingers in the till. There won't have been too many cases like Danny's, where a director came unstuck for putting money back into the till!

In spite of the bank renewing our overdraft facility, six months later the company was once again stretched to financial breaking point. The business just wasn't building momentum quickly enough and the company was effectively insolvent for a second time. We simply weren't selling enough drill bits so I needed to find more cash and I needed to find it quickly.

This time we received some very welcome assistance from De Beers.

CHAPTER 40

The Helping Hand

De Beers was the main diamond supplier for BBL. PDC cutters were the primary component of our drill bits and represented around sixty percent of the product cost. The more drill bits we sold the more PDC cutters we would need to buy from De Beers. We worked closely with them, they liked our technology, and they were keen for us to succeed.

Along the way, Neil, their sales rep, had done everything in his power to ease our payment terms but, at the end of every month, we often struggled to make their payment. When I informed Neil that, once again, we were in dire financial straits, he arranged for Morton and me to come to their industrial product division head office in Shannon, Ireland, to meet their management.

Morton and I flew over the following week. Upon our arrival, Morton was invited to meet with John, their financial controller. I was told that I would not be needed at this meeting so, while they were talking, I was to be shown around the facilities. The factory was quite something to see, especially the huge presses where the synthetic diamond cutters were made. Getting to see, from a safe distance, PDC cutters actually being created, plus all the diamond cutting and sorting facilities, was quite impressive.

I had a brief meeting with the MD and around lunchtime was taken to the directors' dining room for a pre-lunch drink. Morton was already there. I tried to speak with him, but he was busy chatting with John and a couple of other accountants. I had no idea how he had got on in his meeting.

At lunch I sat next to the MD, and Morton sat next to John, further up the table. Morton seemed to be very relaxed and was enjoying the superb lunch and a glass of wine. I was a lot less relaxed. I knew if Morton's meeting hadn't been a success and we didn't get any additional financial support this splendid lunch was going to be the equivalent of our 'last supper'. It went on for an hour. All the while I kept looking over at Morton for some sign of reassurance, but Morton had started drinking another glass of fine wine and didn't seem too bothered.

Towards the end of the lunch I became anxious about our flight home. We were booked on the 2.30 flight to Heathrow, connecting with a flight to Aberdeen that evening. If we missed the Heathrow flight we would need to stay over in London as the next flight didn't leave Shannon until 7.00 pm. I was not keen to pay for a London hotel if it could be avoided.

The manager could see that I was wanting to leave. When I explained my concern, he asked for our travel tickets and gave them to his secretary. "She will take care of your flight," he said. Ten minutes later she returned to say everything had been sorted. "Well I guess we have a night in London," I thought to myself, knowing we had already missed the 2.30 flight.

Once we'd enjoyed a nice cup of coffee and the lunch finally ended, the manager said we had better be on our way. "Our driver will take you over to the terminal whenever you are ready," he said. (Great, I thought, we will just sit there for the next four hours until the 7:00pm flight departs.)

Ten minutes later we arrived at the terminal, drove through a security gate, out onto the tarmac and stopped next to a private jet. The driver said, "You still have time to visit the duty-free if you like. The pilot is ready to fly you to Heathrow as soon as you wish to leave."

Wow! We got on-board and away we went. Back then, a private jet could still land at Heathrow and that is exactly where the De Beers plane was heading.

Once we were on-board, I finally got to speak to Morton and he told me De Beers had been amazing. (Apparently, Neil and Phil, De Beers' chief engineer, had put in a good word for us.) John had agreed to extend the repayment on some of our debt until we were more solvent and offered to supply us with diamond cutters on consignment until they were actually assembled into a drill bit. These two actions were most helpful and put us on a much stronger financial footing.

Until Morton told me how his meeting had gone, I wasn't entirely sure we weren't going to be asked to leave the plane … somewhere over the Irish Sea! I had always been open and honest with De Beers about our financial position and this relationship had now paid off.

Upon our arrival at Heathrow, we were met by a VIP hostess and she escorted us from the private lounge over to the main terminal. We checked in for our scheduled flight to Aberdeen and made it home that evening just as we had planned.

On another occasion a couple of years later, I needed a little more help from De Beers. Once again it was to do with our finances. This time Derek, my bank branch manager, called to say that his bosses in Edinburgh had reviewed our overdraft facility and, rather than giving us the increase we had asked for, they proposed to reduce our current facility by twenty-five percent. (The bankers in Edinburgh knew there weren't any guarantees in place so they were calculating their exposure based on the performance of the business.)

Probably the most important job I did as MD was to manage our cash flow. I always knew exactly how much money was coming in from outstanding invoices and I always knew what our spending commitments were. The fixed cost for wages, rent, utilities, and so forth, was a significant number but there wasn't much I could do about that. The money we spent on building new product was a variable. As soon as I saw that our sales were down, I would stop as much production as possible to make sure we stayed within our overdraft limit. I usually knew six weeks in advance if we were heading for trouble so I took what action I could, then called Derek to let him know what I was doing. He was made aware of the potential problem and I promised to keep him posted going forward.

I had an excellent relationship with Derek. I always kept him fully informed and over the years he had always done his best to support me. This time however, the matter had been taken out of his hands.

I immediately got on the phone to John in Shannon to let him know what had happened. If the facility was reduced we would not be able to make our next payment to De Beers. John was disappointed with my bank's action and suggested that he should come to Aberdeen to investigate.

He and his assistant arrived a few days later. After reviewing everything with Morton, he was satisfied that our accounts were in order, just as he had expected they would be.

I arranged for us to meet with Derek.

Derek was ready and waiting. He even had his finest china tea cups out, which didn't always happen when I came to visit him on my own. John immediately asked why the bank had decided to reduce the BBL facility. Derek started to explain about the new bank structure, whereby Edinburgh was reviewing all business overdrafts and decisions were no longer being made by the branch managers.

John told Derek he was disappointed that he hadn't been able to convince Edinburgh that BBL was well managed and had excellent financial governance. This put Derek on the back foot. He agreed that I had always kept him well informed and that we were excellent clients.

After a few more minutes of back and forth, John looked over to his assistant and said, "I think I have a solution.

My signing authority is more than Roy's overdraft. Why don't we take over his facility, then he won't need to deal with this bank at all."

Well that wasn't what Derek expected to hear. Instead of getting to continue business with a lower risk account, suddenly he was on the brink of losing our account altogether. "Let me just speak to Edinburgh one more time," said Derek. He left the room and returned ten minutes later to say that the facility, including the requested increase, would be fully reinstated.

The meeting ended. As we left Derek's office, John's parting remark made it clear that he didn't want to fly to Aberdeen to deal with my overdraft again. John turned and gave me a big wink. He had been bluffing about taking over the overdraft, but had got us the result we needed to have.

I was once again very thankful for De Beers' assistance. After taking John back to the airport, I couldn't help thinking, if he ever decided to give up working as a financial manager, he could probably have a great career as a poker player.

It turned out to be the last time I ever needed to speak with John about our overdraft and the last time we ever had any difficulty with our bank facility. From then on, BBL started making money and we managed to keep our finances in line and to pay our De Beers account every month.

Even though De Beers supported us up to the hilt, we never did have a formal supply contract or exclusive agreement with them. De Beers' cutters were simply the best on the market, so they were the ones we preferred to use. However, their cutters were expensive and some of their competitors occasionally came to us with offers to sell us cutters at a lower price. A few of these companies sent samples of their product, so from time to time we would trial other cutters to see if they were useable.

One time we were sent half a dozen sample cutters from a Chinese manufacturer. When I saw that they were offering to sell their cutters at a sixty percent discount to the cost of a De Beers' cutter, I had to trial these to see if they were useable. If they were good enough to use, we could reduce our manufacturing cost significantly. This would give us a big price advantage over our competitors. On the other hand, if our competitors were to use these cutters and we didn't, we would be priced out of the market.

We took two cutters and subjected them to a standard wear test. The result of the test showed that their cutter quality was excellent.

I called Phil and explained my problem. Based on how good the Chinese cutters had performed and the significant cost saving available, I would probably need to source cutters from China, not De Beers.

Phil asked if he could have a look at one of the Chinese cutters. A week later he called me back to confirm that the cutter we'd sent him was indeed as good as one of theirs. In fact, it *was* one of theirs. The Chinese supplier had sourced a few De Beers' cutters and had sent these to me for testing!

Had I purchased the Chinese cutters, BBL would almost certainly have had a number of below par drill bit performances. This could have made a serious impact on our business. Phil said he knew the Chinese manufacturer and was aware that the quality of their product wasn't quite there yet. Once again the open relationship had paid off.

I have never worked with a more supportive supplier than De Beers. The company produced an excellent product and their managers always went the extra mile to help me out. They were a great group of people and we simply would not have made it without them. With their help, BBL survived and the company slowly started to become stronger.

CHAPTER 41

The Company Cars

At home things were going a lot better. Neva had settled into her routine as a doctor and academic, and both Janna and Elise were attending school. Everyone seemed to be in a better place. Even my strimmer was working well so I was getting to enjoy a few more games of golf. In a lot of ways it felt as though the most difficult times were behind us.

I was still very busy and occasionally still got stressed, but I was enjoying the challenge of managing BBL and working with my team to solve the various problems which kept coming our way. On the other side of town, Oilphase continued to do well but Keith hadn't managed to stop the lawsuit action. In fact, Expro's management was looking for ways to turn up the heat another notch.

In order to show that the single-phase sampling concept was already in the public domain, Keith cited a twelve-year-old patent owned by an oil company.

Having had his patent attorney examine the patent to make sure Oilphase wasn't in breach, Keith mentioned to him that it might be a good idea to purchase the patent as the oil company who owned it wasn't using it and were prepared to sell. Ownership of the patent would ensure that there was no chance of any patent infringement issue going forward. The patent attorney said, "Why would you want to do that? I've already confirmed for you that your technology isn't in breach. It would just be a waste of money." When Keith suggested that it would prevent anyone else from buying the patent and claiming that Oilphase was in breach, the attorney replied, "That's Hollywood, this is Scotland. That doesn't happen here."

After Keith's lawyer passed this information on to Expro, the outcome was not what Keith's patent attorney had expected. Keith's prophecy would come back to haunt him.

Within BBL, the success with our drill bits in the North Sea led to various attempts to find sales opportunities internationally. After one year, the Nigeria distribution arrangement had not gone well and we were no longer selling any drill bits there. Only a few of the drill bits from the first shipment had been sold and only a few more had been ordered. For whatever reason, the business never really got much customer support. The distributor decided he wanted out of the business and asked if I would buy back his stock. I declined. I couldn't afford his drill bits and by then a lot of his stock had been superseded. The agent was very disappointed that I wouldn't help him out, but, he did eventually managed to sell his stock as a job lot to a local oil company. After the drill bits were sold Dennis left Nigeria and returned to look for a new job in Aberdeen.

In Aberdeen Chris was doing a great job. Some local customers were getting excellent results with our drill bits and had become repeat customers. Within a short period of time Chris needed help to cover all the potential clients and recruited two more sales engineers. There were then three of them making sales calls.

Norway was our closest international market and as some of our UK customers were also active in the Norwegian side of the North Sea, we thought this country would be the easiest new market to target. Also, the wells in the Norwegian sector were being drilled through similar rock formations, so our UK data base was a useful reference. Chris made a couple of trips there and managed to sell drill bits to both a Shell and a BP engineer who had used them in the UK. In spite of the fact that both these runs were successful, Chris couldn't manage to sell bits to any Norwegian oil company. He concluded that we wouldn't be successful in Norway until we hired a local sales engineer and opened an office in Stavanger.

Having made the decision to open this new office, I engaged a professional head-hunter to find a sales manager. After an extensive search, a lot of interviews, and several trips to Stavanger, we hired Geir. Geir was a highly qualified sales engineer working for a direct competitor. He didn't come cheap. (Very few things in Norway do come cheap.) The day after agreeing to join BBL, Geir handed in his notice. He was immediately asked to leave his office and told to hand over the keys to his company car. He was also told that he would not need to work his one-month's notice, but he wasn't allowed to start work for BBL until that time had passed.

Since he had no car and had four weeks to wait before he could start working for us, Geir called to ask if I would buy his new company car straight away. He wanted to use his free time to go away for a short holiday. I agreed to his plan and a few days later he collected a new BMW and headed off for a driving holiday in Europe.

I didn't hear from Geir for two weeks, then one day he called from Germany to say that his car had been stolen. He hadn't even started working for us and already I needed to replace his company car! He caught a flight back to Stavanger and I ordered a second new BMW for him. Fortunately the first car had been insured, so we would recover the loss, but buying a second car was still going to impact on my cash flow.

After a week at home, while still waiting to start work, he found an office to rent, ordered furniture, a computer and some office supplies. When the four weeks were finally up he was ready to start.

As a new employee the first thing he did was come to Aberdeen for a two-week training session. He needed to learn about our products and become familiar with the track record we had built up with our UK customers.

Finally everything was ready for Geir to start selling to clients in Norway. Away he went to introduce himself and our drill bits to the various oil companies. After only two weeks of selling, and not having made a sale, his previous employer called him with an offer of re-employment as their sales manager, together with a big salary increase. He accepted the job and the next day, a Thursday, he called me to say that he was leaving BBL on Friday.

I couldn't believe it.

"What do you want me to do with the car?" Geir asked. "And by the way, the police just called to say that they've recovered the first BMW in Germany and will have it returned to Stavanger next week."

Two cars, a two-year office lease, furniture, computer, office supplies and now no employee. Bloody marvellous! I was very disappointed but realised that there wasn't anything I could do to keep Geir.

The most annoying thing was that we now had a competitor in Norway who knew everything about our business and all the success we were having in the UK. In more ways than one, my venture into the Norwegian market had been a costly failure. Even after selling both cars the two-month exercise left me with a loss of around sixty thousand pounds.

We tried to make use of the office by sending a sales engineer over from Aberdeen for a few weeks at a time but the Norway business never took off. A Norwegian drilling engineer explained our problem to me very clearly when he said, "Why would I use a drill bit from BBL when we have a drill bit manufacturing company in Norway?"

I had been working on the assumption that Norwegian oil companies would accept suppliers on merit. In business, however, the Norwegians tend to look after their own national suppliers first. The fact that their local manufacturer didn't make a similar product to ours, or have the track record we had, was irrelevant.

CHAPTER 42

The New Tax Disc

For a small company such as BBL dealing with regulation changes in employment law, Health and Safety, and implementing new controls to keep our quality accreditation up to speed was always a challenge. Regular reviews and meetings were needed to make sure we complied with all the latest changes. These tasks were necessary but they took a lot of time and were a constant hassle.

On a personal level I had some admin challenges of my own. In the UK thirty years ago you needed to get a new paper tax disc for your car every year. The government sent you a renewal form in the mail and you then needed to have the car inspected to certify that it was roadworthy. Having received this MOT (roadworthiness certificate), you took that document, together with your car insurance and the government renewal form to the post office to purchase your new tax disc. Sounds simple, but my company car, my wife's car, my daughter's car and our motor home all needed taxing. Four vehicles with four different sets of documents. It was all made a little more difficult by the fact that the tax disc renewal date for three of our vehicles were due at the same time, and the insurance renewal on each vehicles also coincided with this due date.

Getting all the MOTs done in time and then coordinating all the paperwork was just too difficult. I made many trips to the post office, only to be sent home because I'd taken information from the wrong vehicle or some other piece of paper wasn't exactly correct.

I ended up stressing about this tax-disc exercise so much that my wife finally said, "I'll do it. It's really very simple. You're just not careful enough to make sure everything is correct before you go to the post office." Off she went, only to return home, angry, twenty minutes later because something had been incorrect. (Apparently the insurance document she'd taken didn't take effect until Monday and it was now Saturday so the postmistress said that she would need to come back on Monday.)

I located the current insurance document and then went back to get the tax disc. Just to be sure I had a better than even chance of success, I went to a different post office, the one in Mannofield, on the corner of North Deeside and Cranford Road. I went in and joined the queue. When it came to my turn, I took all the papers out of the plastic sleeve I was carrying them in and handed them over one at a time. I waited for the rejection I was certain I was about to get, but, to my surprise the postmistress took a tax disc out of her book, printed my registration number on it and handed it to me together with all my papers. "Next," she said, indicating that my job was done. Just like that. It had only taken two minutes and I was ready to leave with my new tax disc. I was amazed. I put all the papers back into the plastic sleeve and with a glow of self-satisfaction walked outside just as a huge gust of wind came by.

In an instant, the tax disc was blown out of the plastic sleeve, flew across the road and attached itself to the grill of a passing car. I stood there in disbelief as the car continued to drive along the road and disappear from sight. The car and my new tax disc were gone. I starred at the empty road for a while, then took a deep breath and went back into the post office.

When my turn came, I tried to explain to the postmistress that I needed another tax disc because the one she had given me ten minutes earlier had been lost. "Nothing I can do," came the reply. "If you have lost your tax disc you need to go to the DVLA office in town to report the loss. They will issue you with a new one."

Off I went to the DVLA. After a fifteen-minute wait, I explained to the lady what had happened and she went off to check her records. "We don't have any record of you buying a new tax disc," she said.

"That's because I only just bought it an hour ago and the information is still at the post office in Mannofield."

"You can make out a 'lost disc' form and once the information from the post office gets lodged at head-office in Swansea, they will receive our form and you will be sent a new tax disc in the mail," she replied.

"I can't go home without a tax disc," I said.

The lady kindly wrote a note confirming that my new disc would come in the mail within a couple of weeks.

Almost three hours after leaving the house I arrived back home.

"Would you believe it," I said "I finally got all the papers correct and the post office ran out of tax discs! Here is the letter they gave me saying the new disc will arrive in the mail in a couple of weeks."

My wife replied, "How is it possible that the post office can be so inefficient? No wonder this country is in such a mess!"

"If they didn't have a disc, what took you nearly three hours?" she asked.

"It's a long story," I replied.

CHAPTER 43

The Big Surprise

By 1993, the drill bit business was gaining momentum and BBL was seen as a credible competitor in the market. The company's technology had been recognised with an Offshore Achievement Award in 1992 and a number of oil companies including Shell, BP, Mobil, Marathon and Amerada Hess had all written about outstanding BBL drill bit runs in their internal publications. Some of the best testimonials included a report by Mobil North Sea saying that a BBL drill bit drilled twice as fast as the drill bit they used on their previous well and that they only needed two BBL drill bits to drill the same footage which usually required four drill bits. In its September 1993 in-house publication, Amerada Hess reported that the use of BBL drill bits saved them an estimated three hundred thousand dollars by drilling a section with one drill bit at a rate of penetration sixty-eight percent faster than the drill bit used on the previous well.

The Parliamentary Under-Secretary of State for Energy, Colin Moynihan, came to pay us a visit and I was interviewed for a short clip on the BBC *Money Programme*. Things were moving ahead very nicely.

With the success we were having in Aberdeen, even though Nigeria and Norway hadn't worked out, I was still keen to look for sales opportunities internationally.

The Middle East was a sizeable market for PDC drill bits and Chris had already generated some interest from one oil company drilling there. He had gone to Dubai to follow up a sales lead and eventually made a sale. After a very successful drill bit run, this led to more sales opportunities so we decided to open an office and enter the market in Dubai on a full-time basis.

Chris was keen to work overseas, so he immediately offered to take the assignment himself. Like a lot of people in the industry, the financial reward for working as an expat was a big attraction.

In Aberdeen, the UK sales manager, John, who had been hired months before Chris relocated to Dubai, took over as the international sales manager. John came with a lot of experience and a lot of new enthusiasm to drive the business forward. Once again we managed to find an excellent employee who would make a big difference to our business. Paul, another excellent sales engineer on our staff, then moved up to be the new UK sales manager.

In the Middle East, foreign companies like BBL are only allowed to conduct business transactions if they use an agent to represent them. Back when Chris sold our first drill bit in Dubai he found an agent and, through this company, we were able to invoice the first drill bit sale. I flew over to Dubai and together with Chris, formalised this agency agreement in order to facilitate future sales.

There were potential customers in Qatar, Oman, Kuwait and Abu Dhabi, so we needed to appoint agents in each of these countries as well. Iran and Iraq we would leave for later. With each appointment I needed to visit the agent to finalise the formal engagement. This often meant nothing more than exchanging gifts (usually a Cross pen) and listening to a presentation about how well connected the agent was to the ruling sheikh and his family. For the most part, all the agents were similar. They didn't actually get involved with the business, but they collected ten percent from every invoice raised.

I particularly remember my meeting to appoint the agent Chris selected for Qatar. There weren't many agents to choose from, as the 'big boys' had already been signed up by our competitors. I flew to Doha with Chris to meet the agent with whom he had spoken, but hadn't met. We arrived fifteen minutes early and were shown into a huge office to await his arrival.

All the furniture and fittings in his office made a statement of size and power; tall double doors when you entered, a large desk standing on a nine-inch plinth, large portraits of the sheikh and presumably other family members on the wall and sizeable Arabian artefacts around the room.

We took a seat on a large sofa in the lounge area of the office.

While we waited, a man-servant came into the office and we were offered a cup of tea. He advised that our sheikh was running a little late.

Ten minutes later a secretary came in to tell us that the sheikh knew we were there and was on his way to meet us. He would be arriving in ten minutes time. The next time the secretary came through, she announced that the sheikh was in the building and would be coming to meet us very shortly.

The build-up was such that I was expecting nothing less than Lawrence of Arabia, or Attila the Hun to come bursting through the doors on his camel. You can imagine my surprise when both doors were finally flung wide open and in walked 'Casper the Sheik'.

Our sheikh was less than four-feet tall and was dressed in a full white dishdasha (robe) and ghutrah (headscarf).

Mr Sheikh scurried over to his desk, climbed up onto the plinth, then up a little step to perch himself in his chair. Sitting there on a cushion in that huge chair just looked silly. As I looked at him I could not rid myself of the image of the Mad Hatter's Tea Party. As I attempted to suppress a bad case of the chuckles I found that I couldn't speak.

Chris sensed my predicament and took the initiative. He walked over to the desk and handed Mr Sheikh the pen in the nice gift-wrapped box we had purchased. Mr Sheikh expressed surprise and delight at receiving such a wonderful gift. He then opened his desk drawer and pulled out a similar nicely wrapped box, also containing a pen, and handed this to Chris. On our behalf Chris expressed his wonderment at receiving such a thoughtful gift.

Chris then told Mr Sheikh how honoured we were that he had agreed to be our agent, and how pleased we would be to pay him ten percent of any invoice we would raise for the sale of drill bits in Qatar. I still hadn't spoken.

With our formal business now concluded Mr Sheikh climbed down off of his chair, came over and reached up to shake my hand. The handshake sealed the deal. He was now officially our agent. Chris could see that I needed to get out of the office pronto, so he explained that we were meeting a client and would need to leave. I managed another handshake and a quick 'goodbye' as we left.

An hour later I still hadn't got a grip of myself. I needed to go back to the hotel before I could meet anyone else. I know it shouldn't have been so funny. It just was.

Chris worked hard and was soon making the occasional drill bit sale. Unfortunately, the business never did build enough momentum. We carried on with our office there for a couple of years but eventually decided that the competition was just too strong. It wasn't that their drill bits were performing better than ours, they simply had more 'stroke' to secure the sale. Partly this had to do with who their agent was, but mostly it had to do with the fact that they were offering a lot of products and services in addition to selling drill bits, and the bit sales were often included as a part of their directional drilling packages.

A few years later, this 'packaging trend' would become a big problem for us in Aberdeen as well.

When it became apparent that we were not building up the business, we eventually decided to close down the Dubai office. Chris wanted another expat contract, so he decided to stay in Dubai and go to work for a competitor rather than move back to Aberdeen.

Our BBL venture into the Middle East market didn't make much of a contribution to our success, but it did let me visit a part of the world which is as bizarre as it is interesting. To me it didn't seem to make sense to build huge cities in the middle of the desert, where the summer temperatures can get to be over 45 °C. However, for many years this region has been the world's fastest growing urban development. Dubai and Abu Dhabi have become cities on steroids which are now home to some of the most amazing property developments in the world, including the world's tallest building, man-made islands, an indoor snow skiing resort and just about everything else imaginable.

Just about everything in the Middle East is the biggest and best.

CHAPTER 44

The Candid Camera

Back in Aberdeen, Terry, a customer who had occasionally used our drill bits decided to give us a 'serious' trial on a well being drilled in the southern part of the North Sea. Terry arranged to take three BBL bits out to his drilling rig and, if necessary, planned to use all three of these to drill the three thousand foot length of the 12¼-inch wellbore section. Unfortunately, he set the drilling parameters for the drill bits above the limits our drill bits were designed to withstand. By pumping drilling mud at a pressure higher than our drill bit could cope with, our first drill bit 'washed-out' after drilling only a short distance. This bit was tripped out of the well and then replaced with the second BBL drill bit. Employing the same practice as before, after drilling only a short footage, once again, the second drill bit suffered the same failure.

This was happening over a weekend, so on Sunday morning I received a call from the rig telling me about the two failures and asking if I wanted them to run the third drill bit. I declined. To have two failures one after another was really bad. If the two failures were our fault, I knew that they could not be invoiced and I wasn't prepared to risk giving away a third drill bit as well. Not knowing about the extreme operating conditions, I feared the drill bits must have been faulty and that we had a serious manufacturing problem. I would need to find the reason for the failures before I could think of running any more BBL drill bits for Terry, or for that matter, for any other customer.

I immediately called Jim, my production manager, and instructed him to examine all recently manufactured drill bits in stock and review his quality controls. I then called Chris and asked him to look at the drill bits on consignment with other customers and consider if these needed to be recalled. Apart from the loss of revenue from Terry's two drill bits, it was a disaster.

We carried out a post-mortem as soon as the two washed-out drill bits were returned. Although we had already recalled a few drill bits from other rigs, I was almost relieved to find out that Terry's bits had been used incorrectly and that the failures were not due to a manufacturing problem. Our drill bits were designed to perform their best under normal, not extreme, pressure applications.

Terry had not intentionally set out to destroy our drill bits. We knew there was a pressure limit above which our drill bits would not cope and our sales engineer should have made him fully aware of these limits. He should have declined the sale had he known Terry was planning to work out-with those parameters.

Even after I knew the reason for these failures, they were still failures and our competitors were quick to let their customers know about our bad result. Just as the business was building momentum we were stopped dead in our tracks. I decided not to invoice Terry for the drill bits and accepted the financial loss as well.

Because the trial went terribly wrong we never did get to show Terry what our drill bits could really do for him. I was doubly disappointed as he and his wife Janice were good friends of ours.

I don't know if it was meant to be, but a year or so later, Neva and I were on a golf outing in Turriff with Terry and Janice. They were playing in the foursome ahead of us. The layout of the Turriff course is such that, after playing the second hole, players need to walk a short distance back down the fairway to reach the third tee box.

When I prepared to hit my drive at the second hole, I had already seen Terry play his second shot and start to walk towards the green. When my ball was airborne, I looked up again and was surprised to see Terry pulling his golf-trolly back towards me! We all shouted 'fore' a second or two before my ball hit him. I heard a 'crack' like the sound of a breaking stick, when the ball struck him on the head just above his right eye. Terry grabbed his head and sank to his knees. We all ran up the fairway expecting the worst. By the time we arrived Terry was getting back up. He had a nasty lump on his head but said he was okay. I think I was more in a state of shock than he was.

Terry managed to carry on playing but said it was quite eerie to play golf with Janice being so nice to him. Definitely not the norm. Janice was quite outspoken about her golf and about Terry's shots, should he be unfortunate enough to play a poor shot when they were partners. On this occasion she complimented him on every shot.

What was not such a good result was the bogey I took on the second hole. My perfectly driven ball had finished off the fairway in the rough.

Another oil company, Philips Petroleum, had an active drilling programme and were achieving record rate-of-penetration drill bit runs. Their drilling manager, Norm, was very focused on setting records and having his company recognised as the 'Best in Class' operator in the North Sea. Norm even went so far as to have a brochure printed to promote their achievements, highlighting the number of record-breaking bit runs they were having. Their new brochure looked great and featured a large photo of one of our drill bits on the front cover and again inside. This was immensely valuable publicity for BBL.

There was only one problem. Although we had tried hard on many occasions to get Norm to try one of our drill bits, the bits he had used for all the record breaking runs were not manufactured by BBL. The drill bits he'd used were made by a competitor.

When I spoke with the lady in Philips' London office who had produced the brochure, I thanked her for featuring our drill bit. She said that our drill bit was the prettiest and blue was her favourite colour, so that was why she'd used our photo. I told her I was pleased that she had and offered to help her circulate her wonderful brochures. She sent me one hundred copies which our sales team happily distributed to all our customers in Aberdeen. We also wanted to help Philips to be recognised as the 'Best in Class'.

I wish I could have recorded the phone call Chris received from the sales engineer who had sold Norm all those record breaking drill bits. He wasn't happy. He simply couldn't work out how we managed to get our drill bit on the brochure when he had sent the lady in London a specially selected photo of his drill bit.

Although I hadn't done it deliberately, I never felt bad about taking advantage of the situation. Norm and I were both coaches for girls' softball teams. His team always won the league and his daughter was a better player than my daughter. I marked the brochure down as a small win for Elise and me.

As we were always trying to get business from Norm and his drilling engineers, I would occasionally meet or have lunch with some of them. They had eight or nine engineers and were one of the first companies working in Aberdeen to employ a female drilling engineer. Penny was a very pretty American girl. She and her husband Bill both worked for Phillips in the Aberdeen office and were both on the rota to work offshore from time to time. I got to know them both.

There weren't many other women working offshore in the UK section at the time, so when Phillips contracted a drilling rig they specified that the accommodation block had to provide suitable facilities for Penny should she be assigned to work on that rig. In order to comply, on one rig they simply got the welder to partitioned off one shower cubicle. Penny said the modification the welder had made was pretty makeshift and didn't appear to be as private as she thought it should be.

I had a good laugh when Penny told me the story of her last two-week tour of duty. While on the rig, all the rig hands were very aware of her presence and always paid her a little more attention than she might have preferred. She was the only female on-board. One pretty girl and forty rough and ready oilmen.

One day as she was walking back to her room after taking a shower, a roughneck stopped her and asked if she had any nude photos of herself. She was mortified!

"No, no, I do not," she replied.

"Would you like to buy some?" he asked.

It was probably just a joke, but for her own peace of mind she got the welder back to fill in a few of the gaps.

Penny was a pioneer in the UK sector of the North Sea. While there were never a lot of female drilling engineers, eventually there were women doing other technical jobs such as mud logging as well as non-technical work. Eventually all rigs and platforms needed to provide for women on-board.

In Aberdeen, BBL was the first company to hire a female drill bit sales engineer. In response to our advert, Karen, a geologist who had worked offshore, applied for a job as trainee sales engineer. She was the best qualified candidate and got the job.

I was concerned how she would handle selling to male drilling engineers. It turned out not to be a problem. Karen got on just fine and kept away from lunching with the drilling engineers unless it was in the company of others. She was good at her job, had a nice friendly personality and the drilling engineers liked dealing with her. She became a successful sales engineer and an excellent member of our team.

While women working on rigs in the UK was unusual, in Norway it had been commonplace right from the beginning. In fact there were a number of women on platforms doing a variety of jobs. On one installation they even ran a disco for their evening entertainment.

One day, someone in head office in Stavanger decided their disco should not function on a Sunday night, apparently for religious reasons. When the staff on the platform replied to say that, for the same reason, they didn't think it was appropriate for them to work on a Sunday, the decision to stop the disco was quickly reversed.

"Please disregard the last instruction," came the reply.

CHAPTER 45

The Oilphase Story

The main reason for drilling a well is to establish if there is a reservoir containing a commercial volume of oil or gas. Even if the find wasn't commercial, if oil or gas was present, getting a good sample for analysis could provide valuable information.

As Keith had predicted in his original business plan, one of the nice aspects of the sampling business was the onshore storage of oil and gas cylinders containing samples. This oil or gas sample became very valuable to the oil company as there wasn't any means of getting another one once the well had been completed. Often oil companies didn't send samples to a lab for analysis straight away, so they were held in storage and every time Oilphase did a sampling job offshore, a few more cylinders would come back to their storage facility. This meant that the company started every month with invoices to customers for cylinder storage and every month the number of invoices increased. I was amazed how long some companies would continue to store samples simply because they couldn't make up their mind to have them analysed or discarded.

From where I was sitting at BBL, the sample storage business looked like a much nicer business to be in than selling drill bits. At BBL I started every month without any revenue until the first drill bit was sold.

A few months after Keith had been persuaded by his patent attorney not to buy the single-phase patent from the oil company, he received a Sheriff Court Order instructing him to stop using his single-phase sampling tools because they were in breach of that very same patent. When Keith received this, he could hear the wise words from his patent attorney still ringing in his ears. He had taken his advice not to buy the patent because, "that's Hollywood, this is Scotland. That doesn't happen here."

Apparently, when Keith's lawyer had forwarded a copy of the patent to Expro as part of the Oilphase defence against the lawsuit action, Expro's patent attorney must have taken a look at it. Their attorney took the opposite view to the Oilphase patent attorney and was convinced that it did cover the technology Oilphase was using. On the strength of this belief, Expro purchased the patent from the oil company and proceeded to raise a Sheriff Court Order instructing Oilphase to stop using their single-phase sampler in breach of the patent they now owned.

Keith was really annoyed that he had listened to his patent attorney rather than follow his own instinct and buy the patent for Oilphase in the first place. He now had a second legal action to defend.

I guess Expro's patent attorney must have read the Hollywood script, not the Scottish script.

When the Court Order had first been served on Oilphase, Expro made this fact known to customers and suggested that they could be party to the court action if they continued to use Oilphase. For a full year Keith had to contend with this issue and often needed to explain to customers what all the fuss was about. One or two clients decided not to use Oilphase until the matter was resolved so it did have some financial impact. Keith ignored the order to stop offering services with his single-phase sampler, however, he was aware that he might need to pass over any profits from the sampling service to Expro should he lose the case, and also, once again Keith needed to convince to his bank manager, Douglas, that the bank should continue providing Oilphase with funding support. The Court Order hadn't stopped Oilphase, but it certainly wasn't helpful.

The Oilphase patent attorney was confident Keith would win the case and eventually this did happen, but only after a lot more aggravation and more legal fees. It took nearly a year before the case was finally settled in favour of Oilphase.

Meanwhile, another challenge Keith had to deal with was in the court of the Inner House where he challenged the award of a 'discovery process' order against Oilphase. The Inner House is a court hearing where a group of judges review a ruling which has been made independently by one judge on his own. In this case, a judge had ruled in favour of Expro's request that Oilphase forward copies of all correspondence about single-phase sampling to Expro. This covered all documents, records of conversations, copies of invoices, and a lot of other information about the design and manufacture of the single-phase sampling tool. This is know as a 'discovery process' order.

Keith and Graham felt this demand was unacceptable. In particular they objected to passing over all customer information and tool design drawings to an aggressive competitor.

Keith engaged Nigel, a Queens Council, to challenge the ruling. After hearing the case, the group of judges overturned the decision made by the single judge and ruled in favour of Oilphase. The 'discovery process' ruling was overturned. This result was quite unique and a major success for Oilphase. It was probably also the turning point in the lawsuit action. From then on things started to move in favour of Oilphase.

After having been in business for four years, the 'breach of implied term of contract' lawsuit was still outstanding and was the only action not yet settled in favour of Oilphase. Then, one day out of the blue, we were informed that Expro had dropped the case and it was all over.

At first we couldn't understand why, after fighting us so hard for so long, they had given up. We were aware that Expro was looking to list on the London Stock Exchange at the time and made the assumption that the company's advisors wanted to clear out anything which could be a distraction to potential investors. Whether or not that was the reason, I don't know. The legal actions would have cost a lot of money so that might also have been a factor.

Regardless of the reason, Expro withdrew the lawsuit and we were delighted the affair had finally come to an end.

In our view the 'breach of implied term of contract' had never been a valid case. However, this lawsuit had served a purpose. It was probably intended to make life difficult for us and Oilphase. In the end it did exactly that. Not a very nice thing for someone to do, but business is business so I guess Expro's management just saw it as an astute competitive move.

Interestingly, throughout the time of the action, Schlumberger continued to use Oilphase as their sub-contractor. Keith always kept them fully informed so they probably saw the various actions for what they were.

We briefly contemplated filing a countersuit, but Keith didn't want to have anything more to do with any legal actions. He just wanted to go back to doing what he enjoyed doing most, running the business.

In the end, Expro paid Oilphase's claim for legal costs and that was the end of the matter.

There is a saying, 'if it doesn't kill you, it will make you stronger'. For four years, Keith was the one who took all the pressure and did all the work. I know it left a bitter taste, as it did with me, but I'm sure it did make him stronger.

Keith returned to his day job and went on to build a successful company. Oilphase continued to establish itself as the market leader in the single-phase sampling business.

However, over the five year period that Oilphase had been in business the market had been changing. Rather than contracting Oilphase directly, oil companies now preferred to award one contract to their main service provider and have that company subcontract auxiliary services such as sampling. Schlumberger was the main company using Oilphase as a subcontractor on jobs in the North Sea and around the world. In fact, by 1995 Oilphase was so closely linked to Schlumberger that seventy-five percent of its work was coming on the back of Schlumberger contracts.

Schlumberger liked working with Oilphase and really liked the technology they had. So much so, that they finally said to Keith that they needed to have the single-phase sampling technology in-house so they could incorporate it into some of their other downhole tools.

In 1996, the CEO of Schlumberger approached Keith with a proposal to buy Oilphase. During their conversation he also confirmed Schlumberger's intention to develop competitive technology should Oilphase not be for sale. The message was pretty clear, sell or face the possibility of losing subcontract work with Schlumberger sometime in the future.

Soon afterwards, with the assistance of a professional advisor, Keith, Graham and I entered into negotiations. From the outset, the intention was to get as good a price as possible and negotiate as good a compensation package for Keith and Graham as we possibly could. A deal was done, and in September 1996 Schlumberger purchased Oilphase.

Once the sale was agreed, Keith and Graham stayed on to run the sampling business for Schlumberger and I retired as chairman.

In the end, none of us felt that we had sold Oilphase as well as we might have done, but then again, we weren't unhappy with the deal we made at the time. With the benefit of hindsight, I think we could have done a lot better had we used a broker who specialised in selling oil service companies and had we considered other potential buyers. We never did know how anyone else might have valued the business.

It was unusual for Schlumberger to have bought a business as small as Oilphase, but they were very pleased they had. Once it acquired Oilphase, Schlumberger went on to make an outstanding success of both the company and the technology.

Today, some Schlumberger managers still recognise Oilphase as one of the best acquisitions the company ever made. In fact one Schlumberger manager told me that he thought they would have paid what they'd paid just for the company name. I knew we had undersold the business; I hadn't quite appreciated that we'd actually given the company away and just sold the name 'Oilphase'! Even though it might have been a bit of exaggeration, I thanked him for sharing this with me. I can't say that it made me feel very proud of my negotiating skills.

Ten years on, the sampling component has grown to become a meaningful part of Schlumberger's business and, based on the profit contribution, a measurable portion of their market capitalisation. The same core business we started all those years ago is now fully integrated and much bigger. I am very pleased that Schlumberger has made it such a success and am proud that the technology and the name Oilphase continues to be recognised throughout the industry. Within Schlumberger, Oilphase is now a worldwide brand.

Keith, Graham and a lot of very hard working, clever people built Oilphase. I was delighted to play a small part and to know that I made the single most valuable contribution, even if it was only coming up with the name.

CHAPTER 46

The Best Seats

As we continued to internationalise BBL, there were two other occasions where we didn't have much luck with our company cars. When we decided to open an office in Point Noir, West Africa, we employed a new salesman for the posting and sent off a container with his personal belongings, office furniture, and a left-hand-drive jeep. Six weeks later David, who intended living there with his wife, was in Point Noir when the container arrived.

Unfortunately, the arrival of the ship coincided with the very day a war broke out. The container was offloaded one day and loaded back onto the ship the next. After all the work we had put into trying to select the best and safest location to start our West African business our plans went up in smoke. The new office was cancelled and David flew back home.

When we got the shipment back six weeks later, I found there were not a lot of people interested in buying a rusty left-hand-drive jeep which had been floating around the Atlantic for three months. We eventually sold it for very little money at a car auction.

Around the time we gave up on Point Noir, we were also focused on an opportunity in Venezuela. Lake Maracaibo had been a busy oil patch for decades and was once again a hub of activity. Three Venezuelan national companies and a few international oil companies had all started new drilling campaigns there.

When we opened our Maracaibo office, we imported two cars from America; one for Victor, our Venezuelan manager, plus a second car for the salesmen to use. Both cars were brand-new and Victor's car had nice leather upholstery.

One day Victor came out of his house and found that the car was still there, but the car seats were not. All the seats had been stolen.

Victor got an orange crate out of his garage and sat on this to drive to the police station to report the theft. He 'negotiated' with the police to establish how much he would need to pay to get a replacement set of seats. A fee was agreed and two days later he got a phone call to say that they had found the thief and recovered his stolen seats. Victor drove back to the station … still on his orange crate … to collect his seats. The seats he was given were not leather and they were the wrong colour, however, they did fit his model car, so Victor was pleased to accept them and went home happy.

Victor explained that this type of theft was not uncommon. Apparently, someone with the same model car had wanted an upgrade to leather and had made arrangements to have Victor's seats stolen. I wasn't sure Victor should be negotiating with the police to get new seats, but apparently that was how it was done. According to him, someone else would be arriving at the station on an orange crate that very day to negotiate a fee for their replacement seats.

When Chris, (one of our new Aberdeen sales engineers, not Chris the sales manager) went to work in Maracaibo for a few weeks he had a much more terrifying car experience. Chris and Victor met for lunch at a popular restaurant on the edge of town. As was the case with many restaurants, this one had an armed guard at the front door. The guard was there mainly to keep an eye on the cars in the car park, but his presence would also deter any thieves from coming in to rob the diners.

On this occasion two banditos had come. One managed to surprise the guard and held a gun to his head while the other went inside to do the robbing.

Once inside, the thief ordered everyone to get down on the floor. Like everyone else, Chris and Victor did as they were told. The thief then went around the tables taking money from people. When he came to Chris's table he yelled at him to hand over his car keys. Chris didn't understand Spanish so he opened out his pockets to show that he didn't have any more money. The thief wasn't happy and made a fuss to see if Chris was concealing anything, which he wasn't.

After only a few minutes the bandit made his escape. Victor said to Chris "You were very brave not to give him your car keys!" Chris admitted that he had no idea what the guy was saying. He would happily have given the man his keys. They were lying where he had left them, on the table under his napkin. The thief simply hadn't seen them there. Chris suddenly realised that he was probably very lucky not to have been shot.

Our local sales trainee Andre was not so lucky. Late one evening he was riding home on his motorbike when he stopped at a red light. A man with a gun jumped out from the side of the road and ordered him to hand over his bike. He refused and tried to speed away. The thief fired his gun and the shot hit him in the back. While the bandit made off on the motorbike, Andre was left lying where he had fallen.

A short while later a doctor happened to come along the road and saw Andre lying by there. Fortunately for Andre, he stopped his car, saw that he had been shot and immediately took him to the nearest hospital. The doctor saved his life.

Sadly, Andre had known how ruthless thieves could be in Venezuela and yet had foolishly tried to escape. It was a bad mistake to have made.

Andre survived but lost the use of both his legs.

Over the years, just about everyone I spoke with who had been in Venezuela had a story about a theft or a kidnapping. One common story involved wives being taken hostage. Usually two or more thieves would find their way into a house. The thieves would first help themselves to any money and valuables and then take the wife away and demand a ransom. If everything went to plan they would drive the wife out of town and leave her with enough money for a bus fare back home. If things didn't go to plan and they didn't get their ransom, or the police got involved, things could turn ugly. As long as everyone stayed calm, no one got hurt. If something went wrong, however, the thieves weren't afraid to use their guns.

It was hard to comprehend that this could happen in a civilised country, but most people knew Venezuela wasn't entirely civilised, at times it was a bit like the Wild West.

Apart from these hiccups, the office we set up in Maracaibo was reasonably successful. The drill bits were performing well and some international oil companies as well as one national oil company were using them on a regular basis.

Unfortunately this success didn't last.

I had a pretty good indication that our local agent wasn't entirely trustworthy when I was in Venezuela on a sales trip. Victor, Jim (the production manager from Aberdeen) and I went to visit a client whose office was on the other side of Lake Maracaibo, some fifty miles away. We arrived at the office and, before going inside, Jim stopped to have a cigarette.

As we stood outside a car passed by with our company logo in bold lettering on the side. "Funny," I said to Victor. "I didn't know we had more company cars. I thought there were only the two in Maracaibo." Victor didn't know about the car either. Even he was surprised. The next day we investigated and found out that our agent was using our import licence to bring in other vehicles. As long as they were seen to carry our company logo, the tax inspectors considered them to be part of our fleet. That car and possibly others had simply been sold into the local market with the BBL livery still attached.

The more I saw of Venezuela the less I understood how the country managed to function. The women all looked like models for blue jeans while the men looked like extras for a cowboy movie, and they all appeared to rely on some kind of shady deal to make their living.

I never could figure out how the Venezuelan economy actually worked.

CHAPTER 47

The High Court

After all the legal actions I had been involved with at Oilphase I didn't want anything to do with a court action ever again. Unfortunately it didn't work out that way.

In 1996 BBL was on a roll. The drill bit business was going well and we were looking for other countries where we could sell drill bits as well as looking for ways to expand the business by adding other products which employed elements of the drill bit technology.

Although everyone on the team contributed to the success we were having, no one had more impact than Mike and Jim who were both top performers. I felt I needed to make sure they were both committed to staying with BBL longterm, so I decided to give them both an equity holding in the business and provide them with scope for further advancement.

I set up a new division, 'BBL Downhole Tools'. Jim moved from being our Production Manager to Managing Director of the new division, Mike became his design engineer and Mitch was brought in to lead the sales effort. They were a strong team and the three of them worked really well together.

A new manufacturing facility was set up in Arbroath, south of Aberdeen, to manufacture the first new product for their division, called a Reamer Shoe.

When drillers couldn't lower the casing into the well as far as it needed to go because of well-bore restrictions or ledges, it was an expensive problem. When this happened, all the lengths of casing had to be removed from the well one at a time so that the restriction or problem ledge could be attended to by re-drilling.

A Reamer Shoe is designed to be attached to the bottom of the first joint of casing. It has an off-centre nose profile and cutting structure all around the side and shoulder areas. By rotating the casing, a driller could use this tool to open up a wellbore restriction or get the end of the casing to slide off a ledge. This would enable the casing to move down past the obstruction.

The Reamer Shoe was seen as an inexpensive insurance policy. Even if well-bore problems weren't expected, it was always nice to know that it was there if needed. It became very popular and, when it was used, some oil companies credited it with saving them a day or more off the time it took them to construct their well.

As Jim started selling Reamer Shoes he realised there were particular oil-fields in different parts of the world where casing running problems were common. These oil-fields were his prime market target.

With his small team it was impossible to cover every country so when Jim happened to meet the manager of another Aberdeen company who was selling their products in Colombia, South America, he approached him about becoming the Colombia distributor for the Reamer Shoe. It looked like a good deal for both companies. Their company salesmen were already travelling to Colombia on a regular basis so, selling our Reamer Shoes along with their own products would help offset some of their sales costs. Shortly after his initial discussion a distribution agreement for Colombia was agreed.

From the very first trip the arrangement worked well. We received a number of orders and the distributor received some nice commissions. Unfortunately, once the manager saw the revenue we were getting from our product he decided he wanted more.

After selling Reamer Shoes for nine months his company copied our design and started manufacturing a similar product. They simply ignored the patent application we had in place and the non-compete clause they had agreed to.

When our agent copied our technology, I experienced the outcome people fear the most when they allow someone else to market their prized technology. We had simply been too hasty. We should have built a trusting relationship with the companies management before ever giving them access to our new product.

Jim was not able to convince them to stop what they were doing so we had to take legal action.

After Mike designed the Reamer Shoe, he had contacted a patent attorney to draft a patent and arrange for it to be filed. Having a 'patent applied for' appeared to make the case against our former distributor pretty straightforward. However, nothing is straightforward.

On the day of the hearing at the High Court in Edinburgh, I arrived at 10.00am in time for a quick review with our Queen's Council (QC). The case was due to be called at 11.00am. My learned QC, who was costing me one thousand pounds per hour, was wearing his fanciest wig and finest robe. He was ready to go and I was sure we would win.

As soon as I arrived he took me aside and said, "Roy, we have a problem. I spoke with your patent attorney last night for one final briefing and went through each of the questions I will be putting to him in front of the judge. Your patent attorney didn't give me the right answers."

"What are you saying?" I asked.

"Well, your man wasn't so sure that the patent application he drafted for you is as strong as it needs to be, so, if I ask a specific question about one crucial aspect of your design he will not give me a definitive answer."

"Oh dear," I think I said. "Everything relies on him defending the patent he drafted for us."

"Yes, that is correct. If the judge decides that the wording of your patent does not make it illegal for these guys to copy your product you will lose the case," said my QC.

"Where is my patent man, I would like a word with him," I said.

"Well, he called this morning to say he wasn't coming to Edinburgh to defend your case," said my QC.

I said, "Holy crap."

My QC agreed with my sentiment. "However, I have some good news, the defendants QC has come to me with an offer to settle out-of-court. Apparently, he pointed out to his clients that it will cost them five hundred thousand pounds or more for costs and damages if they lose the case, so they have offered a settlement. They have offered you a sizeable payment and an undertaking to modify their tool so it can't possibly infringe your weak patent," said my QC.

I didn't have my patent attorney to take the stand and, had he been there, he would not have adequately defended the patent he'd written.

Had our opponents known that he hadn't come they would never have offered an out-of-court settlement. I would have had to concede defeat, walk away from the court action and pay all of their costs as well as any court costs. However, they didn't know that my patent attorney wasn't there. I had no choice.

My QC went back and negotiated a settlement.

I was very angry with my patent attorney. He had hung us out to dry. He had taken our money to draft a patent and had done such a poor job he couldn't even defend his own work.

As for a patent itself, other than acting as a deterrent, I discovered that patents only have true value once they have been successfully defended in a court of law.

When it was all over, I realised how exposed we had been. Without much patent expertise ourselves, there was no way of knowing how to choose a good, competent patent attorney. Once a choice had been made, we had to depend on him totally and when he failed to draft a strong patent we suffered the consequences.

My attorney made himself even less popular when he sent an invoice for the preparation work he had done for our court action. I thought about not paying this bill but then considered the time and money I would need to spend fighting a battle against the legal firm for whom he worked. It would be a fight I wasn't going to win. I sent his payment.

I often wondered how many of other clients of his had found their patents weren't as strong as they needed to be. Most people would probably never find out. I had just been unlucky … I had found out twice. The same attorney who gave Keith the recommendation not to buy the single-phase patent, had drafted the Reamer Shoe patent.

However, having had two bad patent experiences didn't stop us from moving forward. We put it behind us and moved on.

CHAPTER 48

The Feeling of Success

In 1996 we opened three more international offices to sell drill bits. Two in North America and one in Australia.

The Canadian office in Calgary was a little different from the others we had opened. (I'm not even going to count the office we opened in St. John's Newfoundland. We hired a local salesman, brought him to Aberdeen for training and, as soon as he returned to St. John's, he typed out his resignation letter on his new computer. He had already received and accepted a better employment offer while he was still with us in Scotland!) In Calgary, we appointed an agent who had a company offering various oil-field products. This agent, Kathleen, had agreements with other suppliers so I was able to confirm that she was trustworthy and a good person to do business with.

Most of the oil companies Kathleen was selling to were drilling shallow gas wells. These wells only took ten days or less from start to finish. The drill bits they used to drill the main section of the well didn't wear out on one run so they could be used a number of times on different wells. Once they were worn they were sent back to Aberdeen to have the worn or broken cutters replaced. After this refurbishment we would return the drill bit to Calgary for another two or three runs. Effectively Kathleen's business was a drill bit rental business. It was a good business for her as she rented the drill bits out, one well at a time. For us it was not so good as we weren't selling many drill bits.

After a while it became obvious that the cost and turnaround time for getting drill bits refurbished was becoming an issue for her, so we agreed to set up a facility in Calgary. Having the ability to refurbish her own drill bits did take away some revenue, but it also took away a lot of hassle. The refurbishing arrangement worked well and, as Kathleen would have needed to make a huge investment, there wasn't any threat that she could start manufacturing drill bits of her own.

Kathleen was an excellent agent and continued representing BBL for some time. Our drill bits worked well and she was getting plenty of rentals. The only thing missing was a decent revenue stream for us.

The other office in North America was in Anchorage, Alaska.

Having had a couple of very good bit runs in Alaska back in 1994, John felt we had a chance to sell more drill bits there. Alaska appeared to be a good market for BBL. BP was one of the two big operators in the area and they were drilling wells in the Prudhoe Bay area on the north coast of Alaska. Dave, a former drilling manager for BP in Aberdeen, had transferred to Anchorage from Aberdeen along with some of his drilling engineers. Both Dave and the engineers had used our bits in the North Sea.

After making a few sales from Aberdeen, John decided we should open an office in Alaska. He was a friend of Dave's and Dave had said, "Provided your drill bits continue to perform as well here as they do in the North Sea, I will see that BBL is given a fair chance to sell to our Alaska drilling engineers." With four drill bit runs already under his belt John decided that he, his wife Vicky and their two girls should leave Aberdeen and move to Anchorage.

Soon after his arrival, John sold some more drill bit and these all worked well. It was a great start and the long term prospect for our business looked good.

However, as I've said before things can change very quickly.

One day, after John had been in Anchorage for nine months he called to say that he had been approached by a competitor with a job offer at twice the salary we were paying him. He didn't want to leave BBL but said that he had to accept the attractive salary he was being offered. I couldn't even come close to paying this new salary, so with much regret I wished him all the best.

When John left, I decided to close down the office. I regarded John as one of the best in the business and felt there wasn't any point sending another salesman over to compete with him. During the time he had been in Anchorage he had built up a good business and a strong working relationship with both drilling engineers and management. Without him, there was no way to take advantage of the great start he had made.

Thus ended yet another attempt at internationalisation.

One overseas venture which was worthwhile was the joint venture we set up in Australia. When we decided we should try to sell drill bits in that part of the world, before John moved to Alaska he travelled to Perth and interview potential partners. John met my good friend Russell from my BJ days and decided he was our man. Russell lived in Perth and knew a lot of potential clients in Western Australia, South Australia, Queensland and Victoria. Russell was looking for the opportunity to start a business of his own and a joint venture with BBL seemed to fit the bill perfectly.

Once Russell and I signed our joint-venture agreement, it didn't take long for him to set up his office and pull together a small team of drill bit sales engineers.

Russell's very first drill bit sale was to BHP, a large Australian mining and oil company, on a well they were drilling in the Timor Sea off the north coast of Australia. BHP was potentially a big customer so the first bit run was important. The company rep said to Russell, "If these oval-shaped cutters and cross-flow jet-nozzles don't perform as you said they will, then you won't get another run with any other operator in Australia … because I'll make sure of that!" Russell was under a lot of pressure. He needed a good result.

The first drill bit run set a new Timor Sea record. It drilled the abrasive Plover formation in one run, the first drill bit ever to do so. It was a great result. The drill bit was still in good condition after the run so it was sent back to Aberdeen to be refurbished and then returned to

Australia. It was then re-run on the next well and once again achieved a similar result. These two drill bit runs were a step-change in the performance of PDC drill bits in the Timor Sea.

After that success, Russell quickly built up a business. He was soon selling drill bits on a regular basis to a lot of oil companies in Australia and, in addition to selling drill bits, Russell was also selling a lot of Reamer Shoes.

Once things got going in Australia, Russell opened offices in Bangkok, Thailand, Jakarta, Indonesia and Kuala Lumpur, Malaysia. Within a year BBL had a good business in these countries as well.

It was entirely down to Russell that we finally had a successful overseas operation.

Back in Aberdeen, the acknowledgment of success continued when an engineering paper was published for the Society of Petroleum Engineers. The author, Rod Begbie, who was a drilling engineer with Amerada Hess, had run many BBL drill bits and most of these had achieved excellent results. He decided it was worth writing a technical paper on the technology behind our drill bits and asked John to work together with him on this. When it was published in 1997 it presented a superb endorsement for our technology.

A copy of an even better endorsement was sent to me by another Amerada Hess drilling engineer. Steve had prepared a memo for circulation to all drilling engineers in the company. An extract from his memo shows just how well BBL's drill bits were doing at the time and how far we had come as a company.

The memo read:

"I have the following comments on BBL bits.

At Hess we have run a large number of BBL bits – 179 in total. I have also run numerous BBL bits when I worked at Shell and Sedco Forex. We have developed a high level of confidence in BBL bits. The quality of the products and the customer service are both of a very high standard. BBL is an innovative company and their bits have a number of unique features which are a benefit to the client.

In general: BBL has a number of advantages common to all their bits. 1. The bit bodies are built from investment castings which allow rework and repair (unlike Matrix bits). Stellite is harder wearing than steel-bodied bits. We often repair BBL bits several times before scrapping them. The bits can be repaired to 'as new' condition for a fraction of the cost of a new bit. One disadvantage of Stellite is that it is more prone to erosion than Matrix. We overcome this by choosing the hard-facing option when we anticipate long and very high HSI (flow rates). 2. The lateral nozzles give a unique cleaning action. The bottom of the hole is cleaned very quickly and efficiently, so ROP (rate of penetration) is generally better. The lateral nozzles create a Venturi effect across the blades, which keeps the cutters clean and prevents bit balling, even in sticky clays. 3. Oval cutters give the same cutter density as small round cutters, but with longer life."

Steve then went on to speak about individual bit models and how well they had performed, naming one model as a 'stunning bit, the best bit in its class'. Steve also mentioned our Reamer Shoe and how well this product worked on a number of wells where it saved them not just a few hours, but 'many days of rig time'.

I really liked his final summary. It read:

"I would have no hesitation in recommending the use of BBL products. BBL is a small, innovative company, which keeps customer satisfaction as its main priority. It does not have the powerful marketing organisations of some of the big companies, but it offers real solutions and applies genuine engineering rather than the 'gimmicks' which are sometimes offered by others. If you require any further information, including bit run details, please do not hesitate to contact me."

When I received a copy of Steve's memo I was very proud of what my team had achieved. We had certainly come a long way from a most precarious beginning.

Around the time all this was going on, I was approached by two companies about the possibility of acquiring BBL. I hadn't thought about selling the company as I felt there was still a bright future ahead. As well as the drill bit success, the Downhole Tool Division was growing on the back of its Reamer Shoe. However, I agreed to travel to America to meet with the owners of two companies to see what was on offer. I asked Morton to come with me.

First we went to Houston where we met Bob, who had a drill bit business quite similar to BBL's, focused on the US market. His company was in fact owned by a venture capital group. He had sold the company to them a couple of years earlier and now managed the business on their behalf. I hadn't appreciated that was the case before agreeing to our meeting and decided pretty quickly that I didn't want to end up in a similar position. I didn't want to manage my business and have some financial people in Houston asking how much money we were making every month. I had 'been there, done that' when I was working for BJ.

After spending the afternoon with Bob and meeting some of his people, Bob arranged for Morton and I to have dinner with him and his backers. The financial people had prepared an offer and intended to hand this to me after our meal.

Everything went to plan. We enjoyed a very nice meal and then they gave me the envelope. I had no idea what BBL might actually be worth or what someone might consider paying for the company. After all the tough years I'd had, I was just pleased to realise that it actually had a value. I opened the envelope and saw that they were offering a price which valued the business at six times EBITDA, (earnings before interest, tax, depreciation and amortisation). Not bad I thought, but I wasn't blown away. It was a similar valuation to the ones I'd received when I sold Exal and Oilphase.

The timing of handing me the offer coincided with some breaking news in America. At that very moment on the restaurant TV, Bill Clinton was retracting a previous statement he'd made about his relationship with Monica Lewinsky. I had expected my hosts to be on the edge of their seats awaiting my response to their offer, however, they were far more interested in the detail of the Monica story than they were to my reaction. I suddenly thought, "this really isn't a big deal for them, it's just another offer for another company."

Anyway, I had said to Morton that I wouldn't make any decision on the night and left the dinner without giving them any indication of interest. I still had another offer to consider the following day which they weren't aware of.

The next day, Morton and I travelled north from Houston to Forth Worth to meet with Marvin. His company was Gerhart RBI. Marvin was seventy years old when we met and as full of energy and enthusiasm as any thirty-year-old. He was enthusiastic about everything he was doing. Apart from running his drill bit manufacturing business he was building an airplane in his factory. Marvin had an idea for a revolutionary propulsion system which he intended to demonstrate on his new plane. He certainly wasn't afraid of new technology. He was an inventor and, during his time in the oil service industry, he had developed many new tools and held numerous patents.

Marvin liked BBL, and liked the innovation we had. He hadn't given a lot of thought to acquiring the company and simply asked me how much I would like to sell the company for. I wasn't really looking to sell and didn't have any idea what price I might accept, so we just sat and talked about what he was doing in his company and what I was doing in mine. It was a very special meeting. Marvin is a legend in the oil industry and it was fascinating just to spend an hour with him.

Towards the end of our meeting, Marvin stood up, closed his office door, then came back as said, "Roy I want to show you something."

He had my attention. He reached behind his desk and pulled out a piano accordion. He then sat down beside me and played a couple of tunes.

"I'm just learning how to play, and I wanted you to hear how I'm getting on," he said. I was very impressed. What a lovely man with such enthusiasm for life. I thought, I'm fifty years old. If I can have the same drive as him when I'm seventy I'll be doing pretty good!

No progress was made regarding a sale but, neither Marvin nor I were bothered, we had become friends.

As Morton and I were leaving the building, Marvin's secretary bid us farewell. "I hope he didn't embarrass you and take out that old squeeze-box of his," she said.

I said he had and that I had enjoyed it immensely.

Although the trip to Houston and Fort Worth didn't make me any richer, having had two people approach me to buy my business certainly made me feel great. The first seven years in BBL had not been easy. I knew we were making progress, and that the team had built a strong company against some formidable challenges, but that was the first time it actually dawned on me that the company must be worth something.

When I returned to Aberdeen my managers were all keen to find out whether or not I was planning to sell the business. I hadn't told anyone the reason Morton and I were going to America but somehow everyone knew and they were hoping it wasn't going to happen.

Ironically, while I was away there was an article in the local newspaper about the sale of a Belgium bank called BBL which was bought by IMG for $5.5 billion. One of my managers doctored this article to make it read as if I'd sold my company for that amount. He attached a little note to say that he thought I'd got a fair price and couldn't blame me for having sold out.

I felt good and the future looked bright.

CHAPTER 49

The Oil Price

Unfortunately, just as we were getting used to some good times in the industry, everything changed. In the summer of 1997 the oil price started to fall. It stood at twenty-five dollars per barrel and was forecast to go much lower. As the oil price continued falling, oil companies started to cut back their drilling programmes and by the beginning of 1998 this was impacting on all the oil service and supply companies, including BBL.

After John moved to Anchorage, I promoted Paul to be the international sales manager and Mark moved up to be the UK sales manager.

When Paul was preparing his sales budget for 1998, he and his sales team called on customers to ask about their drilling plans for the coming year. They came back with some grim news. The expected drilling activity for 1998 was going to be fifty percent down on 1997.

Working on the assumption that, in the coming year, our competitors would be selling very aggressively to maintain their market share, we would need to reduce our prices by ten or twenty percent and, even then, we were likely to sell only half as many drill bits as before. Meanwhile our production costs were forecast to rise. I set about preparing our budget on that basis. Not surprisingly the outcome was not good. When Morton printed out the final draft it showed that we would make a sizeable trading loss for the year.

I didn't like what I saw. There was no guarantee that the oil price would recover in one or two years' time and there was no way we could survive a prolonged slowdown. The company simply wasn't in a financial position where we could lose money and stay in business. It didn't make sense for us to manufacture drill bits which we couldn't sell for a profit and scaling down wasn't an option. BBL simply wasn't big enough to down-size and still retain the core expertise needed to remain viable. With less than half the revenue we were destined to fail. I told Paul I would sell the company or, if necessary, sell the technology and close the company down, rather then watch us slowly bleed to death.

Paul went away to think about what could be done. The next day, he came back to say he had the answer. "Wow, I wonder what this might be," I thought.

Paul said, "All we need to do is raise our prices by five percent and we can just about survive on the lower level of sales. He showed me the numbers and sure enough, with a five percent price increase and a few cost savings we could break even.

"Great," I said. "How are we going to get our customers to agree to a price increase when our competitors are going to be offering discounts?" I knew how American companies tended to work, their top priority was to retain market share, and discounting prices was usually their first move.

"That's the clever bit," Paul said. "The oil companies who use our product do so because our drill bit is the best for their application and saves them money. With rigs costing two hundred thousand dollars per day, a few hours of rig time saved quickly takes care of any difference in the price of a drill bit. We have never offered anyone a discount or tried to beat our competitors on price. In fact, the only time we haven't charged full price was when we've had a failure of some sort. I think we should go to all our clients and ask if they will still buy bits from us if they are five percent more expensive and see what they say."

It was worth a try. Paul, Mark and I agreed that we would each visit a selection of managers to get their reaction to a price increase.

Much to my surprise, each manager I spoke with understood our need to increase prices and said they would continue to use our drill bits.

One good customer, Tom, said, "We have just had to give our staff a cost-of-living salary increase, so I fully understand that your costs will also have gone up." When I pressed him for assurance that they would continue to use us, he replied, "We use your drill bits because they work well for us and we will continue to do so as long as that is the case."

"If our competitors come to you with big discounts, will you still support us?" I asked. He said that the discounts wouldn't impact on them making the best engineering decision. His comments were very encouraging.

We received similar, but less bullish, assurances from most other clients. Paul, Mark and I made sure our clients appreciated that we were not going to discount any sales and understood that we would be forced out of business if we didn't get their support.

In 1998 that was pretty much how it worked out. Trading was difficult all year. We sold around half the number of drill bits compared with the previous year but sold every one of them at full price. Our customers had been true to their word and we had been given a share of the business from all of them. By the end of the year we had made a very small profit, and interestingly, that year we achieved the best product margin we had ever made.

On one occasion, I found out that one of Tom's drilling engineers had been offered a drill bit free-of-charge by a competitor. The company had modified the design of a drill bit and offered it to them for a free trial. The engineer declined the offer. "No thanks," he said. "I'm intending to use a BBL bit to drill that section". Our competitor couldn't believe he had just failed to give away a free drill bit. He had to go back to his office and tell his boss that he'd lost a free bit sale to one of ours at full price.

A few months later, I asked Tom if he'd known this had happened. He said he wasn't aware of the specific incident but his engineers all knew that our competitors saw 1998 as their best opportunity to force BBL out of business. Tom wasn't surprised when a free drill bit was offered. He said, "Our engineers decided that it was in our best interest to keep BBL in the game. Your drill bits were working well for us and we didn't want to lose them." I was very impressed that he had taken such a pragmatic view.

1998 was still a difficult year. On a previous occasion when the oil price had fallen I wasn't involved with my own business. When you have eighty employees and their families depending on you to find a way to keep going, it's a different matter all together. I found it very stressful.

One stressful task was having to make four people redundant. I did this right at the start of the year to give us the best chance of survival. Three of the redundancies were from the manufacturing team. With the decrease in production we wouldn't be needing them and couldn't afford to keep them on the payroll.

When I decided to make our quality assurance manager redundant as well, it wasn't a very pleasant task. It was important to have a quality assurance person on the team and David had done a good job for us, however, I simply had to reduce our fixed costs as much as possible in order to give ourselves the best chance of survival. Dave was an unfortunate casualty of this decision. He had been a good employee and was very disappointed to be asked to leave. However, I had decided that, for the time being, we would manage our quality system without a quality manager.

The other action we took was to hold back on any salary increases. I met with the managers and they all agreed to forego a salary increase. The managers also agreed that all the people in the factory on an hourly wage should get a cost of living increase. I was amazed how well this was received. We were one of the very few companies in the service sector to give anyone a pay increase. The guys in the factory knew this and were very impressed. In spite of the difficult time we were having the team morale had never been better.

Over the course of the year everyone did their best to make sure we survived. Everyone worked hard to keep costs down and keep standards up.

Essentially, I employed the same tactic with our employees and customers as I did with our bank and De Beers. It was another example of how important it is to make sure that everyone knows the situation to enable them to help solve the problem. I never actually sat down and thought 'this is a clever thing to do', it just seemed to make sense.

It was during this same year that my relationship with the Venezuelan agent, who had been using our import license to import cars, started to become difficult.

We were still selling drill bits every month and as they were sold, new stock was ordered from Aberdeen. It was a good business apart from the fact that we weren't getting paid. Our agent blamed the oil companies for not paying him. That might have been part of the problem, but I couldn't believe he was being totally honest. When his debt ran up to five hundred thousand dollars I decided we couldn't go any further. I made another trip to Maracaibo to meet with him but unfortunately nothing was resolved.

After the meeting I called on one of the international oil companies we had recently sold some drill bits to and asked for a meeting. I asked their financial controller if he would remit their payment directly to our UK account instead of paying our agent. He was sympathetic and said that he had heard from other suppliers with the same problem. I managed to redirect a big payment and also managed to get a number of our drill bits sent from our agent's warehouse to this oil company. As well as agreeing to remit funds, the financial controller had agreed to have these drill bits returned to the UK for me. In the end I managed to recover a few drill bits and just under two hundred thousand dollars, but had to walk away from the rest.

We were already having a very difficult year, so the write-off couldn't have come at a worse time. I don't think the agent ever had any intention of paying us. We certainly never got any more payments and weren't able to recover any more of our stock.

That year the Venezuelan government also decided to merge the three national oil companies into one single company. It was decided that only the supply contracts with the main company would prevail going forward. We held a supply contract with one of the two companies which ceased to exist so any chance of reviving our domestic business disappeared overnight. The international companies also decided that Venezuela wasn't a sensible country for their investment so they were planning to leave as well.

One more internationalisation venture bites the dust. Our success rate for opening international offices was now one out of eight. (Nine, if you count St. John's …)

1998 had called for a clever and brave solution. Paul had come up with the plan and the team had delivered. The fact that we managed to sell drill bits at a higher price and make a small profit was a magnificent result. Venezuela aside, what we achieved in 1998 made it the most satisfying year ever in my management career.

All our staff and all our customers had made it possible for BBL to get through the most difficult trading year. I was proud of my team and proud of our achievement, and, I was glad when it was finally over. We had survived.

By the end of 1998 the oil price was starting to rise once again and had returned to just under fifty dollars per barrel. It was back to business as usual.

Unfortunately, business as usual had changed. The difficult year had forced oil companies to look at how they were working and find ways to make cost savings. The way some oil companies now wanted to work was to deal with as few suppliers as possible. They worked out that they could be more efficient if they dealt with only a handful of service companies and made those companies responsible for any subcontractors. Unfortunately for us, the selection of drill bits fell into this 'subcontract' category.

Oil companies now wanted to contract a directional drilling company to 'construct' a given section of the well. Their quote would include the directional drilling service and one, two, or however many drill bits they thought they would need to drill the well down to the depth and coordinates specified in their contract. The oil company paid them a fixed price for reaching a very small target a mile or more underground and it was up to the directional drillers to select the best drill bits for the job.

This new way of doing business was a real game-changer.

All our big competitors offered directional drilling services. In the beginning, a few oil company engineers still tried to recommend the drill bits they thought should be used, but they were soon told that their interference would impact on the contract. For BBL this meant that we now had to sell our drill bits to our competitors. Once our sales engineer started giving the competitor information about our product and its performance history, it wouldn't be long before they copied the features they liked and modified one of their own products to compete with ours.

As an independent drill bit manufacturer I could see the new business model was not going to work. Our future was not looking good and I started to think I needed to get out of the drill bit business before I was forced out.

CHAPTER 50

The Spa Treatment

Stress can often creep up without you being aware. My back injury always seemed to flare up whenever I was having a difficult time dealing with business problems. 1998 was one of those occasions.

During one particularly stressful period, my back was giving me so much pain I could only manage to sit in my office for four to five hours per day. Around lunchtime I would need to go home, take some pain killers and rest. A friend lent me a 'back-swing' which is a contraption I could use to hang upside down and ease the pressure on my spine. I could only manage a few minutes at a time before I would start to faint ... that old blood-rush thing again.

One day I never got as far as driving home from the office. I had a back seizure in my office chair. I held onto the armrests and tried not to move as both sides of my back went into spasm. Eventually, in spite of the spasms, I managed to get out of the chair and lie on the floor. Arlene, the office manager, came through to help. She called Neva, who then called Stuart, our friendly GP, who suggested we call an ambulance.

Before the ambulance arrived, Mike came in with an expense cheque he wanted signed. I tried my best to sign my name whilst lying on the floor having spasms but couldn't manage.

Arlene could see that I couldn't manage and said she would sort out some funding for him. Afterwards, Mike felt very bad about this so, I've never stopped reminding him of the occasion.

I was taken to hospital and stayed there for five days until the spasms finally stopped. Chris, the neurosurgeon, said I shouldn't have back surgery and gave me suggestions on how to manage my back a little better. A week later, my back seemed to be okay again so I went back to work.

After the incident Neva felt I needed a break and arranged for us to go away for a few days. Normally a break would involve a round of golf, but on this occasion it was still pretty cold and I didn't think my back would cope with golf so, instead of going to a golf resort, we went to a spa hotel on the North East coast of Spain just south of Tarragona.

Since it was a health spa, Neva decided I should also experience some of the joys of a spa treatment. While she booked herself in for a relaxing massage and a facial, she booked me in for a mud wrap followed by a hydrotherapy session.

I had no idea what either 'treatment' entailed but thought, "How bad can it be?"

When I arrived for the mud wrap I was met by a friendly therapist, who was dressed like a nurse but wasn't. She was wearing a white top and white trousers. She sent me off to the changing room with a bathrobe two sizes too small and paper underpants two sizes too big. I returned holding the robe together with one hand and my paper pants up with the other.

My therapist escorted me into a ten-foot by ten-foot room which had no furniture except for a large marble table in the centre. The walls were tiled from floor to ceiling and there were no windows or other features apart from an open shower fitting in one corner and a hose reel in another. It struck me that this was probably what a morgue would look like.

She draped a large sheet of clear plastic over the marble table and instructed me to get on and make myself comfortable. How I was supposed to make myself comfortable lying on a flat rock I don't know, however she did give me a small plastic pillow so at least my head was somewhat comfortable. Next, two gentlemen also dressed in white tops and trousers entered the room carrying large buckets of warm brown mud.

My therapist took a handful of mud and dropped it on my chest. She then added more mud as she worked her way up to my neck and down both arms. She then started at my ankles and worked her way up. By the time she was plastering mud on my underpants I was sweating like a pig. Everything got covered, touchy bits, tickly bits and everything in between. With four buckets of mud now covering every inch of my body from the neck down, she wrapped the sheet over me from one side, then from the other, and tucked it underneath me. Like a mummy, I was now totally immobile.

"That's it," she said. "I'll now leave you for twenty minutes to relax." She dimmed the lights, turned on some rainforest music, and left the room.

No sooner had she left when my nose started to itch. I desperately needed to scratch but couldn't free a hand from the plastic for fear of falling off the table. I tried to scratch it with my tongue but my tongue was an inch too short.

For the next nineteen minutes, I lay there going through 'itchy nose hell'.

When my therapist finally returned I immediately yelled, "My nose, quick, scratch my nose!" I was obviously in a state of some distress so she came over and scratched my nose. The relief was immense.

"Looks like maybe you didn't get full benefit from the relaxing mud wrap," she said as she unwrapped the plastic sheet.

Next, I was instructed to get off the table and stand near the shower recess. My therapist then took a wash-down hose and started to blast me with water. Mud, water and underpants went everywhere. I darted left and right but she had me locked in her sights. "Stand still," she yelled "You're supposed to be enjoying this!"

After a while she realised I wasn't having the most wonderful time so she stopped and told me to finish washing myself in the shower. I showered and put the bathrobe back on. I felt exhausted. As I left the room I looked back to see an unbelievable mess. Mud, bits of pants and plastic wrap all over the place. This was supposed to be a relaxing experience yet it looked like some kind of carnage had taken place.

As I came out of 'the room from hell' my therapist, who was now being a lot less jolly, met me and directed me to the hydrotherapy room. A similar room to the previous one but instead of a table, this one had a huge stone bath.

There was a lovely smell coming from the bathwater. I tested the water and found it to be pleasantly warm. I was instructed to get into the bath while she went off to get some tea-lights. When she returned, she lit them and placed three on one side of the bath and three on the other side. Once again she turned off the lights, turned on more rainforest music and left the room. This was more like it. I could handle this I thought as I stretched out to my full length in the tub.

Suddenly, without any warning, two powerful jets of water came shooting out from the foot end of the bath directly onto the soles of my feet. I immediately sat bolt upright creating a tidal wave which washed all six tea-lights off the bath onto the tile floor. I heard the sound of breaking glass and all the candles were extinguished. The room was pitch black. As I lay back down another set of jets hit my neck and shoulders followed by a sequence of jets from both sides. The cycle of jets was relentless.

Because the water level was now below the level of some of the jets, there was water flying in all directions. I managed to work out which jets were the main offenders and for the next fifteen minutes used my hands, feet and other body parts to block these off as best I could.

When my not-so-jolly therapist returned, she turned on the light and couldn't believe what she saw. There I was in the altogether on hands and knees fighting a losing battle against the jets. There was water on the floor and broken tea-lights all around the bath.

She had a look of shock and anger on her face. I told her what had happened. I couldn't get out of the bath because of the glass, so she called for one of the bucket men to come and clean the floor so I could make a safe exit.

Once out of the bath and fully dressed I came back to reception to sign for my treatment. My therapist was still looking rather annoyed. After I signed my bill her parting remark was, "I don't think you're quite ready for spa treatments. I think you should stick with golf."

When I asked Neva why she had booked these treatments for me, she said, "I've never had a mud wrap and was keen to hear if you would recommend it." I was happy to give her my recommendation.

I've never had these treatments again, although I have had a few massages and quite enjoyed those. Maybe I should have started with massages and worked my way up to mud wraps and hydrotherapy rather than doing it the other way around.

CHAPTER 51

The Drill Shoe

Fortunately selling Reamer Shoes wasn't affected by the changes in the way the drill bit business was heading. Reamer Shoe sales were increasing and our Downhole Tool Division was doing well.

Shell Peru had heard about the Reamer Shoe from one of their colleagues in the North Sea. As they were frequently having problems running casing, they decided they wanted one for a well they had just started to drill so, one afternoon, Jim got a call from the Shell procurement man in The Hague asking for a Reamer Shoe to be sent to Peru the following day. Jim called his freight forwarder and tried to arrange the shipment.

The freight forwarder called back an hour later to say that KLM, who flew from Amsterdam to Lima, Peru, wouldn't take the item of freight. Jim reported this back to his contact in The Hague. As Shell was one of KLM's biggest accounts, he said he would take care of it. A short while later he called Jim to say that the freight could go on a flight the following day, but, it had to be accompanied by a passenger.

Knowing that he held a valid passport, at 7.00 pm Jim called his production supervisor, a Glaswegian also named Jim, asking him to come to the office. Arrangements were made for 'Glasgow Jim' to fly with the Reamer Shoe to Lima. Having packed his overnight bag, Jim was picked up from his home at 2.30 am and, together with the Reamer Shoe, driven one hundred and twenty miles south to Edinburgh airport. At Edinburgh he boarded the 6.00 am flight to Amsterdam, connecting with his flight to Lima. More than twenty-four hours after leaving home, he and the Reamer Shoe finally arrived at Lima's international airport.

The Reamer Shoe was in a crate weighing over fifty kilos. Jim couldn't lift it off the baggage carousel, so an armed guard came to help him and then escorted Jim and his crate over to an inspection room. Inside the room the guard presented Jim to his companion, a female customs officer. Neither the guard or the customs officer spoke any English or could understand any Glaswegian. While the customs officer inspected Jim's passport, the guard set about breaking open the crate. Although he had nothing to hide Jim became very nervous. Scenes from the film *Midnight Express* started flashing through his mind. Fortunately, no one in the factory had decided to play a little prank on him by sticking something suspicious inside. Jim was very relieved. The customs officer could see that Jim was anxious about something and reached for a pair of spandex gloves. She put these on and gave his overnight bag a thorough examination. Although Jim wished he'd packed some nicer underpants and maybe taken a less trashy book, once again there was nothing illegal to be found.

Eventually, an English-speaking person came into the room and more questions were asked. It just didn't seem to make sense that someone would fly half way around the world, deliver a fairly innocuous looking steel tool, and then plan to fly home again the next day. There just had to be more to the story, but they couldn't find anything.

After three hours of interrogation, Jim was eventually allowed to go. He went through to the arrivals hall, called the Shell number he had been given, and waited for someone to come. Eventually a Shell rep arrived to collect the tool and take him to his hotel.

In his hotel, while drinking a beer, he declined an offer from the barman for some company. The barman had offered him a girl for one hundred and fifty dollars. When he wasn't showing any interest the price came down to one hundred dollars for two girls! Jim left the bar, had a quick meal, then headed upstairs and locked his door. Apart from being woken by what sounded like distant gunfire, he managed to get a good night's sleep.

Jim spent the following day at Shell's office passing on information to various drilling staff about how to use the Reamer Shoe. He then took a taxi back to the airport for his evening flight home.

At the airport, although he didn't see anyone in particular, he felt he was being watched. He was very relieved when he finally boarded his flight and was sitting comfortably in his seat as the plane lifted off the runway. Twenty hours later he arrived back home.

For a 'wee loon' from Glasgow it had been an interesting four days.

After the patent case against our former distributor, we were approached by Weatherford, a large American international service provider who was interested in marketing our Reamer Shoe in any country where we weren't selling it ourselves. Weatherford offered a variety of services to the oil industry and our Reamer Shoe fit nicely with the range of casing products and services they were providing. It looked like a good move so we decided to give it a try. This time the distribution agreement had stronger safeguards which prevented them from making a copy-cat product. It was a good arrangement and started off very well. Weatherford were soon making regular sales and contributing to our monthly income.

Meanwhile, Mike was busy inventing his next product. Russell had a customer in Thailand who was regularly having difficulty getting casing into their wells. The top few hundred feet of their wells were drilled through an unconsolidated rock formation. Once this section was drilled and the drill bit removed, sections of the wellbore would often bridge-over or simply collapse. Often they couldn't get the lengths of casing down beyond a certain point because of this blockage. Having a Reamer Shoe helped, but it was designed to enlarge the wellbore or move the end of the casing off an obstructing ledge. It was not designed to drill a new wellbore as was now required. The Thai customer asked Russell if we could modify a Reamer Shoe so that, if necessary, they could actually 'drill' the casing past an obstruction. Effectively, they wanted to be able to drill a new wellbore as opposed to just reaming the existing one.

Mike considered the problem and wondered about designing a drill bit which could be attached to the end of the casing. Instead of just drilling through an obstruction, the entire top section of the well could then be drilled with the casing itself. There would be no need to first drill the well in the conventional manner. It sounds like a simple and obvious solution, but there is more to it than you might think.

Casing is not intended to be used for drilling. The threaded connections on most lengths of casing are designed for vertical-loading strength and pressure sealing. These connections are not designed for the torque loading required by a drill bit. If too much torque is applied, the casing connection could over-torque causing it to 'twist-off'. If that happened and the connection parted, a fishing job would be required to recover the section of casing which had parted. This could be a very costly failure.

Knowing that the top section of the wells only penetrated through very soft rock formation, Mike felt that, with care, it would be possible to drill this rock with very little torque being applied.

Mike was also aware that the drillers could rotate the casing using a 'Top-Drive' assembly. (A top-drive is a piece of equipment which attaches to the top of the casing thereby enabling the driller to rotate and drill with the casing.) With Mike's new *Drill Shoe* fitted on the end, the drillers could use the casing to drill the entire well to the depth required, completely eliminating the need to first drill the well with a drill bit on drill pipe.

Once the casing reached setting depth a normal cement job would be performed to cement the casing in place with the Drill Shoe still attached.

The clever aspect of Mike's design was to construct the Drill Shoe so that it could be drilled-out with another drill bit. Once the cement had set, the drill pipe with any conventional drill bit attached, would be run inside the casing. This drill bit would drill right through the Drill Shoe, pass out through the bottom of the casing, and then carry on drilling the rock section below. The construction material used and the way the Drill Shoe body was designed were what made it so clever.

When Mike's Drill Shoe was first introduced in Thailand it was a big success. Our sales people had been told about its limitations. The drillers were instructed to proceed with care. Should they experience any torque whatsoever, they were told to back-off until virtually no torque was being applied. They were aware of the possibility of 'twisting-off' and knew the potential cost of such a failure. Everyone knew that just one failure during the first few jobs could destroy the credibility of the Drill Shoe and, were this to happen, the new product might never be accepted.

The Drill Shoe worked really well. For the drillers, it removed the problem caused by wellbore obstructions and for our Thai client, the cause of one of their most frequent well construction problems had been eliminated.

Over the following two years, the top sections of nearly eighty wells were drilled with a Drill Shoe. Most of the jobs were in the Gulf of Thailand although there were also a few jobs elsewhere. All the jobs were successful and more and more customers were becoming interested.

Weatherford's management was aware of our Drill Shoe performance and liked what they saw. They saw a huge market potential.

CHAPTER 52

The Unsung Heroes

By the beginning of 2000, we had built a strong relationship with Weatherford. They liked our Downhole Tool Division and thought a lot of Jim, Mike and Mitch. They were impressed with the success of the Reamer Shoe and thought our new Drill Shoe looked very interesting indeed.

I could see that our drill bit business was going to continue to struggle as more and more oil companies decided to go with the contracting option, effectively making BBL a subcontractor. The less often oil company engineers were selecting the drill bits themselves, the more difficult it would become for BBL. I could only see this situation getting worse.

I decided that I should try to sell the company. Jim, Mike, Neil and Russell were all shareholders and they also thought that it was a good idea. Once I'd made this decision, I discussed it with Gordon, my solicitor, and he recommended I speak with Simmons International. Simmons was the most active broker for mergers and acquisitions in the oil service sector, both in the North

Sea and around the world. They knew all the big service companies and were well placed to sell businesses to these companies. After meeting with Colin and Eddie, I was convinced that they could do a good job for me.

Colin showed me examples of businesses which had been sold in the previous twelve to eighteen months giving me an idea of how BBL might be valued. From his list of deals, it appeared likely that a market value for BBL would fall in the ten to twelve EBITDA multiple range. I felt it would be a great result if they could achieve this for me.

I agreed to Simmons's fee and appointed them to broker my sale. I then added an incentive whereby they could earn an even bigger fee if they were able to sell BBL for an EBITDA multiple above twelve. For every point above twelve, their fee would increase significantly. Colin and Eddie liked my proposal and thought it was a good motivator for them to get the best deal possible.

Together with Eddie and his team, I helped prepare the 'Descriptive Memorandum'. This document set out in detail the business and technology BBL was offering to sell.

Eddie suggested that we market BBL to a range of potential buyers but I felt uncomfortable about letting a lot of potential competitors know all our business secrets. Everything BBL had to offer fitted nicely with Weatherford's business and we already had a great working relationship with them. I wanted Simmons to focus on selling BBL to Weatherford first and focus the Memorandum specifically on the value BBL could add to Weatherford. Only after the option of a sale to them had been eliminated would I consider looking for other potential buyers.

I agreed that Eddie should offer Weatherford an exclusive, time limited, option to buy BBL.

Weatherford came back with a positive response. They were pleased to have exclusivity and started looking at the information we had prepared. At the time, Weatherford was working on a much larger acquisition, so the purchase of BBL was not at the top of their list. Their acquisition team had to remain focused on the deal in hand until it was completed. It wasn't expected to take long but, in the end, this took another five months to complete so nothing much happened with the purchase of BBL while we waited our turn.

Eventually it was our turn and Weatherford made an offer. It wasn't quite as good as I had hoped so Eddie and Colin started negotiating. They kept working the price higher and higher until they were convinced they had secured the best possible deal.

Bernard, the Weatherford CEO, and Gary, the Vice President of the company's Drilling Division, came over to Aberdeen to meet with me. It was an important day and I had everyone on notice to make sure we made the best impression possible.

When my visitors arrived, Arlene brought in some coffee made from luxury coffee beans purchased especially for the occasion. I closed my office door and made sure Arlene knew we were not to be disturbed.

Bernard and Gary spoke about how all the BBL staff would be retained post-acquisition and commented on the exciting opportunities Jim, Mike, and Russell would have within Weatherford. It was all sounding pretty good. Then my phone rang.

I couldn't believe Arlene would be putting a call through unless something very serious had happened. I picked up the phone and waited to hear the worst.

It was my eldest daughter Janna on the line. She was going out that night and called to ask whether I thought she should wear her blue dress or the black dress she had recently purchased. I suggested her blue dress would look nice and quickly ended the conversation.

I could see that Bernard and Gary were somewhat perplexed that I would take a 'social' call to give advise about the colour of a dress in the middle of our meeting. Bernard must have thought I was a very cool customer, or maybe he thought the phone call had delivered some kind of coded message.

You would think Arlene would have known better, however, she did exactly as she had been told. Arlene knew that I had a golden rule which was, if either of my daughters called they were never to be put on hold or told to call back later. "If ever they call, always put the call through," was my instruction. Janna's call just happen to come at a rather inconvenient moment. I didn't explain my reason for taking the call to Bernard and Gary, but I wish I had. I'm sure that they would both have understood and approved.

After further conversation, when I still hadn't agreed to the sale, Bernard finally remarked, "Roy there is a saying which is very appropriate for this occasion … you can only sell your peanuts when the circus is in town."

I got the message and, subject to a couple of very minor changes, I agreed to sell the company. I had agreed to sell BBL to Weatherford for a price which equated to an EBITDA multiple of 17.4! An absolutely amazing price.

Colin and Eddie had done an exceptional job. The sale price was far more than I had expected. The increase in price above the twelve multiple covered far more than Simmons's fees plus all the other fee notes. Simmons had added nearly thirty percent to the price I would have accepted.

The man who helped me through this selling process was my lawyer Gordon. He is a superstar. During the twenty-five years I have been in business, Gordon walked through many potential disasters with me. He always had my best interests at heart and gave me the advice I needed whenever I faced a difficult situation. He was always there.

Gordon's contribution was always much appreciated. In recognition of this I awarded him a medal for his role as my 'Unsung Hero' at a birthday celebration where I gave public recognition to a number of important people in my life. On the occasion of the sale to Weatherford, once again he took charge of the process and guided me safely over the finish line.

My other star was Arlene. Arlene was the office manager. She made sure things ran smoothly. One fortunate thing about the drill bit business was the fact that our clients were all oil companies. There was never a question about whether or not an invoice would be paid. Some paid slowly and some paid quickly, but over the ten years I never had one bad debt. (The distributor in Venezuela was the one exception ….)

The biggest problem I had from one week to the next, was managing cash flow. Arlene was the one who chased up the payment of invoices and delayed the occasional outgoing payment to make sure we stayed within our overdraft facility. I think she stressed about this as much as I did, but always tried to give the impression that everything was under control.

Arlene had been the very first person to become a BBL employee back when Danny started the company in 1989 and she was still there when the company was finally sold to Weatherford in 2001.

During the years of her employment my hair had turned from brown to grey. Surprisingly, hers had turned from grey to brown.

CHAPTER 53

The Weatherford Way

The completion date was scheduled for Tuesday 3 July 2001. Gordon and his team had prepared all the documents and when the day arrived, they were ready to go.

A few weeks before, as we were getting the last documents together, one of the issues we had to finalise was merging Russell's holding in BBL Australia into a holding in BBL. This required a bit of negotiation. BBL Australia was making a healthy contribution to our profit and Russell and his team had been a big help with the development of our technology and getting new products into the market place. Weatherford had indicated that they valued our technology and intellectual property more than our sales organisation so, I didn't want to leave it to Weatherford to make an independent valuation of Russell's share of the Australian company, which they considered to be a sales organisation … I felt Russell should share equally in the overall value of BBL. It was in Russell's best interest as well as our own to merge everything into BBL before the sale.

Russell agreed to my merger proposal on one condition. That condition was that he was excluded from any warranty to do with Venezuela. I and all the other shareholders had to agree to a number of warranties including one which stated that we had not left any liabilities behind in Venezuela or any other country where we'd previously had an office. Russell was aware of all the difficulties we'd had in Venezuela and wasn't entirely sure there wasn't something still lurking around which could come back to haunt us. We, of course, had to warrant to Weatherford that we had made a clean exit and they would not be liable for any costs relating to BBL's business activity there. The warranty issue became a sticking point. I tried to explain to Russell that he couldn't choose the parts of BBL he didn't want to be a part of. To share in the ownership of all the technology he also needed to share in the ownership of everything else – the good, the bad and the ugly.

Gordon discussed this issue with Russell's lawyer in Australia but couldn't get him to accept the 'all in' concept. Eventually I agreed to exclude Russell from the Venezuela warranty and we merged the two businesses on that basis before going to completion. At the time it irked me a little that I needed to do this, but Russell and I had far too much good history to let it become an issue.

On completion day Jim, Mike, Neil and I gathered in the boardroom of Paull and Williamson, the legal firm Gordon worked for, together with Weatherford's legal team. A local legal representative Russell had appointed, to observe proceedings and sign the documents on his behalf, was also in the room. We were all ready to sign on the dotted line and finalise the sale. The completion process took a long time. The last documents were finally signed and the sale completed at 3.30 in the morning. We left the office on July 4, American Independence Day, just as the sun was rising for the break of the new day in Aberdeen. All very symbolic I thought. I felt wonderful. I had come to the end of a long, hard, successful journey.

Mike decided we should speak with Russell in Australia to include him in our moment of achievement. When Russell answered his phone, Mike congratulated him on the part he'd played in the creation of BBL and confirmed for him that his funds were winging their way to Venezuela as he spoke. Mike and Russell were good friends. I hope Russell appreciated his sense of humour.

In the fullness of time, no warranty issue ever arose with Venezuela or any other country where BBL had been active, or for that matter with any other aspect of the deal. Weatherford got exactly what the sale document said it had paid for.

Once the deal was done, I stayed on with Weatherford for another year to assist with the integration of BBL. This didn't work out particularly well. Weatherford had a 'matrix' management structure whereby managers and engineers around the world answered to different vice presidents. For example, Mike was an engineer so he answered to the VP of engineering in Houston, and our production manager, Bill, answered to a manufacturing VP in Houston, while Paul was responsible for sales so he reported his monthly revenue to the manager of Weatherford's business unit in Aberdeen. Suddenly the link between the manufacture of new drill bits and volume of drill bit sales disappeared. My effort to help the BBL staff settle into this structure wasn't making any difference.

Various Weatherford managers around the world decided that they also wanted to start selling drill bits and needed to have a stock of drill bits at hand to get into the market.

The production facility in Aberdeen wasn't big enough to keep up with demand so it was relocated and expanded. Lots of drill bits were being produced and flown to warehouses around the world. It was chaos. As could have been anticipated, these new drill bits were not getting sold. Very few regions actually had qualified staff who could engineer a drill bit sale, so most drill bits were going offshore and then being returned unused. Some managers didn't seem to realise that without proper applications engineering, it was unlikely that their drill bit would be selected.

I tried to explain how the drill bit business worked and how crazy it was to be building drill bits which weren't being sold, but it would take nearly eighteen months before this message hit home. By then, the amount of money tied up in inventory would make Weatherford think again about whether or not they even wanted to be in the drill bit business.

After working alongside the Weatherford people for only a few weeks, Jim found that he simply couldn't work in the big company environment. It wasn't working for him and he couldn't see how it could change so, in spite of having a very attractive salary and generous share options, he resigned.

This was a big disappointment for Weatherford as they had big plans for Jim and for the products he was selling. It was only after Jim left that I discovered the reason Weatherford had paid such a high price for BBL. Apparently, a report had been produced for management indicating that the Drill Shoe product could ultimately have a market potential of five hundred million dollars per year. I couldn't believe it. The reason Weatherford had actually bought BBL was primarily to acquire the Drill Shoe and the Reamer Shoe. They weren't really interested in the drill bit business at all. Hence the reason they were so disappointed when Jim resigned.

Possibly the engineer who prepared the internal report hadn't fully understood the Drill Shoe technology. He certainly hadn't factored in the limitations of the Drill Shoe and the need for it to be sold by drill bit engineers. When they allowed non-qualified people to sell the product, there was a high risk that the product would be misapplied. It wouldn't be long before there was a disaster.

The first 'twist-off' happened a month later. A Drill Shoe had been used for the wrong application. After the failure, the oil company was not happy and took Weatherford to task for having misapplied its product. Their claim cost Weatherford a lot of money.

Immediately Weatherford became wary of the Drill Shoe and decided to rethink where and how they would sell the product. It took some time before they got to grips with the technology and were ready to bring the product back onto the market.

CHAPTER 54

The Ice Bucket

Two months after selling BBL, my wife and I were out with a group celebrating a friends birthday.

It was Monday night, 10 September 2001. I sat at the end of the table and wasn't really getting into the chat. For whatever reason it was then that it suddenly struck me what I had achieved when I'd sold BBL. I started to think about all the difficult times I'd had and how lucky I'd been to have had so many employees, managers, business partners, suppliers, bankers, lawyers and friends help make BBL a success. It seemed strange, but it was the difficult times I could remember the best. The drill bit failures, the financial problems and many other things which had gone wrong along the way. There had been a lot of good times as well, like the first month we achieved two hundred and fifty thousand dollars in drill bit sales back in January 1994, but I struggled to remember many other success highlights.

The things which made the BBL achievement so memorable and so enjoyable had actually been the difficult times. Getting my team around me to deal with seemingly unsolvable problems and then working together to find the solution was what it had all been about. Even before BBL, with Exal and Oilphase, the difficult times were the occasions I now recalled. Those were the times that made my adventure in the oil patch such a wonderful experience.

I reached over to the ice bucket and poured myself a glass of champagne. I'd been a very lucky guy, from my days in Roma to my time in Aberdeen, from Dope Bucket to Ice Bucket, it had been one heck of a journey. I loved every minute and wouldn't have have changed a thing … although I could quite happily have done without the litigation … I just sat there in my own little world drinking champagne and enjoying the feeling of success. I thought about some of the amazing people who had come into my life and how lucky I'd been that Dad had introduced me to the oil industry in the first place. Silently, I drank a toast to my Dad.

Postscript

The following day, I took one of the Weatherford managers down to Arbroath to show him the manufacturing facility there and introduce him to the staff. After our visit, we went to a hotel in town where we were about to enjoy a local delicacy. They were serving haddock which had been cured in a smokehouse and is known as an Arbroath Smokie.

It was three in the afternoon and we had just sat down to a late lunch when I received a call. It was from Russell who was in Beijing on a sales trip.

"Where are you," asked Russell.

I explained where I was and that we were about to have some lunch.

"Do they have a TV there?" asked Russell.

I confirmed there was one in the bar.

"Turn it on right now and watch what is happening. I'll call you back later," he said and hung up the phone.

I couldn't understand what Russell was on about and didn't even know what channel I might need to watch. Anyway we went through to the bar and turned on the TV. I couldn't believe what was happening. It just didn't make sense. Airplanes were flying into buildings, there was news of hijacked planes, one was heading towards the Pentagon another was thought to be flying towards the White House. It was just incomprehensible. Fire engines, people jumping out of buildings, buildings collapsing. Total chaos and the reporters couldn't explain how or why.

We left Arbroath and drove home, trying to pick up more news on the radio.

I completely forgot about the euphoric feeling I had had the night before. Suddenly my adventure seemed insignificant when the entire world was changing and September 11 was happening.